Boys Don't Try?

"What do we want for our boys?" Matt and Mark explode myths, challenge some of our preconceptions, and suggest alternative routes to success in our raising and educating of boys. And they don't dodge the most sensitive issues.

This is a thoughtful, balanced, thoroughly researched, eminently sensible, and practical consideration of how we can support boys to be their best in the classroom and beyond it. It recognises and addresses the pressures boys are under as they make their journey towards manhood. Mark and Matt skilfully demonstrate that if we help boys in schools we will improve education for girls, too.

Each chapter is structured according to the story, the research, the solutions: this is positive and forward-looking, asking not only "what's not wanted?" but "what's wanted instead?" and so focusses on the future rather than only the past and present.

The authors explain honestly, courageously and with humility how and why they have rethought their own perceptions of "the boy problem" to come to a more nuanced and carefully considered understanding of why boys behave in certain stereotypical ways and how they can be encouraged, motivated, and inspired to be their best selves. I learnt a huge amount from this book, and I suggest you will, too.

Jill Berry
Former head, now leadership consultant

This is a fabulous book. It's going to be a must-read for any teacher, leader, or parents who have ever had concerns or questions about boys' attitudes to school, to learning, to sex, to each other. *Boys Don't Try? Rethinking Masculinity in Schools* is impressively ambitious in its scope, tackling a range of key issues with a brilliant blend of the personal and the analytical with a clear, helpful, repeating structure: the story, the research, the solutions. Matt and Mark speak from experience, acknowledging their biases and changes of heart; both have voices of conviction and an absolutely authentic desire to find real answers to difficult problems. The final "other voices" chapter illustrates this perfectly.

I loved reading this book and I know thousands of others will too.

Tom Sherrington
Author and education consultant

Having just read *Boys Don't Try? Rethinking Masculinity in Schools* by Matt Pinkett and Mark Roberts, I have found myself with a sore neck. Why? Because I found myself nodding in agreement page after page. Like many teachers, at various stages in my career, I have been given really bad advice such as "introduce competition into your lessons to engage the boys" or "don't worry if the boys' work is a bit untidy; that's just the way it is with boys". Matt and Mark address myths like this and use the research evidence, alongside their own experience in schools, to break down many of these widely held beliefs, which serve to do nothing else but compound the problem of gender inequality in schools. Furthermore, they challenge us as educators to reflect on our own gender biases which, whilst uncomfortable at times, is the first step to addressing this problem.

The world of education has needed a book like this for a long time. Evidence informed, written by practitioners, and not pulling any punches. It gets to the heart of a really serious issue that permeates our education system and should be read by anybody who works in a school.

Shaun Allison
Author, deputy head, and Director of Durrington Research School

Boys Don't Try?

There is a significant problem in our schools: too many boys are struggling. The list of things to concern teachers is long. Disappointing academic results, a lack of interest in studying, higher exclusion rates, increasing mental health issues, sexist attitudes, an inability to express emotions... Traditional ideas about masculinity are having a negative impact, not only on males, but females too. In this ground-breaking book, Matt Pinkett and Mark Roberts argue that schools must rethink their efforts to get boys back on track.

Boys Don't Try? examines the research around key topics such as anxiety and achievement, behaviour and bullying, schoolwork and self-esteem. It encourages the reader to reflect on how they define masculinity and consider what we want for boys in our schools. Offering practical quick wins, as well as long-term strategies to help boys become happier and achieve greater academic success, the book:

- offers ways to avoid problematic behaviour by boys and tips to help teachers address poor behaviour when it happens

- highlights key areas of pastoral care that need to be recognised by schools

- exposes how popular approaches to "engaging" boys are actually misguided and damaging

- details how issues like disadvantage, relationships, violence, peer pressure, and pornography affect boys' perceptions of masculinity and how teachers can challenge these.

With an easy-to-navigate three-part structure for each chapter, setting out the stories, key research, and practical solutions, this is essential reading for all classroom teachers and school leaders who are keen to ensure male students enjoy the same success as girls.

Matt Pinkett is a Head of English in Surrey with a personal and professional interest in gender in schools. Matt has written for a number of publications on this topic – and others – and also writes a blog in which he discusses teaching and masculinity.

Mark Roberts is Assistant Principal at a mixed 11–18 comprehensive school in Devon. Previously, he worked at an inner-city comprehensive for boys in Manchester. Mark writes a blog about teaching English and is also a frequent contributor to TES on subjects including pedagogy, behaviour, leadership, and educational research.

Boys Don't Try?

Rethinking Masculinity in Schools

Matt Pinkett and Mark Roberts

Routledge
Taylor & Francis Group

LONDON AND NEW YORK

First published 2019
by Routledge
2 Park Square, Milton Park, Abingdon, Oxon, OX14 4RN

and by Routledge
52 Vanderbilt Avenue, New York, NY 10017

Routledge is an imprint of the Taylor & Francis Group, an informa business

© 2019 Matt Pinkett and Mark Roberts

British Library Cataloguing-in-Publication Data
A catalogue record for this book is available from the British Library

Library of Congress Cataloging-in-Publication Data
A catalog record has been requested for this book

ISBN: 978-0-8153-5017-0 (hbk)
ISBN: 978-0-8153-5025-5 (pbk)
ISBN: 978-1-351-16372-9 (ebk)

Typeset in Melior
by codeMantra

Visit the eResources website: www.routledge.com/9780815350255

M.R. - For Joe, Angus and Ned, three boys who try to do their best. And for Harriett, without whom this book wouldn't exist.

M.P. - For Lily: you are such sweet thunder. And for Donna, whose love keeps me strong when I am weak.

Contents

Foreword

A brave book this. To tackle the landscape of boys' underachievement in education is brave. It is brave because this is a well-documented field, brave because the endemic underachievement seems to be intractable, and brave because the authors propose some answers.

This book will open up some really important conversations across the sector. The achievement of boys has long been a concern and considerable research and brainpower has gone in to trying to work out why. In this important work, Matt Pinkett and Mark Roberts unpick a raft of reasons why many of the strategies developed to engage, cajole, and induct boys into learning have not worked.

The pace and intellectual energy in this book are largely driven by accounts from the authors' school experiences both as pupils and professionals. Based on this, they tackle some of the behemoths of the educational landscape and some of the most sensitive subjects involving teachers' attitudes towards gender. And in the hands of Pinkett and Roberts, two English teachers in secondary schools, this is a triumph. This work leaves no stone unturned, no taboo untackled. In sharing their personal stories, combining these with an astonishing range of research, they unpick the tricky, messy stuff of boys' underachievement and assemble arguments which are both scholarly in their erudition and elegant in their simplicity.

When I reflect on some of my own practice with boys both as a professional and a parent, I wish some of the insights from this book had been available to me as a young teacher and leader, because they would have equipped me with the language to challenge what I understood at a deep level to be wrong and which I could only articulate clumsily. There are fascinating insights, for example, into juvenile jibes about boys' mothers, something I noticed was more provocative than many other crude insults when I was head of year. Elsewhere, there are some harsh observations – the fine line, for instance, between the blurred boundaries of banter and bullying, amusement and abuse, humour and harassment. And this is just the teachers. Some tough messages for us all.

In particular, Pinkett and Roberts highlight some of the misconceptions about boys' engagement. As English teachers, they look at these issues through the lens of what has worked, what has appeared to work, and what has fallen off the perch in their practice. This analysis is substantiated with their own experiences as students, so that their professional gaze is mediated through their adolescent selves. It frames the inadequacy of attempting, for example, to make material relevant to boys' own interests and preferences. Their suggestions neatly unpick the cheap tricks and quick wins and make a powerful case that privileging challenge, love of the subject, and authentic discussions are the deep, lasting legacy. Not a pseudo activity in sight.

There are searing insights into the systemic bias against children from low-income households: in maths, for example, "low income pupils are more likely to be judged as below average than higher income pupils". This is despite the fact that pupils from low income and higher income backgrounds had scored equivalently in tests. These observations seek not to cast blame but to shine a light on deeply held cultural assumptions about what children in general and boys in particular are capable of. And the narrative is completed by offering suggestions, some of them counter intuitive. For example, Pinkett argues that the current approach to raising the attainment of disadvantaged pupils focuses too greatly on what disadvantaged pupils are doing, rather than how teachers teach them.

And the commentary on so-called "hard to reach parents" is worth its weight in gold. Here, they show what is possible through imagination and humanity. The book is laden with observations, mined from wide ranging research, such as the finding that boys have very limited language to describe emotions.

If there is a single theme throughout the book, it is challenge: a call to challenge our perspectives as professionals, to unearth our hidden assumptions about boys, to check our language; a challenge to senior leaders to reframe the current lens through which they view most boys' underperformance; a challenge to open up to talking about emotions; and finally a challenge to ensure that every child, whatever their gender, has a curriculum they can leverage to become fully human.

Mary Myatt
19 November 2018

Acknowledgements

We want to thank all the teachers, academics, and experts who have taken the time and effort to help us rethink masculinity in schools. Without your time, passion, patience, and support this book wouldn't have happened.

Throughout the whole process of writing this book, we've been lucky enough to work with a supportive, dedicated, and professional team at Routledge. We'd also like to thank the anonymous reviewers who gave us much to think about during the initial stages of the book's development.

We are very grateful to the contributors to Chapter 10; their excellent essays provide insights that we couldn't possibly have provided.

We're particularly grateful for the invaluable feedback, comments, and ideas from everyone who read various versions of the manuscript, especially Tom Sherrington, Jill Berry, Shaun Allison, Vivienne Porritt, Vic Goddard, Alex Quigley, Ben Newmark, Sarah Ledger, and Helen Carter. Huge thanks go to the incomparable Mary Myatt for her unending wisdom and support, and for the excellent foreword to this book.

As well as those he engages with on Twitter, Matt Pinkett would also like to thank those teachers who are relentless sources of support in "real life", especially Maria, Ed, Bubz, and Alastair. I won't ever forget what you've done for me.

Introduction

They do try, of course.

Well, some of them do. Despite the national trend of boys' relative educational underachievement in comparison to girls, there are many boys who try very hard at school and achieve great success as a result of doing so.

However, it must be said that for every boy who tries to succeed, there is another boy who tries to fail. These boys try to avoid completing work. Sometimes, they try too hard to impress popular peers and forget about trying to impress their teachers. Occasionally, they try to hurt and humiliate each other; and try to belittle and demean girls or female teachers. Or they try to hide how they are feeling behind a mask of bravado. As this book will illustrate, when boys behave like this, they are actually trying to aspire to an outdated, but nonetheless widespread, idea about what it means to be a "real man".

A tale of two blogs

The genesis for this book began with a couple of blogs. In January 2016, Matt Pinkett wrote a blog post entitled *Balance for Boys*, arguing that

> ...teachers across the country are so focused on addressing, combating, and undoing the deplorable wrongs inflicted on women in society, media, and literature for centuries, that they're inadvertently alienating the boys.

A few months later, Mark Roberts knocked out a blog called *Boys' Engagement in the Classroom*, containing wisdom such as:

- Boys love competition (group vs group, homework league tables, etc.)

- Is there an alpha male in the group? Win them over and the others will probably follow

- Sometimes the timetable is against you. Try negotiating rewards for hard work e.g. P5 Friday 45 minutes of solid focus = 15 minutes of more relaxed learning.

We wince as we read these now.

One blog saw it fit to blame feminism for boys' academic underperformance; the other spouted stereotypical mumbo jumbo and encouraged lower expectations for boys.

Gradually, we've had to rethink some of our beliefs about masculinity. Especially the ones we articulated so clumsily in our respective blogs. The truth, as we realise now, after two years of discussion, rethinking and readjustment is that boys' relative lack of academic success is nothing to do with feminism at all, or a lack of engaging ploys to grab boys' attention, but a wide range of complex contributory factors. This book will examine these factors in the nuanced way that the subject requires. Throughout, we will invite you to rethink masculinity in schools, as we did.

The problem with boys

Boys underperform at all key stages of primary and secondary education compared to girls. Boys are more likely to be excluded from school. Boys are less likely to go to university; boys are less likely to become apprentices; boys are less likely to find paid work between the ages of 22 and 29. And when these boys become young men, they are three times more likely than women to be victims of suicide. They also belong to the gender that makes up 96% of the UK prison population.

These are startling statistics, especially given that there are no significant differences in male and female cognition. And yet, as we shall discover throughout the book, teachers largely see girls as obedient and hard-working, but view boys as disruptive and uninterested in their education.

The fallacy of boys' engagement

Training courses for teachers, aimed at raising boys' attainment in boys have proliferated, peddling the fallacy that there are specific techniques that can be employed to engage boys, reinforcing ideas about gender difference, and playing on fears of "the boy problem". This book will show that boys are just as capable of academic success as girls, whilst also highlighting key areas of pastoral care that need to be acknowledged by schools in order to combat the side effects of a brand of masculinity that leaves many boys floundering.

What about the girls?

We are limping – too slowly, but limping nevertheless – towards female equity in areas like education, careers, and the right to go through a life without being sexually abused or harassed. Some will rightly question the need to address the boy "crisis" when in fact it is women who are more likely (despite the grim statistics about boys cited above) to be illiterate, poor, and victims of sexual abuse.

However, it's our belief that in tackling the serious issues faced by boys in education, teachers can go some way to tackling the serious issues faced by girls, both in schools and out in what adults persist in calling "the big bad world". We should avoid futile and meaningless boys vs girls narratives and recognise that when boys struggle educationally, it also has a direct, adverse effect on girls. *Boys Don't Try?* hopes to offer useful advice that will help boys but also help girls as well.

Tender masculinity

So, what do we want for our boys? Do we want our boys to talk about their feelings, even if those feelings are anger and frustration? Do we want our boys to be chivalrous, even when chivalry is tied to the belief that women are damsels-in-distress? Do we want our boys to be vulnerable, even when vulnerability can expose them to pain? These are complicated questions, but there is a simple answer to the question, "What do we want for our boys?"

That answer is: tender masculinity.

In a blog post entitled *In Praise of Tender Masculinity, the New Non-Toxic Way to Be a Man*, Terra Loire explains that tender masculinity is a "necessary antidote to our media portrayals of men" as macho tough guys with all the emotional depth of a vacuum floating in outer space. Loire suggests that if you ask the following questions of a man, and can answer in the affirmative, then he embodies tender masculinity:

- Is he invested in all of his relationships, not just romantic ones?

- Does he express his emotions in a healthy way?

- Is self-awareness a concept he's comfortable with?

- Does he commit to personal growth?

- Are boundaries something he is aware of and respects?

- Is he unafraid of male intimacy – for instance, can he express affection for male friends without making a gay joke?[1]

The ultimate aim of this book is to produce boys who turn into men, of whom we can proudly say "yes" in answer to these questions.

What about toxic masculinity?

"Toxic masculinity" has become a popular term of late. When we first heard it, it struck us as a timely phrase for a dominant strain of masculinity that defines being a man through the qualities of toughness, emotional coldness, aggression, predatory heterosexuality, and unblinking homophobia. The metaphor seemed particularly apt, summing up the way that traditional ideas about manhood have destructive consequences for boys. We liked how "toxic" hinted at the pernicious effects of these beliefs, gradually poisoning the victim, unnoticed until it is too late.

But now we've changed our minds.

Now we think, like its subject, the term does more harm than good. Males have enough on their plates – the ones they are constantly spinning in an effort to meet the demands of being a "real" man – without being seen as some sort of disease, contaminating those who they come into contact with.

Non-tender masculinity

So what term, to refer to negative aspects of masculinity, might we use instead? Let's remove the appealing but exacerbating metaphor of toxic masculinity and label this condition differently. Let's use a term that addresses the issues faced by modern males without heaping further opprobrium upon their shoulders: **non-tender masculinity**.

This is preferable to toxic masculinity because its very usage directs us towards a more desirable alternative: the tender masculinity we should desire for all our male pupils. It doesn't imply that masculinity is an infection; the last thing we want is boys seeing themselves as noxious contagions of little positive worth. We'd like it if every reader of this book could use the term non-tender masculinity, rather than toxic masculinity, to reduce the stigma that being male carries in some circles, without shying away from the unkind nature of certain male behaviours and attitudes.

Stories, research, and solutions

Each chapter of *Boys Don't Try?* features an easy-to-navigate three part structure: the story, the research, the solutions.

When we first discussed the idea of writing a book about boys and schools, we knew that it would involve our own experiences of education, as pupils and teachers. We also realised that our lives outside of school offered rich insight into the masculine condition. It's easy to look down upon anecdotal evidence, with its subjective limitations, but we feel it helps to frame the subsequent debates that rely on the use of research evidence. We make no apology for telling stories about the experiences of boys in education. The anecdotes we use may provide only insights; yet without these insights, we think the solutions to the problems we discuss would be harder to pinpoint.

At the same time, we acknowledge that narratives about masculinity and education can only act as a launch pad for further investigation of the complex issues we cover. By engaging with a great deal of high quality research, we provide a solid foundation that can help leaders and teachers move away from the popular but highly damaging "commonsense" approaches to solving "the boy problem" in our schools. These "intuitive" answers to engaging boys miss the point and make things worse. Our argument is based on a body of evidence that gets to grips with topics such as anxiety and achievement, behaviour and bullying, schoolwork and self-esteem.

A summary of the book's content

In Chapter 1, you'll discover why some of the most common myths about teaching boys are not only wrong but actively damaging. You'll see the problems caused by using specific techniques to "engage" boys, which imply, erroneously, that boys are somehow different from their more successful female peers.

The experience of disadvantaged pupils in the education system is addressed in Chapter 2, helping you understand why disadvantaged boys perform so badly compared to their more privileged peers. You'll find out how decisions made by schools – such as the groups pupils are taught in – worsen rather than alleviate disadvantage gaps.

In Chapter 3, you'll learn about the effects of peer pressure on boys, and how the influence of peers can have a particularly profound and destructive impact on boys. This chapter will look at ways that schools and teachers can attempt to tackle the issue of teaching boys who would rather gain acceptance than achieve good results in school.

Chapter 4 looks at on boys' mental health, with a specific focus on suicide, anger, and self-harm. In this chapter, you'll be offered practical, useable advice on how you can encourage boys to talk about their feelings, and what you can do when they just won't. You'll see how a proactive approach is required in order to ensure the mental well-being of the boys in your school.

Reading Chapter 5 will provide you with a new insight into how teacher's expectations of boys and girls have a significant effect on their attitudes, self-belief, and outcomes. You'll also gain a greater understanding of how gender stereotypes negatively influence the way we deal with boys' behaviour in class.

By lifting the lid on boys' often disturbing attitudes towards sex and females, Chapter 6 explores the impact of pornography on young boys. You'll also see how sex and gender education are important factors in breaking down the foundations of misogyny found in schools across the UK.

Chapter 7 will take you into the classroom, addressing the way that the resources we use in lessons shape our ideas about gender roles. This section will also provide answers to two key questions regularly thrown up during debates about boys and underachievement: *do boys need to be taught by male teachers?* and *would boys do better in single-sex environments?*

From Chapter 8, you'll gain a more nuanced appreciation of why males are more likely to commit acts of violence, using the essentialist vs socialisation debate as a backdrop. You'll see what can go wrong when schools deal badly with incidents of aggression and be given a detailed explanation of violence-intervention programmes that can reduce physical displays of aggression in your school.

The first part of Chapter 9 looks at the often damaging nature of boys' relationships with each other, providing you with a detailed understanding of the blurred lines between banter and bullying. It also addresses the thorny issue of what happens when "banter" between staff goes wrong. The second half of the chapter looks at how you can develop positive relationships with boys in lessons, giving hands-on advice about how to ensure a warm, calm and insistent presence.

In Chapter 10, we introduce other voices from the world of education, giving you insight into areas beyond our experience. Stories about boys and boyhood shared by people whose experience of masculinity in schools goes beyond our own, will enable you to build up a bigger picture of the full range of viewpoints and responses to masculinity in schools.

What about behaviour?

You might be surprised to notice there isn't a chapter entitled "behaviour". Surely, you might be thinking, that's the area where teachers struggle most with boys? Actually, behaviour is the spine that holds the book together. Each chapter offers insight into how you might avoid problematic behaviour by boys, with lots of helpful tips along the way to help you address poor behaviour when it happens.

The aim of the book

This book is written for classroom teachers and school leaders. We both know what it's like to teach a five period day, bookended with wet morning playground duties and even wetter after-school CPD[2] sessions. The advice we provide is intended to be practical enough to bring about short-term enhancements to your classroom practice and begin improving the culture of your school. Yet, we are realistic enough to accept that this book grapples with huge societal concerns; we recognise that simultaneous incremental shifts are required to bring about lasting change to the way schools think about masculinity and education. Throughout the book, you'll see that while we've been able to provide you with "quick wins", we've also been honest enough to point out that certain solutions involve a long-term strategy to truly shift the sands of gender in schools.

Notes

1 Loire, T. (2017) *In praise of tender masculinity, the new non-toxic way to be a man.* Available at: https://electricliterature.com/in-praise-of-tender-masculinity-the-new-non-toxic-way-to-be-a-man-7bb4f0159998 (Accessed: 24th September 2009).
2 Continuing professional development.

The engagement myth

Mark Roberts

The story

You meet them at the door. Come on in lads. Take a seat. Pens out.

We're doing things differently today boys, you tell them. You know they've done LOADS of writing recently. You know they're tired of extended writing. You can tell they've had enough of analysing quotations from the book they've been reading. The book they've been reading, which is perfect for them. Perfect for them because it is boy-friendly. Boy-friendly because it is full of action and features things that they're interested in, like gangs, guns, and girls.

You put them in groups. You give them a whopping piece of A3, and felt tip pens fatter than a German sausage. "We're having a competition". Each group gets an extract from the book. You want them to come up with the best PEA paragraph[1] possible.

The Writing World Cup

You make eight groups: perfect for a quarter-final scenario. At the end of the first round, you adjudicate. You put the best four through to the semis, with the four losers going into the "play offs". You whittle four down to two. The class look on entranced as you hand over a couple of nightmare quotations for the Grand Final. One group of boys really raise their game. They produce a paragraph that is precise, perceptive, worthy of any prize. As the winners hold aloft their bumper box of Maltesers, you imagine being interviewed about the group's victory:

Interviewer: The boys have done good Mark. How does it feel to have used their competitive natures to spur them on to such Olympian achievements?

Mr: I'm chuffed to bits Alan. They gave me 110%. I'm literally over the moon. This is probably the proudest moment of my managerial – sorry, I mean teaching – career so far...

How to teach boys (part I)

Teaching boys is straightforward.

This is what I was told as a trainee teacher. There were solid strategies to follow. Top tips to implement. Sure fire ways of guaranteeing engagement in every single lesson. These strategies were logical. They were common sense. And boy, did they work for me.

Towards the end of my PGCE year, I found myself in a job interview, at the school where I did my second placement. An inner city comprehensive for boys in Manchester, it was located in an area of very high deprivation. The vast majority spoke English as an additional language. Well over half of the school received free school meals. A challenging school.

As you can imagine, most of the questions were about engagement and behaviour. To be honest, I found it relatively easy to answer these: all I needed to do was parrot back the advice I'd been given in university and explain how I'd adapted these strategies in my practice so far. I got the job. The school was the perfect fit for me. I understood boys because I grew up in a house with three brothers. Back in the day, I was even a boy myself. From the moment I leant over the desk to shake the hand of the interviewers, I knew that things were going to be fine.

And things were fine. I implemented my boy-friendly strategies and tested out my top tips. My lessons were popular. The Writing World Cup was just one example of the many boy-friendly engagement-guaranteeing lessons I knocked out.

My most memorable lessons

As an NQT[2], if a researcher, interested in what pedagogical approaches work best when teaching boys, had asked me to describe my best lesson, I'd probably have plumped for the Writing World Cup lesson.

Or maybe the one where I dressed up as a news reporter and started the lesson "in role". Microphone in hand, my best American accent deployed, I described the scene of devastation as the Twin Towers fell. This lesson, spurred on by an Ofsted inspection that had downgraded my previously Outstanding teaching to Good, was intended to showcase the "wow factor" and "oomph" that the inspectorate had found lacking in my practice. I was teaching poetry – Simon Armitage's "Out of the Blue" to be exact – and this was designed to introduce context but also tick the "creative, innovative" box that had suddenly appeared on the Outstanding lesson content descriptors.

Or possibly I'd have mentioned the lesson where we put paper helmets on and lobbed scrunched up balls of paper at each other, to get an idea about the conditions of trench warfare. Or the one where kids launched scrunched up balls of paper at me, containing questions for me to answer.

And if this same researcher had asked my pupils to recall the most memorable lesson I'd taught them, they'd probably say one of these.

Winning ways to engage boys

Funnily enough, the question about their most memorable lesson was asked of teachers and pupils by Michael Reichert, Ph.D. and Richard Hawley, Ph.D. – the writers of *Reaching Boys Teaching Boys*[3] – in an effort to find the "most concrete and most useful data bearing on boys' success in school". Their research involved polling nearly a thousand teachers across 18 boys' schools from countries which included the UK, United States, Australia, and South Africa. They asked teachers to describe a lesson "they consider especially effective with boys". Amongst this array of educators, the authors found certain recurring themes. According to their teachers, the lessons that boys liked most included the following features:

1. The opportunity to get up out of their seats and move around

2. Competition

3. Students teaching each other

4. Using technology

5. Games, role-play, or debates

6. Topics that are relevant to their lives

7. Surprising events or some other kind of novelty.

The boys – who were asked to recall a particularly memorable lesson – concurred with their teachers. Yes, they said, this is the kind of learning that we like.
  What did these trends look like in reality, then? They looked like this sort of thing:

■ Mastering stage swordplay during a *Romeo & Juliet* module

■ Acting out the process of cell division

■ Dissecting squids during biology. Then using the ink to draw things with. Then turning these cephalopods into calamari. Science, art, and cooking in one lesson.

Now these lessons, just like my celebrated offerings, sound ideal for boys. They sound fun. They sound engaging. They certainly sound novel.

How to teach boys (part 2)

In 2014, I decided to do something radical. In search of a new challenge, I got myself a job at a mixed gender comprehensive. This capricious act meant I would now be teaching *girls* as well. It also meant relocating to Devon. The new school was in an affluent middle class area but had a significant intake from local villages that followed the region's pattern of rural deprivation. The English results were below where they should be, given the entry data. Boys in particular were massively underperforming.

I was under no illusions that the main reason I'd been given the job was my reputation as the "boy guy", the answer – no, the panacea – for the school's boy-fuelled nightmares. The first year, I'd sort out English. The following year, I'd spread my magic fairy dust over the rest of the college. And the funny thing is, that's what started to happen. The results for boys began to improve. Oddly though, they also did for girls. I put that down to girls being compliant. It was obvious that they'd just gone along with the boy stuff.

Towards the end of that first year in Devon, I wrote a blog – my first ever – on how to improve progress through boys' engagement. And to bring things full circle, I was also asked to deliver more CPD[4] sessions on – yes, you've guessed it – boys' engagement. Things were going exactly as they should be. My strategies continued to bear fruit.

Not long after writing that first blog, I had an epiphany in the shower. My epiphanies always happen in the shower. Suddenly, I was struck by a thought. In fact, it wasn't sudden; it had been niggling away in the back of my brain for a few months, including while I was writing my boys' engagement blog.

What happened is I realised that all of my views on how to teach boys were actually garbage.

Well, not all of them. But a fair chunk. Especially the boys' engagement strategies that had been the bedrock of my teaching practice.

What were these strategies then? And why were they such rubbish? Before I share with you what really works, let's start by looking at three prevalent boys' engagement myths, which are not just flawed but actually contribute to boys' poor academic outcomes.

The research

Engagement myth 1: boys like competition

The logic behind this boy-friendly strategy is simple: boys like competition, therefore, making activities competitive will make them more motivated to learn. It's a no-brainer, right? Chuck in a few prizes, reward points, or even good old-fashioned bragging rights, and the most reluctant of lads will get stuck in. After all, male pride is at stake. For many years, this was fundamental to my quest for maximum engagement. My best lessons, including the legendary Writing World Cup, featured competitive elements. The resulting engagement, to my eyes, was evidence that boys were spurred on by a traditional battle for victory.

The reasoning behind this is logical, compelling and catastrophically wrong. Rather than encouraging boys on to greater efforts and achievements, this motivational tactic in many cases has the opposite effect, particularly for the very boys who are most in need of a boost to their confidence.

Martin Covington[5] has argued that in Western cultures, "ability" is a "commodity" that has a widespread value and as such carries high status. In schools,

Covington contends, academic ability is prized above other abilities. The particular emphasis placed on "intellectual" ability has a profound impact on an individual's self-worth. Put simply, the feelings we hold about our academic ability and the judgements others make about our academic ability directly affects our self-esteem. For Covington, there is nothing quite like a good set of grades to boost our self-worth levels. Conversely, there is nothing like a collection of Es and Fs glaring at us from a report sheet to obliterate our self-worth.

This seems rather obvious: success builds success. Of course pupils feel better when they get good grades. Of course they feel awful when they don't. But where Covington's argument gets really interesting is when he applies this self-evident knowledge to the competitive backdrop of our education system. In most countries, exams are set up in a manner that is inherently competitive. Unlike, say, a driving test – where if you meet a required standard you pass – many summative assessment regimes are organised and administered to ensure that only certain percentages can achieve a desired "pass" mark. Many thousands will "succeed", many thousands more will not. Some people think this is a good thing, others feel that the bell curve is unfair.

Whatever your views of the rights and wrongs of the hierarchical nature of education outcomes, there are clear consequences for the self-worth of individual pupils. If you don't believe me, next results day, try telling lachrymose Pupil X, who got a D, that their grade is just as much of an achievement as their mate Pupil Y, who got a B. You may well talk about different starting points, and how much progress Pupil X made over the course, but your rational words will provide no solace. Pupil X will still feel like a loser compared to Pupil Y.

Failure as a protection strategy

As we shall discover in Chapter 3, male pupils are more likely to do less work through a desire to fit in with the peer group. But they also, according to Covington, withdraw from academic work as a "self-worth protection" strategy. This is a paradox that many experienced teachers will recognise: only by guaranteeing failure – through a palpable, public lack of effort – can boys avoid a more damaging brand of failure. Through not trying their hardest, pupils avoid injury to their perception of self. To the fragile male adolescent mindset, trying hard and still failing is the worst of both worlds. Indeed, further research[6] suggests boys are more likely than girls to self-sabotage their academic outcomes in an effort to protect their sense of self-esteem.

So what's the link between self-worth protection and using competition as an engagement tool? Well, first, the education system itself is inherently competitive. Male pupils in particular are more likely to self-handicap when confronted by the competitive realities of "pass or fail" examinations. Why then, would you want to increase the competitive content by introducing further competition into the classroom? As Carolyn Jackson[7] has noted, the strategy of increasing competition in the classroom, in an attempt to engage boys in learning, "is likely to exacerbate the adoption of defensive strategies on the part of many boys". Think back to my Writing World Cup. As a teacher, my self-congratulatory focus was on the smiles of the winners and the impressive work they'd been inspired to produce. What I hadn't focused on, and what I think about now ruefully, is the well-hidden feelings of dejection among the defeated multitude. The runners-up may have found comfort in a near miss that left their egos relatively undented, but the first round knockouts suffered serious self-worth depletion.

Unintended consequences

What you see as fun little games may well be, on a daily basis, further corroding the delicate confidence of those pupils with the lowest levels of self-worth. But why is a spot of seemingly harmless competition so damaging to boys in particular? Research suggests[8] that most boys are very competitive, that the outcome of competition matters more to boys, that boys are more bothered about outperforming their peers than girls are. Oh, and according to Covington, boys are also more concerned about whether they belong to the "high ability" club. This toxic combination results in boys downing tools in a textbook show of self-destructive behaviour: *if I haven't tried, I haven't really failed.* The worst possible scenario of course, for this fragile psyche, would be to have really tried – to have rolled up one's sleeves and given it the proverbially innumerate 110% – and to still have failed. That really would be a defeat, to stretch the cliché, to leave a boy feeling gutted.

Because, after all, boys can get their competition fix elsewhere with far less risk to their ego. They can fight. They can accumulate girlfriends. They can stand victorious on the sports field. Indeed, in the sporting arena, most boys can rest assured that even if they lose to a fellow male, at least there is only a slim chance of *losing to a girl*. And this fear – this stupid, pathetic, Neanderthal, misogynistic, self-defeating fear – is all too real to boys who want to be part of the dominant, overtly masculine in-crowd. To this warped but ridiculously common mindset, losing to a girl means much more than losing. It means undertaking a process of emasculation, of losing one's manliness.

The academic arena and the classroom specifically offer, to these boys, the greatest danger to a boy's sense of self-worth and belonging. Little wonder that many opt instead for the sanctuary of the dunce act, ducking detentions and messing about. The biggest victims of this disruption are, of course, girls.[9] And "feminine" boys who break the rules of masculinity by studying hard and competing with girls on equal and fair terms. Boys who are terrified of failure not only harm their own progress, therefore, but also make a futile attempt to drag the competition down with them.

On the surface, bringing competition into the classroom is a common-sense approach to hook boys into learning. Peel away the surface of this well-meaning approach and we find a solution that causes many more problems than it solves.

Engagement myth 2: make learning relevant to boys' interests

I want you to imagine an environment where many boys feel uncomfortable. They can't be themselves. They feel pressurised to live up to a preconceived notion of how their gender behaves. The work they are expected to do – and to do well if their self-worth is to remain undamaged – is seen by their peers as "feminine". For many boys, this is *your* classroom.

Now think about a classroom that tackles this disregard for school by making the learning *relevant* to boys' lives. By making the topics they study boy-friendly. By making the curriculum based, as much as possible, around the things that boys like doing. Then, surely, boys will put their apparent aversion to academic endeavour to one side and feel compelled to do their best.

At my old school in Manchester, I devoted a few years of my life to this crusade. My mission was simple: take the things "the lads" were interested in – gaming and grime, football and fighting – and squeeze as much of that content as I could into my lessons. Reviews of the latest first-person shooter; interviews with Tinchy Stryder; Premier League reports; extracts from a biography of Muhammed Ali; exposés of inner city gun crime. As long as they were reasonably well written, and contained the odd pun or rhetorical question, they were fit for the photocopier. Other texts were selected for their boy-friendliness as well. War poetry, fight scenes from Shakespeare, books with gadgets and explosions. Wherever possible, we chose contemporary novels over "inaccessible" texts. Hello *Gangsta Rap*, see you later *Great Expectations*.

There are many problems with this approach:

A. Boys get bored eventually, even of things that normally interest them

In the excellent *Why Don't Students Like School?*[10] cognitive scientist Daniel T. Willingham gives one example of why the quest for relevancy is a colossal mistake:

> … I don't think content drives interest. We've all attended a lecture or watched a TV show (perhaps against our will) about a subject we thought we weren't interested in, only to find ourselves fascinated; and it's easy to get bored even when you usually like the topic…The content of a problem…may be sufficient to prompt your interest, but it won't maintain it.

The novelty of reading about Arsenal vs Chelsea in a lesson piqued the interest of my pupils. But as soon as the grim reality kicked in – that I was still going to make them analyse language – their enthusiasm began to wane. They were happy to discuss the key events – the penalty that wasn't, the 30-yard-screamer that was – but as soon as I started rattling on about the clichéd use of "outfought and outthought" and the definition of "profligacy", they realised they were getting an otherwise normal English lesson.

B. Boys will remember the "relevant" part but forget the actual learning bit

The logic behind this teaching method is straightforward: make the content relevant to pupils by giving them first-hand experience. The problem, as Willingham points out, is that the fun, engaging activity is likely to leave pupils thinking much more about the experience than the knowledge. Think back to the science lesson I mentioned earlier in this chapter. What if pupils remember the process of smearing the squid ink around on paper, or the taste of the calamari, more than they did the key part – the anatomy of the squid?

I once observed a maths interview lesson where the teacher hooked the pupils in by appealing to their stomach. Pupils had to work out, using $A = \pi r^2$, whether it was more economical to buy one 16" or two 10" pizzas. This candidate certainly stimulated the senses, producing an elaborate takeaway menu resource. The boys solved the problems, the bell went and they trooped out for lunch, salivating. I asked them the following morning if they'd enjoyed the lesson. Absolutely, they told me. Could they explain how to solve the problem? Only one of them could. What they'd remembered were the toppings. Pepperoni. Spicy meat feast. Even the bloody Hawaiian. For Willingham, "memory is the residue of thought". What we think about most is what we remember most.

C. Boys don't all like the same things

Injecting relevance into the curriculum may well grab the attention of some boys but it is unlikely they'll all be satisfied. Imagine a group of boys stood outside a cinema on a Saturday afternoon, deciding what movie to see. These boys happen to be gender-conformists who display their masculinity through banter and bravado. Naturally enough, they *ain't going to see no chick flick.* Even so, there's disagreement about what to watch. Three are petrolheads, so fancy the latest *Fast and Furious*; two are in the mood for a goofball comedy; a couple more vote for an ultraviolent slasher film. In the end, they go their separate ways.

In your classroom, believe it or not, there are some boys who don't like gaming. Some who abhor sport. Some who would rather have their eye gouged out with a rusty penknife than read a grime magazine. As Becky Francis has pointed out,[11] boys are not a uniform, homogenous mass. Indeed, they are as capable of being very different to one another as they of being very different to girls. Also, unless you teach at a boys' school, or in a boys-only grouping, there will be other creatures in the classroom. These are called girls. They may well get sick to bloody death of your attempts to appeal to boys, while their individual interests are ignored.

D. Assuming boys all like the same things reinforces stereotypes

Tailoring our resources to boys is not just impractical, but it's also certain to promote damaging stereotypes about "authentic" masculine behaviour. This essentialist approach perpetuates beliefs that "real" boys like "macho" things such as football, aggression, and heterosexual fumblings. Martin Mills and Amanda Keddie illustrate the pernicious effects of this attitude through an anecdote about an Australian boys' engagement "expert" who, in an effort to get more boys reading, promoted an online magazine full of pictures of "scantily-clad young women draped over cars".[12] As Mills and Keddie explain,

> This form of reading material serves to reinforce narrow definitions of what it means to be a boy [and] rather ironically, serves to reinforce those attributes amongst some boys that have caused them already to disengage with the learning process.

The example given is obviously an extreme. But look around your school library and consider what kind of messages your books for boys section (it might not be labelled as such but there usually is one) is giving out to male pupils. If it makes generalisations about what boys like, then it's probably contributing to the paradox that Mills and Keddie highlight: the very thing that makes boys anti-school in the first place (assumptions about how boys should behave) is being served up as the thing that will get them more interested in schoolwork.

E. It prevents some boys from building cultural capital

Mills and Keddie ask a simple but important question of all teachers: "do we want ... to encourage boys who spend most of their free time playing football to then only read about football?" By appealing to pupils' interests and making the curriculum "relevant" only to their lives, we are limiting their exposure to new ideas, as well as making assumptions about what they will enjoy or what they will be able to handle academically.

The idea of **cultural capital** was introduced by French sociologist Pierre Bourdieu. In his 1979 book *Distinction: A Social Critique of the Judgement of Taste*, Bourdieu argued that we accumulate cultural capital through accessing certain knowledge, behaviours, and skills that is highly valued in society.

This knowledge, Bourdieu contended, shapes how others view our "cultural competence" and determines our social status. For example, a person may be able to impress in a job interview by displaying their appreciation of Wagner's The Ring Cycle, or might gain respect for mentioning that they've read all six volumes of Edward Gibbon's *Decline and Fall of the Roman Empire*. For Bourdieu, society's institutions, rightly or wrongly, value certain types of knowledge, behaviours, and skills more than others. Would the same interviewer be impressed by an encyclopaedial awareness of Abba's back catalogue or an intimate understanding of the works of Dan Brown? Like it or not, pupils from disadvantaged backgrounds generally receive less exposure to ideas that are likely to enable them to accrue cultural capital. In these cases, the school has responsibility to ensure pupils have the opportunity to build up cultural capital to avoid losing out to more advantaged peers.

At secondary school, I was placed in the bottom set for English on behaviour grounds. I was put with a strict female teacher, an ex-police officer who could handle my infantile, disruptive behaviour. As a result, I studied no Shakespeare at school. Not a single line of the greatest words ever written in the English language. Instead, we did texts that were considered commensurate with our "ability". Texts relevant to our lives. I remember studying Barry Hine's *A Kestrel for a Knave*. The novel is a beautiful, devastating piece of social realism about a young lad who grows up in rough Yorkshire mining town, attends a school full of often callous teachers, and is aware that beyond the pit, society offers little hope for working class boys like him. I enjoyed it and am glad to have read it, but looking back now, how did this novel expand my horizons? What did I – a working class lad from a rough mining town in a school full of often sadistic teachers – learn from this experience? Yes, it was pleasing to recognise that books were written about the likes of me – and it's important that disadvantaged pupils experience this sensation at some point during their time at school – but ultimately, it narrowed my scope. Compare this with my first exposure, a few years' later at FE college, to *King Lear*:

> *Mean time we shall express our darker purpose.*
> *Give me the map there. Know that we have divided*
> *In three our kingdom; and 'tis our fast intent*
> *To shake all cares and business from our age,*
> *Conferring them on younger strengths, while we*
> *Unburden'd crawl toward death.*

Initially, I had little idea what these strange words and rhythms meant. There are passages of Shakespeare that I still find difficult. But complexity is part of the appeal. And the rewards, and cultural capital gain, of studying Shakespeare are immense. So next time you think that the boys in your class won't be able to grasp certain molecular formulae, cope with complex global ecosystems, or manage with you speaking in a foreign language for the majority of a lesson, it might be time to think again. A much overlooked, but very important point is that the negative impact of the search for a relevant boy-friendly curriculum doesn't just further disadvantage many working class boys; it also has an adverse effect on the working class girls who may well have had fewer opportunities to accrue cultural capital. The engagement through relevancy strategy does these girls no favours either.

F. It encourages low expectations of boys

As we shall see in Chapter 5, low expectations of boys contribute to their lower educational outcomes. Boy-friendly schemes of learning often lack high expectations of what boys can achieve; *disadvantaged pupils need more challenge not less*. Someone had decided that my English group couldn't cope with Shakespeare. When Shakespeare became a mandatory part of the GCSE syllabus, other teachers also decided that Shakespeare was too difficult for "lower ability" pupils.

Instead, these bottom set (often "boy-heavy") groups were fed a diet of comic book Shakespeare, or modern language bastardisations of the Bard's language. By giving boys work that reflects only their lives, we are saying to boys *you're a boy, this is all you can cope with, this is all you need to know about*. Watered-down curricula ensure that boys switch off after the initial sugar rush of relevancy has subsided.

G. It promotes the dominant anti-school masculinity

Boys love weapons, right? So naturally, when they're studying Shakespeare, they'd rather get involved in a spot of sword fighting than sit down and get to grips with the language. What message does this kind of generalisation send out to the boys who would rather read the text than clang about with armour and shields? *Romeo and Juliet* allows the opportunity to talk to boys – especially boys who have been brought up to avoid showing emotions other than anger – about the feelings of the eponymous love-struck male. Why does Romeo believe that falling in love with Juliet has stripped him of his masculine dignity ("O sweet Juliet, Thy beauty hath made me effeminate")? By concentrating on the fight scenes, you are asking boys to concentrate on one obvious, traditionally masculine, aspect of the play. Doing so narrows boys' access to wider and deeper emotions.

On a deeper level, boy-friendly approaches also risk nudging the teacher (willingly or otherwise) into promoting traditional forms of masculinity in an attempt to further ingratiate themselves with reluctant or disengaged boys. Jeffrey Smith[13] explains how teachers in the challenging secondary school where he conducted his research adopted:

> ...survivalist strategies grounded in [a] kind of 'muscular' working class masculinity...The clear objective was to 'win over' disaffected boys by emphasizing similarity and downplaying difference in their classroom practices, positioning themselves as 'one of the boys'.

Acting in a matey manner to try and keep difficult pupils on side is an age old, ill-advised strategy. Yet what makes Smith's interviews so interesting is the fact that some of the teachers – one of whom admits he'll "try anything to grab their interest" – don't just seek popularity, they are willing to embrace a hyped-up version of masculinity to gain credibility with the "tough" boys.

In the past, I have taught *The Fight*, Norman Mailer's account of the Rumble in the Jungle, a famous boxing match between Muhammed Ali and George Foreman. Looking back now, I can see I did this for several reasons. First, I was playing the relevancy card, assuming that the boys would enjoy reading about boxing, a subject several of the louder ones spent time discussing. Second, it's very well written. With its lyrical language and geo-political backstory, it at least offered the opportunity for the accumulation of cultural capital. Third, and if I'm being honest, this was the main reason, it gave me the opportunity to display my "authentic" masculinity. As a young professional teaching a stereotypically feminine subject (the only male in the department no less), breaking up fights in the playground, corridors, and class-rooms gained me respect among the so-called alpha males. Especially the time that I managed to prevent one boy – unbeknown to me, an amateur cage fighter – from assaulting a female teacher. But the kudos came at an expense; I'd unwittingly re-inforced the stereotypical attitudes that so frustrated me during lessons. My own experience at school had been hyper-masculine. Over time, I'd escaped this milieu, but, as a poetry-loving young man, I'd reverted back to my default mode, rather than tackling head-on the overt machismo.

Smith is sympathetic to teachers in challenging schools who adopt this persona (or exaggerate their "natural" characteristics) in an attempt to engage. One female teacher is held in awe by the boys for her forthright, assertive style, which sees her celebrated as being tougher than the lads, someone not to be messed with. Yet, he ultimately labels these educators as "cultural accomplices", teachers who unwit-tingly create a detrimental, Darwinian atmosphere where the toughest are briefly engaged but don't perform in the long run.

Engagement myth 3: boys have different learning styles

When I started teaching, I was given a lesson plan template to use. One box threw me. It was labelled "VAK". "What the hell is VAK?" I asked my mentor. "Visual, Auditory and Kinaesthetic learners," she told me. Ah, that rang a bell now. I re-member it being mentioned during my PGCE. One of the sessions had explained how we all have a preferred way of learning, depending on which of the three senses (seeing, hearing, or touching/moving about) and that we should tailor our lessons to ensure they catered for these preferences. This sounded dubious, but someone had obviously done a lot of research into this, so I carried on diligently filling in the boxes and planning activities to meet my pupils' predilections. V was no problem: I'd prepopulate the section with "PowerPoint slides or film clip" and delete as appropriate. A was a doddle too: I'd just write "reading aloud", which I did most lessons. K was tricky though. I spent ages shoehorning activities into my lessons to allow kinaesthetic pupils to roam about, usually sticking post-it notes on the board. As an English teacher, I couldn't make the link between allowing pupils opportunities for tactile exploration and being good at say analysing poetry, but I dutifully did what I'd been taught. I brought in a sack of spuds and allowed pupils to grope the muddy tubers in preparation for teaching Seamus Heaney's "At a Potato Digging". The kids were bemused by these odd interludes yet enjoyed the opportunity to stretch their legs or poke their mates in the ribs.

Just one slight problem

My reasons for doing this were threefold. First, my observers expected to see it in each lesson. Second, everybody else was doing it. And third, most impor-tantly, boys were far more likely to be kinaesthetic learners than girls. If you

Google something like "boys are usually kinaesthetic learners", you'll be directed to stuff like:

- Touch to learn – boys learn best when instruction involves hands-on activities[14]

- Many boys have a difficult time sitting still to hear the teacher's story, as they are movement-driven in their learning process[15]

- You will have lots of kinaesthetic learners in your classroom … a lot of these will be boys, and guess what? Boys are often the most reluctant learners. Kinaesthetic learners need to use their bodies and move around to help them learn.[16]

So far so good. There was just one slight problem. The learning styles theory is nonsense. As Daniel Willingham[17] notes,

> Dozens of studies have been conducted along these general lines, including studies using materials more like those used in classrooms, and overall the theory is not supported. Matching the "preferred" modality of a student doesn't give that student any edge in learning.

Willingham is probably the most renowned chronicler of the debunking of VAK, but others were also quick to point out concerns about this idea, as far back as 2005 (just before I began my PGCE). In a report for the Department for Education, which looked at trends from schools where boys did well, Younger et al. noted that

> We have found little evidence, for example, to support the notion that the dominant learning style of boys differs from those of girls, and that more boys (than girls) favour kinaesthetic learning.[18]

In fact, when they dug deeper into the data, they found that

> contrary to assertions in some of the literature, the mean scores suggested that, if anything, there was more of a kinaesthetic tendency amongst the girls than the boys.[19]

Discredited but still believed

Nonetheless, more than a decade later, the perception that boys need to experience movement and touch to learn effectively persists and is showing little sign of slinking away quietly to the corner in disgrace. Recently, world-leading experts from the fields of cognitive science, education and psychology wrote to *The Guardian*, warning of the dangers of this widely-discredited but still widely-believed myth:

> research in 2012 among teachers in the UK and Netherlands found that 80% believed individuals learned better when they received information in their preferred learning style. In 2013, research by the Wellcome Trust found that 76% of teachers had used learning styles in their teaching.[20]

Examples of VAK (and other neuromyths such as the learning pyramid) being taught to trainee teachers during their PGCE courses are regularly shared on Twitter, most frequently picked up by Tom Bennett of ResearchEd. The University of Bath's English PGCE page still lists a learning styles module,[21] as does Newman University, Birmingham's School Direct page.[22] Schools are just as guilty. Recently, I sat through a CPD session where a booklet was handed out recommending VAK. I complained and it got yanked, but the damage is still being done in our schools. Boys continue to wander and fondle for no good reason.

The solutions

Advice for school leaders

There are no quick fixes. The idea that making lessons entertaining or tailored to pupil interests will increase focus and improve outcomes is a widespread fallacy. One that is not just attached to strategies about closing gender gaps. Many school leaders still expect to see certain things happening during lesson observations, learning walks, and the like. By obsessing over nebulous concepts like engagement, progress, and pace during lesson observation feedback, leaders often send out dangerous messages to their teachers.

Professor Rob Coe of Durham University has argued that engagement – pupils appearing interested and motivated – is a poor proxy for learning. As is pupils being busy and doing lots of work. This, Coe contends, is because learning is invisible. It's not enough for an observer to say these boys are interested in their work and are completing tasks; therefore, they must be learning stuff that they'll remember over the medium and long term. In their review of research into great teaching, Coe et al.[23] point out the ineffectiveness of "ensuring learners are always active, rather than listening passively".

So what should observers be looking for when trying to assess whether boys are receiving effective teaching? Rosenshine's Principles of Instruction,[24] a summary of four decades of research that links teacher strategies to student outcomes, is a very good place to start. Key behaviours include:

- Beginning the lesson with a brief review of previous learning

- Providing models and examples, with scaffolds

- Including opportunities for guided student practice

- Checking for understanding, using lots of questions

- Ensuring that students obtain a high success rate (approximately 80%).

For many leaders, this will involve changing their expectations of what a good lesson looks like: not expecting the teacher to rely on a creative hook as a starter, not expecting the teacher to explain difficult concepts in only a few minutes, not expecting the teacher to dedicate a certain percentage of lessons to group work or student-led discussion, not expecting the teacher to allow pupils to move around the classroom, not expecting the teacher to prove that progress is being made or that pupils are actively "engaged" in the learning.

One final thing: please stop telling teachers that upping the pace or entertainment factor will improve behaviour in their lessons. Yes, of course torturously drawn-out activities, which could have been completed in a couple of minutes, or badly-worded questions and incompetent explanations, may contribute to pupils becoming bored or distracted. If that's the case, provide feedback on planning, questioning, and delivery of instruction. But advising a nervy NQT that jazzing up their lessons will pull the kids into line does untold harm to their development.

Advice for classroom teachers

Now you might well be thinking *wait a minute. Earlier on in this chapter, you told us your results were really good using your engagement strategies. And with boys who were often hard to teach, due to their challenging circumstances. How was that the case if the strategies you were using were garbage?*

After the original crushing devastation of realising I'd swallowed a load of bunkum for years, I realised something that left me feeling liberated. Joyous even. The answer was obvious. My pupils had done really well *despite* these strategies. Which meant that my other teaching approaches must have *really* worked.

So what should you do to teach boys well?

There is a simple answer to this question. Teach boys in exactly the same way that you teach girls. High challenge. High expectations. No gimmicks. No shortcuts.

Take competition for example.

There's a large amount of evidence[25] to show that one of the best ways of ensuring pupils retain knowledge is through practice testing, in the form of multiple choice questions, practice answers and other forms of quick retrieval quizzes. Significantly, these tests are most effective when they are of a "low stakes" nature. In other words, in this stress-free scenario, it is made clear that students aren't being judged on their performance: there is no teacher's mark sheet, no sanctions for poor performance, no grade attached to the outcome. There are many reasons why pupils memorise information more effectively under these circumstances, but I would contend that the absence of a competitive element plays an important role. Consider the impact of the following:

- Asking pupils to mark each other's tests

- Asking pupils to read out their score out of ten from a test in front of the rest of the class

■ Passing comment on their score as they do so

■ The teacher reading out, or displaying on the board, the test scores of the class, especially in a hierarchical order

■ Highlighting weaknesses of specific pupils

■ Making pupils retake tests for poor performance (as opposed to poor effort).

Now, of course, pupils must take "high stakes" tests (end of unit assessments, mock exams, actual exams) at some point. This is not an argument against that. Yet, intentionally or inadvertently placing a competitive slant onto activities that might otherwise focus on the areas for individual improvement is very likely to further discourage those that are most in need of judgement-free feedback on their performance.

The final word

Hopefully, this chapter has enabled you to understand that hoodwinking boys into learning – through competitive tasks, making activities relevant to their interests and experiences, and believing they will only work for you if you allow them the chance to pinball their way around the classroom – only works for a very short time. If you really want to enthuse your pupils, show them:

■ How much you know about the topics you are teaching them

■ How much enjoyment you get from reading widely to enable you to learn more about the topics you teach

■ How excited you get when they produce excellent work or make impressive contributions or remember a complex bit of knowledge or master a tricky skill.

And that should do the trick.

Notes

1 A formulaic analytical paragraph structure – Point, Evidence, Analysis – used by English and humanities teachers.
2 Newly Qualified Teacher – in the UK, a category of teacher who has completed their initial teacher training and is now undertaking a one-year induction programme while working in a school.
3 Reichart, M. & Hawley, R. (2010) *Reaching Boys Teaching Boys: Strategies That Work – And Why*, San Francisco, CA: Jossey-Bass.
4 Continuing Professional Development.
5 For example in Covington, M.V. (1998) *The Will to Learn: A Guide for Motivating Young People*, Cambridge: Cambridge University Press.
6 Such as Thompson, T. (1999) *Underachieving to Protect Self-Worth*, Aldershot: Ashgate.
7 Jackson, C. (2002) '"Laddishness" as self-worth protection strategy', *Gender and Education*, 14:1, pp. 37–50.

8 See Askew, S. & Ross, C. (1990) *Boys Don't Cry: Boys and Sexism in Education*, Milton Keynes: Open University Press, and Galloway, D., & Rogers, C.G. (1998) *Motivating the Difficult to Teach*, London: Longman.

9 This point might prompt you to ask: if this is the case, should we teach boys and girls separately then? As you'll see in Chapter 7, the apparent advantages of single sex schooling aren't quite what they seem.

10 Willingham, D.T. (2009) *Why Don't Students Like School?* San Francisco, CA: Jossey Bass, pp. 8–9.

11 Francis, B. (2006) 'Heroes or zeroes? The discursive positioning of "underachieving boys" in English neo-liberal education', *Journal of Educational Policy*, 21:2, pp. 187–200.

12 Mills, M. & Keddie, A. (2007) 'Teaching boys and gender justice', *International Journal of Inclusive Education*, 11:3, pp. 335–354.

13 Smith, J. (2007) '"Ye've got to 'ave balls to play this game sir!" Boys, peers and fears: the negative influence of school-based "cultural accomplices" in constructing hegemonic masculinities', *Gender and Education*, 19:2, pp. 179–198.

14 International Boys' Schools Coalition (2008), *Teaching the Male Brain*. Paper presented at the conference workshop by Abigail Norfleet James Ph.D. Available at: www. theibsc.org/uploaded/IBSC/Conference_and_workshops/Toronto_Workshops/James_ TeachingTheMaleBrain-handout.pdf (Accessed: 19th October 2017).

15 Gurian, M. (2006) *The Wonder of Boys*, New York: Tarcher-Putnam.

16 Toward, G., Henley, C., & Cope A. (2012) *The Art of Being a Brilliant Teacher*, Carmarthen: Crown House Publishing.

17 Willingham, D.T. (2009), p. 120.

18 Younger M., Warrington M. Gray J., Rudduck J., McLellan R., Bearne E., Kershner R., & Bricheno P. (2005) *Raising boys' achievement*. DfES. Available at: http://dera.ioe. ac.uk/5400/1/RR636.pdf (Accessed: 27th September 2018).

19 Ibid.

20 Weale, S. (2017) 'Teachers must ditch "neuromyth" of learning styles, say scientists', *The Guardian*, 13th March. Available at: www.theguardian.com/education/2017/mar/13/ teachers-neuromyth-learning-styles-scientists-neuroscience-education (Accessed: 10th November 2017).

21 University of Bath (2013) *Week 6*. Available at: https://wiki.bath.ac.uk/display/sdenglish/ Week+6 (Accessed: 27th September 2018).

22 Newman University, Birmingham website. *Primary and secondary programmes.* Available at: www.newman.ac.uk/school-direct-qts/3990/primary-programme (Accessed 11th November 2017).

23 Coe, R., Aloisi, C., Higgins, S., & Elliot Major, L. (2014) *What makes great teaching? Review of the underpinning research*, Sutton Trust. Available at: www.suttontrust.com/ wp-content/uploads/2014/10/What-Makes-Great-Teaching-REPORT.pdf (Accessed 30th November 2017).

24 Rosenshine, B. (Spring 2012) 'Principles of instruction: Research based principles that all teachers should know', *American Educator*, 36:1, pp. 12–39.

25 See Dunlosky J., Rawson K.A., Marsh, E.J., Nathan, M.J., & Willingham D.T. (2013) 'Improving students' learning with effective learning techniques: Promising directions from cognitive and educational psychology', *Psychological Science in the Public Interest*, 14:1, pp. 4–58.

2 Disadvantaged students

Matt Pinkett

The story

I think boys do worse than girls because they're different. We don't listen enough. I get distracted by other people. Some people can actually distract you when you're trying to do something. Like naughty kids. Some of them want to like, get you involved in something. Also, I don't feel comfortable in lessons because they have stuff I don't know about. So my behaviour drops because I don't like getting stuff wrong. I feel like I've failed. So I get wound up.

Because of my background, I know it's easier to get into trouble. But, I shouldn't use that as an excuse and I should try. Give it a go.

Reading doesn't come to my head, you know what I mean? If I go home and like, I wouldn't not one bit think about reading. I wouldn't like just sit down and read a book cos I'm just not the type of person that'd read.

I don't really know the difference between university and college. I dunno whether I'd go. I don't think anyone in my family has ever gone so it'd be weird for me to go...But, it'd be well good to be the first...I got told you don't have to go to university to do what I want to do–become a plasterer, like my Dad. But my Dad always says, 'Why would you want to do plastering when you could do a better job?' Like a lawyer or something like that. Where you get better money.

Because I know I'm getting nearer to my GCSEs, I know I need to put my head down otherwise it's going to be too late. I should've put head down at the start though.

Extracts taken from an interview with a 16-year-old boy

The research

Our education system is centred on middle class values. Every time a teacher asks a child to write about a time they've been on holiday; every time a teacher comments scornfully on the junk food diets of the pupils for whom this isn't "junk food", but affordable food; every time a teacher mocks a student's use of non-standard English in the classroom; every time a teacher tells a class of kids that £3 for a revision guide is a bargain price; every time a teacher assumes that the parents who don't turn up to parents' evening are lazy and apathetic, rather than considering the possibility that they might be working a second job or putting children to bed in a house with not enough beds: the middle class structure of our education system lies like a luxury duck feather duvet over our schools, cosily warm for those teachers and students who've grown up used to its touch, but stifling and oppressive for those unaccustomed to it.

In 2017, disadvantaged students were 20% less likely than non-disadvantaged students to reach the expected standard in reading, writing and mathematics at Key Stage 2 (KS2).[1] They were also 27% less likely than non-disadvantaged students to achieve a grade 4 in GCSE English or Maths.[2] Much of the mainstream discourse on the topic of working class underachievement seems to take "working class" students to mean *"white*, working class, *and male"* students. This is most probably prompted by the statistics which show that white working class boys do indeed perform worse than any other ethnic group (Graph 2.1).

However, as we can see from the chart below, it is working class boys *and* girls from myriad ethnic backgrounds that are under-performing. Because of this, in the chapter that follows, whilst I will refer specifically to boys where necessary, the suggestions offered here can and should be used in efforts to raise the attainment of all disadvantaged students, regardless of ethnicity and gender.

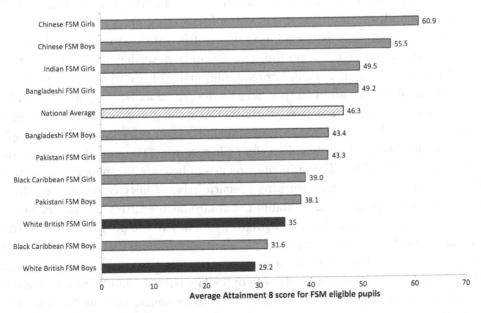

Graph 2.1 Average attainment eight score for FSM eligible pupils from selected minor ethnic groups, by gender.

Free school meals (FSM) and pupil premium (PP)

When teachers, school leaders, and policy makers in the UK refer to "working class", "underprivileged", or "disadvantaged" children, they generally mean those children in receipt of either FSM or the PP. Students receive FSM if their parents receive any one or more of the following:

- Income Support

- Income-based Jobseeker's Allowance

- Income-related Employment and Support Allowance

- Support under Part VI of the Immigration and Asylum Act 1999

- Child Tax Credit (provided you're not also entitled to Working Tax Credit and have an annual gross income of no more than £16,190)[3]

The PP fund is awarded to schools on a per pupil basis and is awarded for all students who have been eligible for FSM in the past six years. Schools will receive £1320 for every primary child on FSM and £935 for all secondary age children on FSM.[4]

The definition of "disadvantaged"

Although much of what's written about social class and underprivileged children and families uses the term "working class", in this chapter, I will use the term, "disadvantaged".[5] This is for two reasons: first, in educational settings, this is the term currently favoured when referring to children in receipt of PP funding. Second, the traditional definition of working class – used to refer to those people belonging to households where the chief earner is employed in industrial or manual work – no longer accurately describes those at the lower end of the socioeconomic scale. For example, many of my friends, who are employed in manual jobs and can therefore be described as working class, earn far more than I do, own more houses than I do (i.e. one), and go on multiple foreign holidays. When I use the term "disadvantaged", I am referring to those people who Michael Savage describes, in *Social Class in the 21st Century*, as belonging to the "precariat" class. Those in the precariat class are the poorest in society. They "are people living and working precariously, usually in a series of short-term jobs, without recourse to stable occupational identities or careers, social protection, or relevant protective regulation".[6] They're the people who live from one pay packet – or income support payment – to the next and for who failure to receive this pay packet or income support payment, would result in disaster. The precariat's life is driven by other peoples' decisions: a landlord's decision to raise the rent, an employers' decision to offer fewer hours, a teacher's decision to see a disadvantaged student as nothing more than the PP label on their annotated seating plan.

Teachers, schools, and class

Before I go on to discuss teachers' attitudes towards the socio-economic status of their pupils, it is first necessary to consider where teachers place themselves in the class structure, because this in itself is telling of the extent to which middle-classness pervades the profession: in a recent Twitter poll by TeacherTapp,[7] 71% of teachers identified themselves as middle class. This means that the majority of teachers will have very little shared formative experience and understanding of what it's like to be a disadvantaged child in early 21st-century Britain.

It's no surprise that teachers exemplify these middle class values when we consider that they themselves are products of an education system that is inherently class-biased and always has been. Despite what policy makers would have us believe, the new educational landscape of academies and free schools neglects disadvantaged pupils no less than the old tripartite system that left so many disadvantaged children languishing in secondary moderns, without hope of ever experiencing an education of the quality provided by the grammar schools that catered for the middle classes. As Diane Reay notes in her exceptional book, *Miseducation*, "academies are more selective than state comprehensive schools"[8] and "within the academy sector, considerably more secondary schools have low levels of FSM students than have medium and high levels".[9] Reay also draws attention to a report by the Academies Commission that reported "academy schools were found to be flouting admission rules by selecting pupils from more privileged families".[10] This is particularly concerning when we consider the rapid growth of academies. As of 2010, there were just 203 academies in the country. By 2016, this number had grown to 5,302, and as of May 2018, there were 7,317 academies in the UK, with academies accounting for 65% of the state-funded secondary schools.[11] The consequences of academisation for the disadvantaged are significant. Academies receive greater funding, per pupil, than state comprehensives,[12] despite the fact that they have lower levels of FSM pupils than state-maintained schools. Clearly, there is a redistribution of funding that takes money from those most in need of it and gives it to those least in need. Not so much a Robin Hood effect, but a Sheriff of Nottingham effect, if you will. What's also concerning is that even in the state sector, schools with less disadvantaged pupils have better funding: In 2015/2016, 84% of local authorities in the least deprived areas saw an increase in funding. This is in marked contrast with local authorities in the most deprived areas in which only 13% received a financial boost.[13]

Unwanted children – the language of education reports

This class bias doesn't just manifest itself in the structure of the school system; it filters down into the very language that shapes educational policy and practice. In her investigation[14] into the middle class bias of educational literature, Karen Grainger discusses the way the language of disadvantaged children has been "treated as a problem for education ever since mass education was introduced in the early part of the twentieth century".[15] One of the reports under Grainger's scrutiny is the "Getting in Early"[16] report, published by The Smith Institute and The Centre for Social Justice. The report seeks to advise schools how they should be "making the most of children's primary school years and intervening where necessary to help all children fulfil their potential".[17] The report, which aims to help schools improve students' ability to communicate, offers some interesting explanations as to why some students may be lacking in their ability to communicate effectively. As Grainger notes, the report states:

> Parents in deprived conditions...may feel alienated from a child they did not want, be depressed by their circumstances or not functioning socially and emotionally because of drugs or alcohol.[18]

As if these ludicrous and shameful generalisations weren't enough, Grainger then points out that the report states "somewhat paradoxically, these emotionally switched-off parents are then thought to be *more* emotional when it comes to discipline".[19] She cites the following example:

> Parents from more disadvantaged backgrounds are particularly unlikely to be able to help their children manage their feelings calm, positive rational ways. They are likely to use punitive, inconsistent and aggressive approaches to discipline, based on shouting, slapping, and even violence.[20]

Perhaps it's easier to realise how shocking this assertion is, if we consider an alternative version:

> Parents from *middle class backgrounds* are particularly unlikely to be able to help their children manage their feelings calm, positive rational ways. They are likely to use punitive, inconsistent and aggressive approaches to discipline, based on shouting, slapping, and even violence.

Publish that in your school newsletter and see what happens.

Teachers: they're only humans after all

We have to be concerned about the very real possibility that the academic and moral deficit model of the disadvantaged presented in reports such as "Getting in Early", is diffusing downwards into the beliefs and attitudes of the policy influencers, school leaders, and teachers that read them. *Surely, no adult, charged with the job of educating the children of the future could actually be biased against disadvantaged children!* I hear you cry. I've got some bad news for you. In 2015, Tammy Campbell, at UCL Institute of Education, published research into the way stereotyping impacts teachers' assessment of pupils' academic ability.[21] The report examined data from almost 5,000 pupils and found that when teachers were asked to make judgements on how students would perform in reading and maths, "Children from low-income families ... appear less likely to be judged 'above average' at reading by their teacher".[22] Also, in maths, "low income pupils are more likely [to be judged as below average] than higher-income pupils". This is despite the fact that pupils from low-income and higher-income backgrounds had scored equivalently in tests. Campbell is keen to stress that the results from the study shouldn't be read as a condemnation of teachers: it is simply the case that "all individuals have a propensity to enact this function [of stereotyping] to some degree: there is no reason that teachers should be exempt, nor unusually prone".[23] In acknowledging teachers' tendency to stereotype, we acknowledge the fact that they are human. Fallible, but human.

To sum up...

■ Students from disadvantaged backgrounds do less well than students from non-disadvantaged backgrounds in SATs and GCSEs

■ The new academy school landscape favours schools with lower proportions of disadvantaged pupils

■ Educational reports can position disadvantaged students as academically and morally deficient

■ Many Teachers stereotype negatively against students from disadvantaged backgrounds

The solutions

Advice for School Leaders and Teachers

There are endless so-called solutions to the problem of disadvantaged underachievement in our education system, and largely they are snake oil remedies offering a quick win. Putting the books of PP children to the top of your marking pile won't solve the problem; withdrawing PP children from mainstream lessons for last minute interventions won't solve the problem; buying a few extra revision guides for PP children won't solve the problem. They won't solve the problem because largely these quick wins focus on what disadvantaged children do, rather than what the teachers of disadvantaged children do. It's *us* we need to focus on. In the rest of this chapter, I'll explore three key areas which schools and teachers can address in an effort to close the disadvantage gap: I'll explain why setting students by ability can impact negatively on disadvantaged children. Then, I'll explain why schools need to foster positive relationships with disadvantaged families in order to ensure the academic success of disadvantaged pupils. Finally, I'll argue for a fundamental shift in the way teachers view disadvantaged pupils and their success.

Rethinking setting

Last year, I was at a garden party when a teacher told me of her joy that in the previous year, a boy achieved a grade 8 in his English Language GCSE. But, in just a split second, my pleasure turned to perturbation, as the teacher followed up her initial pronouncement with, *And he was in* set 6! *Can you believe that?* There was genuine disbelief from this teacher that a boy in the "bottom set" could ever have achieved the grade he did. After all, he was in bottom set and bottom set kids don't get "top set" grades. Worryingly, the teacher could sense nothing wrong in her implicit lack of faith in what this boy could achieve with hard work and effort. She wasn't a bad person; she was just so accustomed to an education system in which students are systematically (and often, *un*systematically) segregated into separate classes based on ability, as determined by prior attainment, and in which the kids in the top sets thrive and achieve, whilst those in the bottom sets often languish into inevitable failure.

In the UK, children tend to be divided into separate classes for different subjects based on either attainment in previous tests relating to those subjects, or, in the absence of such tests, their performance in tests *unrelated* to those subjects. So, a student may be put into top set geography after scoring the highest mark in a baseline geography test taken at the start of the year. Just as likely though, a student may be placed in top set geography based on the fact that he is excellent at reading, writing, and maths, but in spite of the fact that he can't tell an ox-bow Lake from an Oxo cube.

According to a recent TeacherTapp analysis of survey data,

> At Key Stage 1, around 60% of schools tend to group pupils by ability on their tables. By Key Stage 2 this changes slightly and around half of teachers have mixed ability groupings, and around half sit them with people who are alike (either on their tables, or by mixing with other classes/years).[24]

Welcome to the bottom sets

At secondary school, 96% of teachers said that their school uses setting in at least one subject area.[25] These figures are pertinent to the issue of disadvantaged students' underachievement because recent research conducted by Becky Francis (unpublished at time of writing) has found that disadvantaged students are more likely to be in bottom sets. Francis has stated, "we find disproportionate amounts of kids from low socio-economic backgrounds in low sets and streams".[26] Other research backs this up. Dunne et al. found that "social class is a significant predictor of set placement. Pupils from higher socio-economic status backgrounds are more likely to be assigned to higher sets and less likely to be assigned to lower sets".[27] Another study, conducted by Susan Hallam and Samantha Parsons revealed that being a boy, summer born, disadvantaged, or from a single parent family led to a far greater likelihood of being placed in a bottom set at school.[28]

The students from disadvantaged backgrounds hurled into bottom sets are at a double disadvantage: it is well documented that kids in lower sets make slower overall progress than those in higher sets.[29] This is likely explained by two things: first, a self-fulfilling prophecy of failure[30] linked to the knowledge that a group of adults they trust their futures with have decided they're not worthy of anything other than bottom set. Second, the best teachers generally get assigned to the top sets, leaving those in the bottom sets to be taught by teachers with less expertise and less experience. Therefore, the students most in need of the best teachers aren't given them and aren't given the optimal conditions needed to be able to prove wrong, those that have let them down.

So why do we do it?

The enthusiasm for setting is founded upon three main premises. The table below outlines these premises and explains why they're flawed:

Premise	Rationale	Flaw
Setting is easier for teachers	It's a lot easier to meet the individual needs of students in a class full of "grade 8 kids" where kids will generally only struggle with the same types of activities or concepts, than it is to teach a class where the targets students have been tarnished with range from numbers 1–8. This would require differentiation on a grand scale and endless hours slaving away at the photocopier ensuring all kids have a worksheet designed to match their widely differing abilities.	This premise ignores the fact that teaching the disillusioned bottom groups is far from easy. Also, in most schools, pupils within the top set will be working at different levels and will therefore require a certain amount of differentiation. In a top set consisting of grade 7 hopefuls alongside grade 9 certainties, even the grade 9 pupils will be of varying levels of prior attainment. Some will get full marks for the entire GCSE, while others will just scrape their way over the grade 9 grade boundary.
Parents expect setting	Parents know that their child is getting a bespoke educational service that benefits their individual needs. Parents of children in top sets feel that their child is on a fast track to academic success	This is a bad reason for doing anything. Parents wanting to be able to say their 15-year-old son is in the top set for maths, or their 6-year-old daughter sits on the Elephants table, is not a good enough rationale for curriculum plans.
Setting enables teachers to stretch the highest ability students	A teacher teaching a top set can meet the needs of those students' higher intellectual capabilities by presenting them with more difficult material to stretch their understanding of a particular topic without the distraction of having to deal with trifling needs of less able children.	All pupils should be stretched, not just those that have done well in tests aged 11 who have subsequently been placed in higher streams that "pathway" them for the highest grades.[31]

There are other problems with setting that must be acknowledged:

A. Setting doesn't work for the majority of students

For the majority of students, setting actually hinders progress. As the Education Endowment Foundation tells us, "Overall, setting or streaming appears to benefit higher attaining pupils and be detrimental to the learning of mid-range and lower attaining learners".[32] In fact,

> Low attaining learners who are set or streamed fall behind by 1 or 2 months per year, on average, when compared with the progress of similar students in classes with mixed ability groups. It appears likely that routine setting or streaming arrangements undermine low attainers' confidence and discourage the belief that attainment can be improved through effort. Research also suggests that ability grouping can have a longer term negative effect on the attitudes and engagement of low attaining pupils. [33]

But what about the high attainers that setting does benefit? Well, the EEF estimates that students in top sets make one to two months extra progress per year. I don't know about you, but one to two months progress over a whole year doesn't seem to be worth the damage it does to everybody else. Not when great teachers, who have been well trained, will find ways to ensure that all students exceed, regardless of perceived ability.

B. Setting students by prior attainment is problematic

Although it's the most popular method of set allocation, setting by prior attainment isn't without its problems. Performance in an exam is not a reliable reflection of a person's ability in any given subject. For example, a student with excellent writing skills might fail their KS2 SATs writing exam because they're upset that their goldfish died that morning, or because they had a headache during the exam, or simply because they didn't know the 50 answers to the 50 questions in that one exam on that one morning. As a result of this failure, this child may be assigned to a bottom set history class at secondary when in fact they have an excellent grasp of battles, beheadings, and bubonic plagues.

C. Often, set allocation is determined by unfair factors

Is it fair that a student is placed in the bottom set simply because there's only space for 30 chairs in the set above? Is it fair that a student is bumped down a set because a lower prior attainer has a parent on the PTA with a big mouth and a bigger wallet? Is it fair that a student is placed in a lower set, simply because they've fallen out with three girls in the top set? Of course it's not fair. Although I've explained the shortcomings of setting by prior attainment, setting in that way looks positively flawless when we consider the way some students are allocated to different ability sets: the school's timetabling system, staff preconceptions, "social issues", and parental influence are all factors that can unfairly determine the set in which a child is placed.

D. Setting is morally wrong

As Diane Reay points out, students put into bottom sets feel an immediate sense of failure and inferiority as a result of being placed there. Reay provides a number of quotations from children which show that "low sets are clearly perceived to be places of educational failure and despair" (for more detail on pupil perception of setting, see Chapter 5), but none is more heartbreaking than this from a six-year-old in a London primary school:

> They [the Lions] think they are better than us. They think they are good at every single thing and the second group, Tigers there are some people that think they are good and more important than us. And one of the boys in Giraffes he was horrible to me and he said "get lost slow tortoise" but my group are monkeys and we are only second to bottom.[34]

At only six years old, this child already has an acute sense of their own lowly place in the setting hierarchy. The set a child is placed in is rarely forgotten. I bet you can remember the sets you were in at school and if you can't, you probably weren't in bottom set. Still, there are head teachers giving assemblies in which they bang on about "Growth Mindset" and "Carol Dweck" and "the power of yet" who then watch glaringly as these students file out of the assembly hall into bottom sets that destroy their self-esteem.

So what can we do about the problem of setting?

Becky Francis and her team have recently published a guide to good setting practice based on her research. Ideally, schools should move away from setting and adopt a mixed-ability system. Schools that take this approach should do the following:

Mixed-Ability Classes: Good Practice[35]

Practice differentiation. Ensure that you treat each student as individual with their own individual wants and needs. Feedback should be addressed to students' individual needs.
Change in-class groupings regularly. Have a flexible seating plan and give students the opportunity to be exposed to the ideas of a wide range of other pupils.
Have high expectations of all students in the class. Abandon extension tasks and aim high for all students. Every student should be aiming for the same outcomes, which should be challenging. The only thing that changes is the level of help each individual will need to "get it".
Don't over-rely on high attainers explaining to others. Stretch lower attainers by asking them to explain challenging concepts. All students, regardless of level of prior attainment, should be given the opportunity to formulate ideas and consolidate understanding by explaining to others.
Don't establish fixed within-class "ability" groups. Don't have a table that is clearly full of the highest attainers, and others especially for middle and lower attainers. Students know full well the difference between those on the "Lion" table and those on the "Mole rat" table.

Of course, there'll be people reading this now who simply won't be able to get their headteachers to budge on the issue of setting. But never fear! Francis and her team have also provided advice as to how setting should be done, if it must be done:

Setting: Good Practice[36]

Make setting as subject-specific as possible. Geography sets should be allocated based on the results of a baseline *geography* test, not English and Maths grades from KS2.

Group students by attainment only. The only thing that should count towards a child's set allocation is their prior attainment. Not friendship groups, not behaviour, not what their parent thinks is right – just attainment.

Retest regularly and move students between groups. A student placed in a bottom set should not be written off. Teachers should be aware that even students in bottom set are capable of improving, and if they do so, they should be moved to a set that reflects their most recent attainment.

Make sure all students have access to a rich curriculum. All students, whatever their prior attainment, deserve to be taught an enriching and fulfilling curriculum. If top set year 9s are getting quantum physics, bottom set year 9 get quantum physics.

Do apply high expectations to all sets. Every single student, whatever their ability, should be aiming for the highest possible grade.

Don't assign subject expert teachers to top sets. Your bottom sets are made up of kids who understand less than those in the higher sets. It is they who deserve the best teachers.

Don't give less homework to low sets. Give them more. They need it more.

Rethinking disadvantaged parents

Many teachers who work in areas of high deprivation will be familiar with low attendance at parents' evening. When disadvantaged parents do turn up, they're often looked down upon: one teacher told me of her absolute disgust at the fact that a parent from a disadvantaged background sat through a parents' evening appointment twiddling an unlit cigarette in her fingers, as she discussed the educational failings of her firstborn. I can't help but feel that instead of disdain, sympathy and support would have been better. This woman was likely terrified of being in an environment in which she didn't feel comfortable. This isn't unusual. Diane Reay writes that "working class families do not have the same degree of confidence and sense of entitlement that the middle class possess in their interactions with schooling".[37] She goes on to quote Josie, a disadvantaged mother who experiences considerable distress in and about the dealings with her son's school:

> I always found if I went to the class teacher, she'd take it very personal and think I was attacking her. I wasn't. I was just bringing it to her attention in case she didn't know, you know, that in my opinion he's not progressing…I think they took it too personal and felt I was attacking them when really it was so important that I couldn't let it go.[38]

The defensive, angst-ridden, panicked tone of Josie's words reflects an insecurity with education that prevents many disadvantaged parents from going into schools, let alone getting from schools what they know their children deserve. It's worth remembering this, the next time you hear a colleague tut and say, "I knew she wouldn't turn up", when a disadvantaged student's mother misses yet another appointment.

The myth of working class low aspiration

A 2010 white paper called *The Importance of Teaching* stated that "In far too many communities there is a deeply embedded culture of low aspiration that is strongly tied to long-term unemployment".[39] The idea that disadvantaged students and their families have low aspirations will be familiar to many of us. Many of us would have heard a colleague say, or even said ourselves, something along the lines of, *He won't succeed because he doesn't care and nor does anybody at home.* What's strange about the popularity of this narrative is that it's completely fallacious. Actually, disadvantaged kids care rather a bloody lot. A study by Baker et al. found that actually, "contrary to claims often made in public policy debates ... the vast majority of students, including those from highly disadvantaged backgrounds, hold high aspirations for pursuing further academic qualifications".[40] In fact, students from highly disadvantaged backgrounds were *more* likely to judge university to be important than their more privileged peers. Sadly, however, in spite of this, they were still less likely to say, than their more privileged peers, that they would actually attend university. This is either because they wrongly believe they're not capable academically, or because they rightly realise the financial, psychological, and social toll of being a disadvantaged student at university.

As Sonia Blandford notes, "we talk about single parents, or unemployed parents, or low incomes as if that in itself suggests bad parenting and it doesn't – these situations are circumstantial".[41] Blandford goes on to say that schools need to realise that "parents are the first and most enduring educators of their child" and that whilst many parents will face challenges, schools should be working with them for the benefit of their children, and them, rather than peering and occasionally sneering from above.

What can schools do to better engage parents of disadvantaged children?

A report by NFER[42] shows that greater parental engagement has a positive impact on the academic achievement of disadvantaged pupils. They make the following suggestions:

- Take the approach that no family, however hard to reach, is unreachable
- Consult and value the opinions of parents
- Offer universal parent services to reduce stigmatisation

- Provide better access to information about options available to disadvantaged families and provide opportunities to form new community relationships

- Allow for consolidation of learning gained in interventions through regular follow-up activities

- Help parents improve their own literacy, to increase the likelihood of them reading and developing their own children's literacy at home through tasks such as reading.

Abigail Hawkins, an education blogger with over 20 years' experience as a SEND Coordinator, explained to me how she worked to improve parental engagement at her highly deprived inner-city school:

> I spent my first three parents' evenings with no parents at all, despite sending out invitations. For some it was understandable, they had had poor educational experiences themselves, many had even attended local schools...for others they had had negative experiences with older siblings and just felt that the school was "out to get them" or "always bad news".
>
> One year, lucky enough to have several free periods in a row on a Friday morning, I decided to start running a coffee morning. I planned for one hour of "education" and an hour for informal chat, coffee, and bacon buttties. That first week I had 16 parents representing 11 students arrive and coffee morning was born. Some weeks we had families representing just my hard-core 8 who came every week, other weeks we were representing 25 students. It may not sound like a lot, but to go from zero engagement to anything was success!
>
> Each week had a theme which I tried to communicate in advance: one week we had a local company come in to talk about disability benefits and lots of parents came to that one. We had an educational psychologist come in. We did sessions on 'How to create an email account', 'What to expect in English', 'Who's who in school' and lots of sessions on different SEN areas including behaviour management and why schools use sanctions and rewards. The payback was engaged parents who began to attend parents' evenings, spoke about the school in a positive light, and didn't appear at unexpected times expecting me to sort things for them.

Abigail's coffee mornings had other benefits too:

> The parents not only engaged with the school and therefore their own children much better, but they also supported each other. One parent had to attend the hospital for an operation and the other parents rallied around to take her there and organise things for her son with ASD. Another was struggling to organise his benefits and a couple of parents helped him complete paperwork. One parent enrolled on a TA course at the local college as a result of the information and encouragement she was given. The best, for me, was a parent who had to see the paediatrician but struggled to understand what they were

being told. I would usually attend with parents if this was the case, but on this occasion I was unable to. One of the other parents volunteered and stepped in, doing a fantastic job of putting professional talk into layman's language.

Abigail's approach is a perfect example of how schools can foster positive relationships with disadvantaged families that are mutually beneficial. Abigail's school – and countless other schools up and down the country – achieve success with schemes such as these, because they realise that more often than not, disadvantaged families are doing the best that they can with the limited resources available to them. Perseverance – not prejudice – gets results.

Rethinking university

For many schools and teachers, their main aim is to ensure that their students get the grades needed to one day grant them access to university. This is a noble and understandable aim. Teachers, after all, are products of a university education. Of course they'd want their students to achieve the same financial security, job satisfaction and occasional bouts of happiness that come with having a degree-level job. However, as Michael Merrick, a teacher who has written extensively on the topic of class and education, explained to me, for many disadvantaged pupils, going to university isn't necessarily a desirable objective:

> We teach working class kids that in order to continue their education they have to stop being working class. They have to leave behind their families, they have to change the way they talk. They have to stop reading *The Sun* and they have to become middle class. There are plenty of children who would look at that deal and decide not to take it.

This is a sentiment echoed by Diane Reay in *Miseducation*:

> ...striving for success for a working class young person is about wanting something different, something more than your parents had, and that not only implies that there is something wrong with your parent's life but that there is something intrinsically wrong with them. And there is an emptiness to becoming somebody if your parents remain nobodies. What is the point of striving for equality with more-privileged others if the process creates inequalities between you and the people you love, and the communities you were born into?[43]

A complete dismantling of identity is not the only thing that disadvantaged students have to contend with at university: they will also leave university with £14,000 more debt than their wealthier peers,[44] and even when their degree classification is higher, they will be 17% less likely to secure a job than middle class graduates.[45] All of a sudden, university doesn't look like such an attractive prospect for disadvantaged pupils. As teachers, we must be mindful of this: we need to be aware that for some, university will be a difficult experience that may leave a lasting negative impact.

On the outside, looking in

Questioning the idea that university is the only desirable measure of success for disadvantaged pupils does not mean believing that disadvantaged pupils do not want to go to university. Nor does it mean they shouldn't be given every opportunity, and support, to help get them there. But, teachers and school leaders would do well to remember that the transference of knowledge from teacher to pupil is important, not because knowledge grants students access to university, but because knowledge grants students the skills needed to take part in what Ben Newmark, teacher and blogger, calls the "Great Conversation" – the opportunity to talk with others about things beyond the realms of their own experience.

In relentlessly focusing on exam success, and the later university attendance that comes as a result of this success, schools risk alienating the section of disadvantaged pupils for whom university isn't appealing. There's a risk that these disadvantaged pupils, with no desire to attend university, become passive participants of their own education, desperate to learn, but on the outside looking in, as the teacher at the front of the classroom or assembly hall expounds on the benefits of a university education that all should aim for. As Newmark explains, a sole focus on exam success is cruel because:

> It creates an impression that you only study Shakespeare or Hume because it gives you a concrete, almost financial, result. Our subjects are inherently interesting for what they teach you as a human being. Take *Frankenstein*. *Frankenstein* is about love and loss. And it's about how we run away from our mistakes. These are things that anybody can relate to whether they go to Oxford or Cambridge or choose, or have to, because of their life circumstances, to end up pushing trolleys around a supermarket car park.

Probably the worst time of my life

My own experience of University was dreadful. In a blog post from 2017, I explained that "in the three years I spent there I had a nervous breakdown, and ballooned from 14 to 17 stone (in just 8 weeks)". One of the factors behind my negative experience was that I didn't have the means to be part of the "Great Conversation":

> When I got to university, I had no idea what socialism was. Nor did I know what communism was. Or capitalism. I didn't know what right or left wing meant. I'd no idea who George Orwell was. I didn't understand a word of Latin, and Homer had all but passed me by...During seminars, I was frightened into silence as fellow students and professors talked to each other using

words I could not fathom and allusions I could not access. Everyone seemed to know what everyone else knew, and I remained thoroughly on the outside. My GCSEs and my A Levels didn't matter.

As defined in Chapter 1, there are certain items of knowledge that hold higher cultural capital than others, and these are generally those items of knowledge preserved for the privileged. High cultural capital is Beethoven, not Bieber; Dostoevsky, not Dahl; *Troilus and Cressida*, not *Tom and Jerry*. For a plethora of economical, geographical, and social reasons (but mainly economic), it is harder for disadvantaged young people to cultivate a love of German composers, Russian realists, and Shakespearean tragedies. Whilst I wouldn't go so far as to say that my university experience was so torrid because I'd never read *Crime and Punishment* or enjoyed Beethoven's 5th, it's no stretch to say that my experience was largely dreadful because of the simple fact that I knew a lot less stuff than other people.

Life's richest treasures

Schools need to ensure that all students, regardless of their socio-economic background, are exposed to knowledge with high cultural capital. Ben Newmark explained this brilliantly in a blogpost entitled, *The Point of It All*:

> ...a knowledge rich curriculum, based on the best that has been thought and said (and painted, composed, sculpted, danced and so on), is so important. It's the canon, rightfully contested, debated and argued over, that has the best chance of giving pupils the keys that unlock life's richest treasures.

Pleasingly, lots of schools are already taking this approach: students are being exposed to Aristotelian rhetoric and classical mythology in KS3 English lessons; in Modern Foreign Languages, children aren't just being taught the language of a country, but its culture and geography too; in science lessons, students aren't just learning about theories and formulas, but about the important discoveries and famous scientists that have defined the way we perceive the world.

To improve the educational experience of disadvantaged children, schools need to move from being university-focused to person-focused. The sole aim of person-focused schools isn't to produce graduates, but to produce curious, empathic, and kind people with knowledge that enables them to take opportunities – whether it's going to university or working with Dad as a bricklayer – *if* they choose to take them.

Rethinking attitudes

I want to finish by revisiting the Tammy Campbell study mentioned earlier on. The research showed that teachers stereotype negatively against boys and low-income children. It's no surprise that teachers stereotype; they are human after all. However, not all teachers are willing to admit this. This is no doubt because as educators of children, teachers are meant to embody all the saintly aspects of humanity that they wish to cultivate in the students they care for. To admit that they stereotype is to admit that they are prone to the same prejudices they castigate their pupils for. And no teacher wants to admit that.

It's not just a continual drip-feed of gender stereotypes from the media, friends, and relatives that has led teachers to stereotype. The very fact that teachers are teachers may actually make them more likely to stereotype. Campbell poses the theory that "the current concentration on low-income families through the pupil premium may inadvertently imply and contribute to a stereotype that poorer pupils across the board are deficient in ability and potential".[46] The fact that a high proportion of teachers identify as middle class (remember-71%) may further exacerbate this phenomenon.

Changing practice, changing attitudes

Brian Earp of Oxford University has explored a number of ways that teachers might counteract the harmful effects of stereotyping. He refers to these separately as the personal, instructional, and environmental dimensions.[47]

A. The personal dimension

In order to dismantle their stereotypes, Earp states that teachers first need to confront the fact that they hold them. This involves some very honest reflection and I have devised the following task as a prompt for such reflection: Ask yourself, on your own, or in a group made up of individuals you trust, the following questions:

- Do you think disadvantaged students tend to be more concentrated in bottom sets because they are simply less clever?

- Do you think that parents who don't turn up to parents' evenings are less interested in their child's education than those who do?

- Do you think that your disadvantaged students will do less well in their assessments than non-disadvantaged students?

- Do you think that disadvantaged pupils are naughtier than non-disadvantaged students?

- Do you think you have the same expectations of disadvantaged students as non-disadvantaged students?

- Do you think it's important to know whether a student is PP? If so, why?

- Do you think that a child who goes to university is more successful than one who doesn't?

Thoughtful and honest consideration of questions like these can help you to realise that you may hold negative stereotypes about students from low-income backgrounds. Only once you've acknowledged these can you begin the process of building more positive conceptions of these students. This can be achieved by:

- **Being aware of the times your unconscious bias may impact negatively on students and taking steps to protect against it**. For example, you may assume that disadvantaged students haven't done their homework because they're feckless, when in fact, they may not have had the resources (parental aid, confidence, and vocabulary are all resources, by the way) to get it done

- **Exposing yourself and others to cases where stereotypes are contradicted**. For example, if you tend to presume that disadvantaged boys can't write, seek out those instances where a disadvantaged boy has created a wonderful piece of writing and share it with colleagues

- **Not exposing yourself to any information that may trigger an unconscious bias**. Is it imperative that you (or your staff) know which of your students receive PP funding?

- **Making sure that you have consistently high expectations of all your students whatever their socio-economic background**. Be relentless in your insistence that these high standards be reached.

B. The instructional dimension

How we teach plays a large part in improving our attitudes to disadvantaged students. In changing our practice, we go some way to changing our attitudes. Let's ensure that we're critical of class structures when the opportunity provides it. Let's ensure that we're not always talking from a middle class perspective. Let's not assume that everybody knows what it's like to go abroad, have married parents, or a mattress to sleep on. Let's be mindful of the books we recommend, the people we learn about, and the perspectives we view them from. In history, let's humanise the dispossessed. In Physical Education, let's be mindful of the fact that taking part in extra-curricular sports costs time and money that many disadvantaged families simply do not have and let's find solutions that enable disadvantaged kids to take part. In computing, let's not assume that an interest in computers equates to owning a computer.

C. The environmental dimension

We must pay close attention to our environments. Are our corridors filled with countless posters about going to University? Where are the posters about routes to becoming a builder, or a plumber, or a refuse worker? Do our textbooks constantly display images of smiling nuclear families in exotic locations? Where is the reality (for some, for many) of council estate community centres, single parent families, and tracksuits? Do our prospectuses boast proudly of the number of students who have gone on to university, ignoring those who have gone on to become successful carers, shop owners, or tree surgeons?

How about us, as teachers? Research has shown that many teachers are being asked to change their "working class" regional accents in favour of the more neutral, more educated, "received pronunciation" accent.[48] Dr Alex Baratta from the University of Manchester has conducted a number of studies looking at accents, particularly those belonging to teachers. He has found numerous instances of trainee teachers being instructed to shed their regional accents in case students might think them stupid. A recurring theme is of teachers being thought inarticulate if they "drop their Ts". All this is in spite of the fact that in another study, Baratta found that students would prefer it if teachers kept their regional accents on the basis of authenticity. As teachers, especially as teachers from disadvantaged backgrounds, we should be proud of where we come from. Let's keep our accents and show our working class children that accent is a part of who you are and dropping your Ts is not synonymous with being morally or academically lacking.

The final word

The main thing holding back working class students is attitudes. Gimmicks won't change attitudes. Considered and sustained self-reflection changes attitudes. Teachers need greater awareness of the issues of the inequalities inherent in our education system, and they also need to accept the fact that no matter how liberal they think they are, they too may be susceptible to the same class biases instilled through the newspapers they read, the television programmes they watch, and the institutions of which they are a part. Accepting biases is a vital part of the process to eradicate them.

Notes

1 Department for Education (2017) *National curriculum assessments: Key stage 2, 2017 (revised)*, DfE. Available at: https://assets.publishing.service.gov.uk/government/uploads/system/uploads/attachment_data/file/667372/SFR69_2017_text.pdf (Accessed: 11th July 2018).

2 Department for Education (2018) *Revised GCSE and equivalent results in England, 2016–2017*, DfE. Available at: https://assets.publishing.service.gov.uk/government/uploads/system/uploads/attachment_data/file/676596/SFR01_2018.pdf (Accessed: 11th June 2018).

3 Gov.uk (2018) 'Apply for free school meals'. Available at: www.gov.uk/apply-free-school-meals (Accessed: 8th June 2018).

4 Gov.uk (2014) 'Pupil premium: Funding and accountability for schools'. Available at: www.gov.uk/guidance/pupil-premium-information-for-schools-and-alternative-provision-settings (Accessed: 11th June 2018).

5 If another commentator, researcher, questionnaire or survey has used the term 'working class', I'll keep it for simplicity's sake. For the purposes of this chapter, I will retain the term 'middle class' for anybody, barring the aristocratic elite, to refer to anybody who is not what I term disadvantaged. In Mike Savage's new 7-tier model of the British Class

system, it is only the precariat and the elite who differ significantly from the largely homogenous other five groups, whom I term middle class.

6 Savage, M. (2015) *Social Class in the 21st Century*, London: Penguin Books, p. 351.

7 Matt Pinkett, (@PositivTeacha) 'Yeah, so, this is a problem' 8th February 2018 at 3.50 p.m. (Tweet).

8 Reay, D. (2017). *Miseducation*, Bristol: Policy Press, p. 49.

9 Ibid., p. 53.

10 Ibid., p 49.

11 Department for Education (2018) *Open academies and academy projects awaiting approval: May 2018*, Available at: www.gov.uk/government/publications/open-academies-and-academy-projects-in-development#history (Accessed: 4th June 2018).

12 Sibieta, L. (2015) *Schools Spending*, London: Institute of Fiscal Studies with The Nuffield Foundation.

13 Ibid.

14 Grainger, K. (2012), '"The daily grunt": Middle-class bias and vested interests in the "getting in early" and "why can't they read?" reports', *Language and Education*, 27:2, pp. 99–109.

15 Ibid.

16 Gross, J. (2008) *Getting in early: Primary schools and early intervention*. The Smith Institute and The Centre for Social Justice. Available at: www.smith-institute.org.uk/wp-content/uploads/2015/10/GettingInEarlyPrimaryschoolsandearlyintervention.pdf (Accessed: 13th June 2018).

17 Ibid.

18 Ibid.

19 Grainger, K. (2012).

20 (Gross, cited in) Grainger, K. (2012).

21 For further examples of teachers' gender-biased judgements, see Chapter 5.

22 Campbell, T. (2015) 'Stereotyped at seven? Biases in teacher judgement of pupils' ability and attainment', *Journal of Social Policy*, 44:3, pp. 517–547.

23 Ibid.

24 TeacherTapp, *The strange habits of ability groupings*. Available at: http://teachertapp.co.uk/2017/11/strange-teacher-habits-ability-groupings/ (Accessed: 26th July 2018).

25 Ibid.

26 Francis, B. (2017) *What every teacher needs to know about setting*. Audio blog post. TES Podagogy. TES Online, 7th February. Available at: www.tes.com/news/listen-what-every-teacher-needs-know-about-setting-professor-becky-francis-talks-tes-podagogy (Accessed: 25th July 2018).

27 Dunne, M., Humphreys, S., Sebba, J., Dyson, A., Gallanaugh, F., & Muijs, D. (2007) *Effective teaching and learning for pupils in low attaining groups*, Research Report, London: Department for Children Schools and Families.

28 Hallam, S. & Parsons, S. (2013) 'Prevalence of streaming in UK primary schools: Evidence from the Millennium Cohort Study.' *British Educational Research Journal*, 39:3, pp. 514–544.

29 Education Endowment Foundation. (2018) *Teacher toolkit: Setting or streaming*. Available at: https://educationendowmentfoundation.org.uk/evidence-summaries/teaching-learning-toolkit/setting-or-streaming/ (Accessed: 26th July 2018).

30 For more on this, see the discussion on the **Golem Effect** in Chapter 5.

31 Adams, R. (2017) 'Children as young as two grouped by ability in English nurseries', *The Guardian*, 1st December. Available at: www.theguardian.com/education/2017/dec/01/children-two-grouped-ability-english-nurseries (Accessed: 3rd January 2018).

32 Education Endowment Foundation, Teacher Toolkit: Setting or Streaming.

33 Ibid.

34 Reay, D. (2017).

35 Adapted from Francis, B., Taylor, B., Hodgen, J., Tereshchenko, A., & Archer, L. (2018). *Dos and Don'ts of Attainment Grouping*, London: UCL Institute of London.

36 Ibid.

37 Reay, D. (2017), p. 16.

38 Ibid., p. 70.

39 Department for Education (2010) *The importance of teaching*. Available at: https://assets.publishing.service.gov.uk/government/uploads/system/uploads/attachment_data/file/175429/CM-7980.pdf (Accessed: 9th September 2018).

40 Baker, W., Sammons, P., Siraj-Blatchford, I., Sylva, K., Melhuish, E., & Taggart, B, (2014) 'Aspirations, education and inequality in England: Insights from the effective provision of pre-school, primary and secondary education project', *Oxford Review of Education*, 40:5, pp. 525–542.

41 Blandford, S. (2017) *Born to Fail? Social Mobility: A Working Class View*, Woodbridge: John Catt Educational Ltd, p. 54.

42 Grayson, H. (2013) *Rapid Review of Parental Engagement and Narrowing the Gap in Attainment for Disadvantaged Children*, Slough and Oxford: NFER and Oxford University Press.

43 Reay, D. (2017), p. 114.

44 Britton, J., Crawford, C., & Dearden, L. (2015) 'Analysis of the higher education funding reforms announced in summer budget 2015', IFS Briefing Note BNJ 174, London: The Institute for Fiscal Studies, July 2015.

45 Coulson, S., Garforth, L., Payne, G., & Wastell, E. (2017) 'Admissions, adaptations and anxieties: Social class inside and outside the elite university', in R. Waller, N. Ingram & M. Ward (eds) *Degrees of Injustice: Social Class Inequalities in University Admissions, Experiences and Outcomes*, Abingdon: Routledge.

46 Campbell, T. (2015).

47 Earp, B. D. (2010). 'Automaticity in the classroom: Unconscious mental processes and the racial achievement gap', *Journal of Multiculturalism in Education*, 6:1, pp. 1–22.

48 Santry, C. (2018) 'Should there be statutory guidance on acceptable accents for teachers? One leading linguist thinks so,' *TES Online*, 5th April. Available at: www.tes.com/news/should-there-be-statutory-guidance-acceptable-accents-teachers-one-leading-linguist-thinks-so (Accessed: 9th September 2018).

Peer pressure

Mark Roberts

The story

When I was at school, there were only a few rules. These rules were simple, consistent, and upheld zealously:

- Never put your hand up

- Try not to answer questions correctly

- Don't hand in homework

- Avoid showing enthusiasm for learning.

A compliant and popular student, I rarely broke the rules.

School rules ok?

The rules listed above weren't official school rules, of course. I can just about remember a few of those. Standard stuff about black footwear, not swearing at teachers, and not wearing Guns N' Roses or Metallica badges on your blazer. I ignored these rules and was punished for doing so.

No, the rules were informal. These rules were unofficial, unspoken, and deeply intuitive. This list was for boys – well, not all boys, just the popular ones: the hard, the sporty, the non-victimised. Some girls chose to follow these rules. That was fine. That was welcomed. But mostly, these rules were for male pupils. The normal ones anyway. Failing to observe these implicit edicts was a big mistake, leading to hassle, ostracism, and, occasionally, peer group violence.

Even I – a skilful sheep, profoundly attuned to the pervasive culture of indifference, disruption, and defiance – messed up at times. Sometimes, I'd find my right hand had involuntarily jerked skywards during questioning. Before I knew what was happening, and before I'd had time to consider the negative effect on my reputation, I'd be offering an impulsive, fatally correct answer.

At other times, I'd also score far too highly on tests and assessments. Instead of my usual, stunningly self-destructive, and deliberate strategy of getting every question wrong, I would – every now and then, when I wasn't thinking straight – get them all right on a spelling test, trigonometry exercise, or biology paper. This would baffle and infuriate my teachers: one week I'd get two out of 50 on an end-of-unit religious education multiple choice quiz (it would have been zero but I accidentally ticked two correct answers), the next I'd be ranked top of the year group in French, despite being put in the bottom set for "finding the work too difficult".

A sporting chance

Despite my occasional knee-jerk forays into academic excellence, I still managed to avoid becoming a social outcast at school. How did I manage to swerve the usual pariah status bestowed upon the geeks, the swots, the readers? In a word, sport. As a tall boy, with a reasonably stocky, reasonably athletic physique, I managed to hold down a regular position in the school football and rugby teams. I captained the cricket team, inflicting damage on nervy batsmen with my fast(ish) bowling feats. I even won the shot put title one year at sports day.

A solid, dependable beta male, I knew how to stay in with the savage physical specimens at the top of the hierarchy. These beasts were contenders for "cock of the year" status, a strange Yorkshire phrase that referred not to the male appendage, but instead recognised the supreme fighting ability of a nascently psychotic adolescent.

Balancing the two sides of my nature – the sport-loving aggro merchant and the know-it-all voracious bookmuncher – was therefore a stressful act. Mainly because they weren't in balance. My academic/social equilibrium was, as Dr Jekyll (another reputation-obsessed character with a duality issue) puts it, "doomed to a dreadful shipwreck". The laddish façade was an exhausting, burdensome performance, eating away at my true desires – namely, a quiet classroom and the chance to participate in a nice discussion about, say, the difference between a city and a conurbation.

"You could go far"

But mainly, the toll of pretending to be thick for an easy life of acceptance and popularity was too much. My mental health suffered and my behaviour – never great at best – became impeccably outrageous. Exclusions for fighting, bullying, and persistent disruption put even greater distance between me and academic success, and greater distance between me and my parents. Naturally enough, this violent, brutish behaviour earned me greater respect among my most "masculine" peers.

Back in school, between extended periods of truancy and exclusion, some teachers would rumble me. The odd one would make noises about me coming back to do A levels and would tell me, in the sanctuary of their empty classrooms, that if I sorted out my attitude and behaviour I could go to Oxbridge. I appreciated the gestures but I knew deep down that there was no way I was going to do either of those things. I'd tell my mates that I'd been given a final warning about my antics, not friendly and well-meaning careers advice. My friends were impressed, but the teachers were no doubt disappointed when I left school at the first opportunity to do some manual labour instead.

How typical was my experience?

What the hell was I thinking? How much peer pressure was involved?

The term peer pressure is used to describe the negative influence that young people can have on each other, implying that the mere presence of similar aged groups of boys will change their "natural" behaviour. One study,[1] which gave helpful pupil-friendly language to the young participants, defined peer pressure as:

> When people your own age encourage or urge you to do something or to keep from doing something else, no matter if you personally want to or not.

If, like me, you've spent a fair bit of time patrolling the corridors, canteens, and playgrounds of schools, you'll probably think that this sounds about right. Kids, especially the popular, confident ones, influence each other. That's obvious.

But to what extent is this pervasive phenomenon responsible for academic outcomes? And why is it that peer pressure seems to affect the educational performance of boys more than girls?

The research

In his seminal study into attitudes towards school among a group of disadvantaged boys in an industrial town in the Midlands in the 1970s, Paul Willis[2] vividly describes the stereotypically masculine counter-school culture of "the lads". For this small but influential group of teenage boys, non-conformity was the norm. The lads' manifesto was straightforward: avoid going to lessons, avoid doing work, and avoid gaining decent qualifications. Starting to sound familiar? For these lads, school, Willis argued, represented boredom, in stark contrast to the outside world, which offered the hedonistic joys of alcohol, cigarettes, and part-time jobs (which gave them money to buy more alcohol and cigarettes).

Instead of satisfaction through learning, the boys found stimulation through disrupting lessons, repetitive acts of puerile defiance, and petty infringements against school rules, like uniform violations. Further entertainment was found through the harassment and victimisation of a small band of conformist male peers who valued their education and were keen to attain exam results that would enable them to go on to higher education and high-status careers. These well-behaved, motivated pupils – nicknamed "ear 'oles" – were despised by the lads and ridiculed as a matter of routine.

Willis found that a central part of the "lads' counter culture" was a rigid sexism that valued stereotypically masculine traits, such as physical labour and heterosexuality, while denigrating the ear 'oles' supposedly feminine attributes. Doing work to the best of their ability meant the ear 'oles were not only seen as obedient teacher's pets but were also derided for their refusal to display "true" masculine qualities. As a result, the ear 'oles were labelled as "cissies", a pejorative derived from the word "sister" implying that they were a combination of "coward, weakling or effeminate homosexual".[3]

Peer pressure, masculinity, and an anti-academic ethos

The behaviours described in Willis's study, although more than a decade earlier than my time at secondary school, certainly chime with my anecdotal experiences. And any teacher that has had to deal with the wilfully disruptive "minor" acts of defiance that Willis describes (chair scraping, tutting in response to requests to put pen to paper, flicking the ears of other pupils) will recognise that this irritating, self-sabotaging behaviour seems to come more frequently from male pupils. Critics of Willis[4] have, quite reasonably, argued that his sample size (12 boys) is too small for such generalisations about male attitudes to school. They've also questioned his focus on the extremes of the conformity spectrum: the aggressively anti-school "lads" and the academically-driven "ear 'oles", when most pupils within a school setting in that context would usually sit somewhere in between these two outlying groups.

Nonetheless, I would argue that by drawing attention to the extremes, Willis allows us to see the potentially insidious effects peer pressure can have on those in the middle. A middle mass who may well end up walking a daily tightrope between the wrath of the lads and the punishment meted out to the obsequious "ear 'oles".

The lads, it would seem, are not unusual. Similar studies have also highlighted the debilitating effects of having to wear the mask of gender conformity while trying to land some decent academic results.

The significance of sport

More recently, Wayne Martino[5] interviewed Year 11 boys about the effects of peer pressure in a school in Perth, Western Australia. The school in question bore a reputation for sporting excellence, with Australian Rules Football (a high contact game that shares more similarities with rugby than soccer) playing a particularly prominent role in the culture of the school. The pupils who were actively involved in football were known, apparently without irony, as the "cool boys" and enjoyed an elevated social status because of their footballing prowess. Like Willis's disadvantaged "lads", these "cool boys" placed themselves in opposition to the academically successful "squids". Unlike Willis's proletarian sample, however, the "cool boys" were largely the product of middle class backgrounds. While the lads from

the Midlands wear their poor academic grades as a badge of pride, their more privileged antipodean counterparts:

> although loud and disruptive in class…are not usually academic failures.
> Many are successful students but this must be achieved apparently without ef-
> fort and without any visible signs of excessive mental labour or studiousness.

They've got everything going for them

Many teachers I meet and interact with on social media are bewildered by the fact
that middle class and upper-middle class boys often display anti-academic attitudes. *They've got everything going for them – a nice home, supportive parents,
money for revision guides, a quiet place to study – and still they're bloody lazy and
apathetic.* What these teachers – frustrated, dedicated teachers – fail to realise is
that this is a survival strategy. For boys, a safe way to remain part of the dominant
masculine culture is to balance any signs of academic success with a concerted
anti-mental labour stance.

While disadvantaged boys are a key group of underachievers, their middle class
male peers are still also less likely than their female counterparts to achieve to their
full potential because of the influence of a dominant strand of masculinity that
sees school work and high achievement as effeminate and uncool. The rejection of
school work is not just a working class phenomenon then but, as we have seen in
Chapter 2, it affects disadvantaged boys more acutely, because as well as adopting
an anti-school "protest masculinity" they may also lack the cultural capital that
allows their move privileged peers to scrape reasonable results in the end. The
valorisation of physical labour and rejection of mental labour is more likely to be
taken to an extreme by disadvantaged boys. When middle class boys do adopt the
same attitude, according to Martino's interviews, they are more likely to work in
private, albeit far less frequently than their female peers. Tellingly, one of Martino's
subjects admitted that he managed to complete his work and avoid opprobrium,
but made clear that this was only tolerated because he was a sporty boy who also
surfed and was therefore already accepted by his male peers.

The limitations of sport

The work of Jeffrey Smith,[6] who conducted similar research to Martino but in
the very different context of a comprehensive school in a deprived area of a city
in the North of England, illustrates how sport crosses class boundaries in allowing boys to gain entry to the dominant anti-academic masculine club. Member-
ship of this club equals acceptance by the "cool" lads. In both Smith's deprived
context and Martino's more affluent backdrop an elevated, revered brand of masculinity is awarded to those who display skill on the football pitch. The aggressively masculine disadvantaged lads in Smith's study – who display negative

classroom behaviour which is remarkably and depressingly similar to Willis's lads – use football as a way of accumulating "physical capital". In other words, being good at football gains them not just respect, but also bestows upon them the sheen of athletic machismo. Unfortunately, boys who show proficiency on the football pitch, and dream of the riches of the Premier League, are even less likely to value academic qualifications. Speak to any experienced PE teacher or local football coach and they'll tell you countless tales of deluded young males who weren't quite good enough to make it. As Smith puts it, "the possibilities for converting [physical capital] into economic, social or cultural capital are extremely limited".

- **Physical capital** refers to physical abilities and attributes like strength, skill, and beauty that are used in sporting and social contexts. This might include sports and hobbies like tennis and bodybuilding or employment in fashion modelling or sex work

- **Social capital** is comprised of an individual's social networks, friendships, and associations. This could include being a member of a golf club or having gone to university with several members of the cabinet

- **Economic capital** is concerned with a person's wealth and income. So in addition to their salary, this might include things such as inheritance and investments

Yet even sport mad boys – and I was one of them – who are realistic enough to abandon the dream of signing a professional contract recognise the important role that sport plays in boosting one's manly reputation among peers. In the playgrounds of this and other lands, it's a truth universally acknowledged that being good at sport attracts positive attention from popular boys.

This fact has not gone unnoticed by teachers. Given the significance of sport as a factor in dictating how boys are viewed by their male peers, it is unsurprising that since the emergence of the issue of boys' underachievement, teachers have used competition as a way of engaging boys in the classroom. In Chapter 1, we demonstrated how the idea of using competition in the classroom as a way of engaging boys is appealing, plausible, and utterly misguided, with catastrophic consequences for male attainment.

Talking sport

Apart from offering acceptance into the dominant group, sport also provides boys with a safe conversational space to occupy when socialising with other overtly "masculine" boys. Speaking from experience, I can think of innumerable occasions during my teenage years when the topic of sport allowed me to put strained relationships to one side temporarily and at least communicate with my dad and brothers. Sport offers boys the opportunity to talk about feelings: disappointment, elation, anticipation. And, of course, this is a good thing. Yet, often, these heartfelt conversations are anything but. Usually, they act as a proxy for emotional unburdening, a façade that hides genuine feeling. As Jason, one of Martino's boys, puts it "guys are sort of like you can talk to them about personal things but not really like inside feelings that you might really think, you have to sort of go along with the flow". Adolescent boys can talk about their embarrassment at losing a game, or even – whisper it – cry when their team is relegated, but they cross the line of gender expectations when they express their innermost thoughts and fears: namely feelings of shame, guilt, and inadequacy. Indeed, another boy from Martino's sample explains with some eloquence that while sport is a valid subject for discussion, the act of sitting down and talking is otherwise seen as an effeminate and non-masculine activity.

Gender conformity – how boys and girls should behave at school

As we have seen, researchers such as Willis, Martino, and Smith have made clear the link between peer pressure and attitudes towards school and learning. Further research has looked more specifically at the effects of peer pressure on gender conformity.

> **Gender conformity** – behaviour and appearance that matches with society's expectations of a person's gender. In other words, a woman who acts in a stereotypically feminine manner will be conforming to her gender.

A running theme of this research is that young people who see themselves as being typical of their gender are much more likely to gain acceptance and popularity in the often harsh dynamics of school. On the other hand, young people who view themselves as gender atypical – i.e. don't think they fit the stereotypical mould of "teenage boy or girl" – are far more likely to be bullied or teased by their peers.[7] Anyone doubting the significant influence of peer pressure would do well to remind themselves of the time adolescents spend in each other's company. Adolescents spend a much greater amount of time interacting with their peers than younger children. By the time they are at secondary school, adolescents spend nearly a third of their total daily time with their peers. This is double the 15% of time they spend with their parents or other adults.[8] Little wonder that teenagers tend to pay more heed to what their mates are saying.

Peer pressure affects both genders, of course. *Girls have it just as bad, if not worse*, you might well be thinking. Yes, I've seen for myself unpleasant disputes and petty vendettas between some adolescent girls (and boys). Fall outs become meltdowns that often reach nuclear level. Yet, the body of research into peer influences tells us that when it comes to *gender expectations* boys do feel under a greater pressure to conform to widely-held notions of how they, as young males, should behave. Relationship breakdowns between girls may be very challenging, very public, and incredibly hurtful for those involved, but the research suggests that peer group catastrophes are not the norm.

Studies have shown that girls tend to influence their female peers indirectly, using gossip as a roundabout way of challenging perceived unacceptable peer group behaviour.[9] Girls mainly strive to avoid confrontation which, unlike boys, allows girls to learn about "conventional" feminine behaviour without blatantly hurting each other's feelings.[10]

The burden on boys

In gender conformity terms, boys appear to feel a heavier burden of expectation. A study of eighth graders in a middle school in a south western city of the United States[11] found that boys are much more likely to identify as "boy-like" and feel more pressure to conform to these gender expectations than girls.

Other recent research has also found that, from an educational perspective, boys are more susceptible to the negative impact of peer pressure than girls. Unlike most studies into peer influence, which look at small groups of pupils in one school, Belgian researchers Vantieghem and Van Houtte's sample comprised of 59 schools in Belgium,[12] collecting and analysing the views of over 6,000 Year 8 pupils. Like much of the other research, they found that girls' peer groups displayed more studious attitudes than boys' groups, where the emphasis placed on traditional masculine values led to a disregard for completing school work. As in Britain and many other Western countries, there is a Belgian attainment gap, with boys significantly underperforming. On the back of this data, Vantieghem and Van Houtte contend that a strident form of anti-school masculinity – which sees being organised, cooperative, and scholarly as inherently feminine traits – at least partly accounts for the different educational outcomes.

For followers of the gender gap debate, this is well-trodden territory. But what makes this study so fascinating, and of such interest to teachers, is the assertion that "pressure for gender conformity had opposite effects on boys and girls". Among the subjects who perceived themselves as typical for their gender, girls were more likely to work independently and have higher levels of self-efficacy.

> Academic **self-efficacy** refers to a person's belief about whether they can successfully achieve at a designated level in a specific academic subject area (Bandura, 1997).

The benefit for girls

When the girls in the study felt the pressure of gender conformity, their levels of self-efficacy actually *increased*. In other words, being expected to behave like a girl generally made them more "girly", which made them study harder, and made them more likely to believe they would succeed. By contrast, the pressure for gender conformity tended to dent the boys' academic self-confidence and resilience. Now, this is certainly a peer pressure paradox. Being made to act like a typical girl may well cause stress, anxiety, and difficulties with psychological adjustment, but crucially, it appears to help female adolescents work hard and believe in themselves (Figures 3.1 and 3.2):

> girls under pressure could try to emulate the ideal type of typically feminine girl and inadvertently raise their compliance to educational standards, heightening their academic self-efficacy in the process.

The curse of gender conformity for a teenage girl, it would appear, is to be expected to act like a girl and study hard. For boys, the weight of masculine expectation imposes a different set of rules. Ridiculous, self-defeating rules like the ones I used to follow slavishly at school.

Figure 3.1 Peer pressure and boys' attitude to school

Figure 3.2 Peer pressure and girls' attitude to school

Peer pressure and primary school boys

It would seem then that peer pressure and gender conformity go hand-in-hand. But is the phenomenon of boys holding an aversion to mental labour, as a result of pressure for gender conformity, something that only kicks in when puberty kicks in? Emma Renold's research,[13] conducted at two primary schools in a small town in the East of England, suggests otherwise. The study, which spoke to 59 Year 6 pupils, found that "two-thirds of the boys (disadvantaged and middle class) went to great lengths to avoid studious behaviours, *particularly boys who were deemed high achievers*" (my emphasis). As part of their efforts to disguise their ability and favourable attitudes to school, these boys would routinely disrupt lessons, tease others and break the school rules. The alternative – as they made clear during conversations with the researcher – was to leave themselves vulnerable to mockery, name-calling and alienation from the cool kids. Like the older boys in Martino and Smith's research, the primary school boys in danger of being labelled as effeminate swots also establish kinship through aggression and football. One very bright boy, Stuart, stops working hard and learns to play football. As a result, he goes from being an outcast who receives homophobic abuse to sporting hero in the space of a few months.

Stuart's tale is just one story. Nonetheless, despite being an extreme example, it is emblematic of a wider trend in our schools. From a purely academic standpoint, peer pressure and the associated expectations of gender conformity disproportionally affects boys. It affects boys of all social classes (although working class boys still suffer the most). It affects boys from an unexpectedly young age. And, it affects boys of all attainment levels (although higher prior attaining boys seem to feel the pressure most). So what can be done about this? How can schools and classroom teachers even begin to tackle this massive and insidious societal issue?

The solutions

Advice for school leaders

Tackling the iniquitous effects of male peer pressure is not going to be easy. But nothing less than a culture change will improve outcomes for underperforming boys. As Francis and Skelton have put it,

> It's in schools where gender constructions are less accentuated that boys tend to do better – and strategies that work to reduce relational constructions of gender that are most effective in facilitating boys' achievement.[14]

As we explained in Chapter 1, the standard strategies to engage boys are ineffective, because they do not help boys learn and they also perpetuate harmful stereotypes about masculinity. Instead schools will need to challenge head-on the damaging anti-work attitudes held by the dominant strains of traditional masculinity within peer groups. In particular, the so-called alpha males will need to be re-educated about gender in order to enable them, and other boys and girls, to flourish. Let's break the whole school strategies down further:

A. Create an ethos of excellence

To break the anti-intellectual stranglehold within dominant forms of masculinity, schools will need to celebrate and promote male achievement. It hopefully goes without saying that this must be done alongside, not replace, the acknowledgement of female achievement. As we have seen, many boys do not feel comfortable being singled out and praised for academic effort and success, yet at the same time they yearn to feel valued and a sense of belonging. Steps to improve boys' attitudes to work might include:

- Use subtle public recognition of achievements, especially by previous cohorts of boys

While this might lead to initial embarrassment for the first boys to be celebrated, if enough boys are included, then the recognition of achievement will become normalised. This may include prominent displays of boys with their excellent GCSE results or corridor displays of outstanding work done by boys.

- Promote non-stereotypical role models

These may be members of staff, older pupils, or pupils from within the year group. Recognising achievement in areas of the curriculum traditionally seen as "effeminate" is key. The greatest impact may be found by highlighting boys who embrace traditional and non-traditional forms of masculinity: a recent head boy at my school, for example, was both an outstanding sportsman and award-winning poet.

- Establish peer support for literacy

At my school, I've established a reading mentor programme where community volunteers and sixth form pupils give up their time to listen to struggling readers from Year 7 and Year 8. Many of these pupils are boys who are deeply embarrassed about their poor literacy skills. Finding the right reading mentor is key. Spending time in a safe environment with a confident, articulate, and sensitive older male can work wonders for not just their reading skills but also their social skills.

- Get boys involved in anti-bullying programmes

In particular, you should look to involve confident, articulate boys to act as mentors. Research shows that girls are far more likely to take part in anti-bullying mentoring schemes in schools.[15] A school's inability to recruit positive role models into ambassadorial positions effectively says *boys don't care about bullying in this school*.

B. Tackle harmful attitudes about masculinity

It will take time and great effort to allow an ethos of male achievement to develop. Large amounts of boys have an anti-school work attitude that puts them at odds with the values and systems of the school. Some families will reinforce these harmful, traditional notions of masculinity. Dealing with laddish behaviour and attitudes, rather than seeing them as an inevitable consequence of the male condition is a herculean yet vital endeavour.

- Harness peer pressure by changing the mindset of the most influential male pupils

In their article on under-achieving boys, Younger et al.[16] list some approaches that English secondary schools have implemented to try and steer boys away from the shipwreck of stereotypical masculine behaviours. They note that one school:

> developed an explicit policy of targeting key student leaders, those specific individuals within any year group who were seen to be particularly influential, with the potential to influence and lead peer group image and attitude.

By getting these dozen or so pupils on side, the school found that these pupils started to support, rather than oppose, the ethos of the school. Crucially, this sort of change cannot happen overnight. It required senior staff giving up their time and cultivating positive relationships with disaffected males. The impact of these relationships will only be lasting where school leaders – male or female – truly appreciate the nature of non-tender masculinity. If leaders attempt to win dominant boys over by pandering to their traditionally masculine tendencies, then the culture will never change, even if the boys themselves appear to have fallen into line. Some staff may not feel comfortable in this role of course. Imagine a 50-year-old pastoral leader, male design technology teacher, for example, who has carved out a successful career through chats with boys about football and quashing disruption through his impressive physical presence. He may feel uncomfortable moving himself out of this comfort zone. Changing the gender expectations within a school will therefore require:

● Specialist training on gender stereotypes for pupils and staff

There are organisations out there who can train your staff on gender issues. One such group is TIGER, a Bristol based group that deliver workshops that address "gender based issues such as sexist bullying and sexual harassment within the school environment" as well as broader issues of "educational attainment and student participation in traditionally gender biased subjects".[17] This will cost money but, if the messages are implemented and reinforced, will make more difference to the culture of the school than the thousands of reward points that are doled out each year.

● An audit of gender relations in your school

You'll need your staff to be reflective and honest here. You'll want to address obvious things like the gender balance in the middle and senior leadership teams, who deliver the assemblies, and who deal with serious disciplinary matters. But you'll also need to consider less obvious things that contribute to the school's culture. As Kate Myers makes clear, pupils pick up on how staff interact with pupils and, crucially, each other. As we'll discover in Chapter 9, relationships between staff can send out powerful, often dangerous signals to pupils. Implicit messages are just as influential as overt ones:

> We make a special effort to learn some things, but others we pick up and absorb through observing the world around us. Schools may not be able to change the world but they can challenge, encourage and widen horizons.[18]

Advice for classroom teachers

● Slam down hard on displays of non-tender masculinity in the classroom and corridors

What you ignore, you are effectively condoning. What you turn a blind eye to, you are deeming acceptable. What you downplay as mindless banter could well be reinforcing the very beliefs that are undermining the efforts of boys (and some girls) in your class. This may include seemingly tame stereotypical language, such as pupils being labelled "nerds" or "geeks" for completing classwork; homophobic attitudes, like "gay" being used pejoratively to describe anything that is unpopular; pupils mocking or laughing at other pupils for showing enthusiasm about stereotypically feminine activities, such as singing in the choir. You'll also need to:

- Mind the language you use about the subjects you (and others) teach

Have you ever showed surprise in an options interview when a boy has told you he'd like to study textiles or food technology at GCSE. Or when a girl wants to choose construction or A level physics? Do you unintentionally discourage pupils from taking a greater interest in your subject through your words and actions? As Kate Myers notes, departments and teachers can do more to help break down stereotypes about what we learn:

> Are bridging strategies (for example taster courses...) used to encourage pupils to participate in areas traditionally not associated with their gender?...Do all subject areas, particularly those traditionally associated with one gender, offer learning environments that feel safe and attractive for both boys and girls.[19]

You might want to consider what impact you have as, for instance, a female English teacher saying you were "never any good at chemistry" or as a male maths teacher telling your class that you "always hated textiles at school". Like it or not, we are role models and pupils pick up on the subtle messages we give, intended or otherwise.

- Provide opportunities for boys to discuss their feelings

Depending on your subject, and the context, you'll need to consider whether to do this in the public arena of the classroom. But persevering until the mask of macho masculinity slips can develop a greater understanding of, and rapport with, your male pupils. I'm not talking Oprah-style tearful confessions here, merely taking the chance to ask boys how they feel about the representation of a particular character in a novel or whether they think it's fair that we mainly study male figures from history for example.

- Appreciate the particular pressure on clever boys who court popularity

Provide an outlet for them to talk about balancing the demands of scholarship and peer group acceptance. Ultimately, it's down to the school to develop an atmosphere where male academic achievement is seen as laudable, not laughable, but in the meantime you'll make higher prior attaining boys' lives easier by acknowledging their difficult place within peer group dynamics and giving them support and advice to help them navigate the turbulent waters of teen peer group expectations.

- Enforce behaviour systems rigorously

It's no surprise to me that the subjects I tended to do best in at school were the ones where I had strict teachers, whether I liked the subject or not. I remember a blissfully silent French class where the teacher – someone not to be messed with – insisted on minimal noise during writing activities. Compared to the lessons with teachers with weaker behaviour management skills – where I felt obliged to muck about even though deep down I would have preferred to be doing work – this was a haven of tranquillity.

One of the best ways to help out boys who want to work but are cowed by the presence of peer expectations is to create an environment where there is no alternative to hard work. With challenging groups in particular, providing a quiet, orderly environment for those that want to learn (including those who pretend otherwise) is the only way to do everyone a favour. After all, when I walked out of my French teacher's lessons, I had a ready-made excuse – *I had no bloody choice, did I?*

- Give homework careful consideration

The same should also apply for homework: set it and insist on it being done, with immediate sanctions for those that don't comply. That's the ideal and I try to stick to it. But I do have a different take on homework. Forcing pupils to work in your lessons removes the peer pressure excuse, but it's a lot harder for some boys to justify working at home – of their own volition! – to their "cool" anti-school mates. To avoid making this a public thing, you might want to consider how you collect in homework and how you publicly deal with non-completers. I find that quietly circulating the class during an extended activity and collecting work in away from the glare of public judgement works well. Pupils who haven't completed work don't get the chance to showcase their lack of effort. And pupils who have aren't being forced to advertise to the 29 others that they've spent hours scribbling away while their mates were down the park. That doesn't mean pupils who don't regularly do homework aren't tackled of course. But, in my experience, a phone call home or a quiet word with their tutor or head of year can reap greater rewards when peer pressure is hovering in the background.

- Differentiate by stealth

Have you ever noticed how some pupils, usually boys, won't take the feedback and advice you've given them to help them access a task that they'll otherwise struggle with? Furthermore, research has shown that a child's decision about whether or not they want to attempt more challenging tasks is influenced by whether there are peers around and what decisions these peers also make about levels of challenge.[20] It's little wonder then that little Liam pushes away his basic vocabulary handout. After all, this lad is so affected by the fear of seeming different that he'd rather not be able *to read* the work than be given something the others haven't got, even if it will help him learn.

Similarly, if you give pupils optional sections of lessons, like "extension tasks", those pupils who are skilled at doing the bare minimum are going to do ... the bare minimum. For these reasons, challenge has got to be built-in and be non-negotiable. Differentiation has to be subtle. I often give struggling pupils resources that look almost identical to the ones being used by their peers. They are being challenged in the same way – the same ideas, the same expectations of what they'll produce – but they are given an almost imperceptible leg up to get there.

● Any questions?

While we're on the subject, asking pupils to publicly announce that they don't understand the work isn't always a good idea. "Any questions?" after you've explained a task usually elicits no answer. Ask this at a whole staff meeting and you'll often get the same response: silence. Peer pressure glues lips shut and nails hands to the side of bodies. The answer? Know which pupils are likely to misunderstand your explanations and go see them first. If it's obvious several people haven't got a clue what's going on, then go back and explain it better.

I used to give one of my classes the chance to each ask a question before an assessment – one thing each they didn't understand. This was a confident group of outspoken individuals. But not many of them asked questions. Instead, I started giving them post-it notes to write their questions on anonymously. From then on, I could guarantee that every one of them would admit to a misconception. More often than not, the gaps in knowledge were commonplace. The pupils got to feel better that they were all in the same boat and I got some quick feedback enabling me to go over an obvious area of weakness.

The final word

As this chapter has shown, dealing with peer pressure in schools will require a sustained and coordinated approach from leaders and teachers. Many teachers need specialist support and guidance to give them greater confidence when navigating gender matters and the role of peer pressure. In the short term, as influential professionals, they can begin to mitigate some of the damaging effects of the way society socialises boys from an early age. By enforcing high standards and carefully considering pedagogical approaches – while at the same time being sensitive to the burden of acceptance and popularity – teachers can help guide boys through the minefield of gender expectations in schools. In the long run, we need nothing less than a culture shift, to ensure that boys' achievement and tender masculinity becomes the norm in our educational settings. Peer pressure isn't going to go away any time soon but, with the right approach, it can be harnessed and diverted, so that it becomes a force for good that helps improve attainment and reduces boys' anxiety about their role in the world.

Notes

1 Clasen, D.R. & Brown, B.B. (1985) 'The multidimensionality of peer pressure in adolescence', *Journal of Youth and Adolescence*, 14:6, pp. 451–468.
2 Willis, P. (1977) *Learning to Labour*, Farnborough: Saxon House.
3 Green, J. (2008) *Chambers Slang Dictionary*, Edinburgh: Chambers.
4 For a review of these critics, see Haralambos, M. & Holborn, M. (1995) *Sociology: Themes and Perspectives*, London: Collins.
5 Martino, W. (1999) '"Cool Boys", "Party Animals", "Squids" and "Poofters": Interrogating the dynamics and politics of adolescent masculinities in school', *British Journal of Sociology of Education*, 20:2, pp. 239–263.
6 Smith, J. (2007) '"Ye've got to 'ave balls to play this game sir!" Boys, peers and fears: The negative influence of school-based "cultural accomplices" in constructing hegemonic masculinities', *Gender and Education*, 19:2, pp. 179–198.
7 For example, Egan, S.K. & Perry, D.G. (2001) 'Gender identity: A multidimensional analysis with implications for psychosocial adjustment', *Developmental Psychology*, 37:4, pp. 451–463; Jewell, J.A. & Brown, C.S. (2014) 'Relations among gender typicality, peer relations, and mental health during early adolescence, *Social Development*, 23:1, pp. 137–156.
8 Csikszentmihalyi & Larson (1974), cited in Ryan, A.M. (2000) 'Peer groups as a context for the socialization of adolescents' motivation, engagement, and achievement in school', *Educational Psychologist*, 35:2, pp. 101–111.
9 Such as Eder, D.J. & Sanford, S. (1986) 'Adolescent humor during peer interaction', *Social Psychology Quarterly*, 47:3, pp. 235–243; Simon, R.W., Eder, D.J. & Evans, C. (1992) 'The development of feeling norms underlying romantic love among adolescent females', *Social Psychology Quarterly*, 55:1, pp. 29–46.
10 Ryan, A. M. (2000).
11 Kornienko, O., Santos, C.E., Martin, C. & Granger, K.L. (2016) 'Peer influence on gender identity development in adolescence', *Developmental Psychology*, 52:10, pp. 1578–1592.
12 Vantieghem, W. & Van Houtte, M. (2015) 'Are girls more resilient to gender-conformity pressure? The association between gender-conformity pressure and academic self-efficacy', *Sex Roles*, 73, pp. 1–15.
13 Renold, E. (2001) 'Learning the "hard" way: Boys, hegemonic masculinity and the negotiation of learner identities in the primary school', *British Journal of Sociology of Education*, 22:3, pp. 369–385.
14 Francis, B., Skelton, C., Carrington, B., Hutchings, M., Read, B., & Hall, I. (2008) 'A perfect match? Pupils' and teachers' views of the impact of matching educators and learners by gender', *Research Papers in Education*, 23:1, pp. 21–36.
15 Cowie, H. (2000) 'Bystanding or standing by: Gender issues in coping with bullying in English schools', *Aggressive Behaviour*, 26, pp. 85–97, quoted in Myers, K. & Taylor, H. (2007) *Genderwatch: Still Watching*, Stoke on Trent: Trentham, p. 70.
16 Younger, M., Warrington, M., & Mclellan R. (2002) 'The "problem" of "under-achieving boys": Some responses from English secondary schools', *School Leadership & Management*, 22:4, pp. 389–405.
17 TIGER Bristol website. Available at: www.tigerbristol.co.uk/about.html (Accessed: 12th December 2017).
18 Myers, K. & Taylor, H. (2007).
19 Ibid., p. 23.
20 Sagotsky, G. & Lepper, M. R. (1982) 'Generalization of changes in children's preferences for easy or difficult goals induced through peer modelling', *Child Development*, 52, pp. 372–375.

4 Mental health

Matt Pinkett

The story

Although I wouldn't expect the topic to feature on an exam question, *Romeo and Juliet* is about male mental health. At the start of the play, Romeo exhibits behaviours we might now ascribe to the depressed: his father describes his young son's tendency to "... draw/the shady curtains from Aurora's bed" and "Away from light ... private in his chamber pen himself". Then, in a fit of euphoric impulsiveness of the kind observed in the manic episodes well known to people with bipolar disorder, Romeo declares his intention to marry Juliet within just a few hours of meeting her. Soon, his inability to control his anger means that he kills Juliet's cousin, Tybalt. Upon hearing that the murder of Tybalt has earned him banishment from Verona, Romeo seeks out his friend, mentor, father figure, and protector, Friar Lawrence. When Romeo breaks down before him, hysterical with grief at his belief that he will never again see his beloved, Friar Lawrence, in a shocking display of misogynistic callousness, asks Romeo, "Art thou a man?" and tells him, "Thy tears are womanish". It isn't long before Romeo kills himself.

If we fast forward over 400 years from the time *Romeo and Juliet* was written, and traverse from the realm of fiction to the realm of reality, not a lot has changed. Disturbing parallels remain between the imaginings of a 16th-century playwright, and the reality of 21st-century Britain. Still, young men are angry. Still, young men are chided for expressing their emotions. Still, young men are killing themselves.

The research

Before I start, it's important to note that mental health is a hugely complex area, and although in the chapter that follows I limit my focus to suicide, anger, and self-harm as areas of exploration, there are many other complex mental health conditions, each of which affects different individuals in different ways. For people in need of specific advice not covered in this chapter, I recommend Natasha Devon's book, *A Beginner's Guide to Being Mental: From Anxiety to Zero F**ks Given* and the following website dedicated to educators looking for help with issues relating to mental health:

www.mentalhealth.gov/talk/educators

Suicide

It seems almost clichéd now, so often is the statistic cited, to mention that in the UK, 75% of suicides are male. Or that suicide is the single biggest killer, above heart disease and cancer, of males under the age of 40. But, are you aware of these lesser known facts? Did you know that the Irish Traveller boy you teach is almost seven times more likely to kill himself than the rest of the boys in your class?[1] Did you know that statistically, 60% of the gay and bisexual boys in your school have thought about taking their own lives? Did you know that if you teach any boys amongst the most deprived 10% of society, they are twice as likely to die from suicide as those boys born amongst the richest 10%?[2]

In 2016, 90% of suicide victims had a diagnosed mental health condition.[3] According to the Mental Health Foundation, anxiety and depression are the most common of these mental health conditions in the UK, with almost 8% of people meeting the criteria for diagnosis.[4] The Mental Health Foundation also provides the following statistics regarding young people's mental health:

- 20% of adolescents may experience a mental health problem in any given year

- 50% of mental health problems are established by age 14 and 75% by age 24

- 10% of children and young people (aged 5–16 years) have a clinically diagnosable mental problem, yet 70% of children and adolescents who experience mental health problems have not had appropriate interventions at a sufficiently early age.[5]

I got a degree in English Literature and then I trained to be a teacher. Last year, I learned how to fry an egg. But never, at any point in my life, have I ever received any sort of adequate or sustained programme of mental health training. And I'm not alone: a recent survey[6] by teen mental health charity stem4, analysing the responses of 300 teachers working in primary and secondary schools across the UK, found that whilst 78% of teachers say at least one of their pupils has had a mental health issue over the past year, only 19% of teachers said these pupils were getting the help they needed and only 30% of teachers said they had received adequate training to be able to deal with mental health issues. 27% said they have had received no training at all. Given the figures, clearly, current mental health provision is inadequate.

The recent Green Paper, "Transforming Children's and Young People's Mental Health Provision",[7] published in December 2017, might appear to demonstrate government recognition of the need for more professional mental health provision in schools, and the report has some seemingly admirable aims. Where schools are concerned, these are:

- Incentivising schools to identify a "Designated Senior Lead for Mental Health" to oversee mental health provision for students

- The funding of "Mental Health Support Teams" made up of National Health Service (NHS) mental health staff and jointly managed by schools and the NHS. These teams will be "linked to groups of primary and secondary schools and to colleges, providing interventions to support those with mild to moderate needs and supporting the promotion of good mental health and wellbeing".

However, many experts have expressed concern with the plans. Mental health campaigner Natasha Devon has criticised the proposed £300 million of funding for the scheme:

My own view is that £300 million over five years is a drop in the ocean. To put it into context, we spent £5 billion every single year on Trident. We currently spend fourteen times more on adult mental health services than we do for young people, despite the commonest onset age for mental illness being adolescence.[8]

Dr Nihara Krause, founder and CEO of stem4, whilst welcoming of the reforms, has articulated some anxiety regarding the fact that "the full roll out of the designated mental health lead will not happen until 2025", whilst "in the meanwhile there are on-going cuts that are being imposed on Child and Adolescent Mental Health Services (CAMHS), school nurses, educational psychologists, and a variety of children's centres".[9] The fact is there is still not enough being done. Whilst teachers should not be diagnosing, and certainly shouldn't be treating, mental health problems, it's important that they recognise what preventative measures they can take to loosen the grip that depression and suicide has on young people.

Before discussing with how teachers might help reduce rates of male suicide, it's important to explore why male suicide rates are thought to be so high. High male suicide rates might be best summarised by this thesis statement:

Males are more likely to kill themselves than females because they do not talk about their feelings.

Countless research studies have shown that males tend to be less emotionally literate than women. We might define them as "emotionally mute". You probably know one of these emotionally mute males yourself: he's the boyfriend who still makes jokes about his parents' divorce, the father you've known all your life and never seen cry, the brother who punched a wall when he found out about your mother's cancer, the grandfather who hasn't said a word to anyone since Nana died. Unsurprisingly, the emotional mutism of men is something cultivated in childhood. Many studies show that from a very early age, girls are encouraged to display positive emotions such as happiness and internalise negative ones such as sadness and anger. Conversely, boys are expected to show less "tender" emotions and are not stigmatised (as girls are) for externalising negative emotions such as anger.[10]

The research picture is reflected in a story communicated to me by Natasha Devon in which she recalled a small-scale study of students in a primary school. Boys and girls were asked, at aged five and aged seven, "How many feelings do you have?" Whilst girls as young as five years old were able to describe a range of emotions, at the same age boys were only able to describe two: "happy" and "angry". By age seven, boys' emotional literacy had increased by a whopping 50% – they were now able to describe three emotions: "happy", "angry", and "hungry"! As amusing as this is, the study has a concerning ending. These same boys, aged seven, were subsequently asked, "How many feelings does your mother have?" Interestingly (and disturbingly), when discussing their mothers, boys were able to recall the full gamut of emotions, suggesting that these boys, at the tender age of seven, were just unable to reconcile "emotions" with "boyness".

Another explanation for high male suicide rates is the fact that men are simply less likely than women to seek help for mental health problems.[11] This is because, as we saw in Martino's study discussed in Chapter 3, to talk about feelings is to talk about weakness, helplessness, and vulnerability, things which in the masculine world are stigmatised. It's very difficult for any man to be able to admit to a healthcare professional that they are experiencing these emotions. As teachers, it's important that we aim to develop our boys into men who can talk about their emotions, without feeling that they are weak because they are doing so.

Anger

Another factor in male suicide, alongside emotional mutism and a reluctance to seek medical help, is men's anger: "Men are so much more likely to use violent methods of suicide that is tied into anger" explains Anna Mullaney from Campaign Against Living Miserably (CALM), a charity dedicated to preventing male suicide. Whereas females are more likely to use less violent suicide methods, such as overdosing on prescription drugs, men are more likely to use violent methods because violence is what men are taught to use upon things that make them angry, even if that "thing" is themselves.

In their study, *Gender and Culture Differences in Emotion*, Fischer et al. acknowledge that in "many studies on gender differences in emotion ... men report experiencing and expressing more anger and other hostile emotions"[12] than women and they do so because society encourages them to assume a "high status male role aimed at competition, autonomy and power", in which anger is a necessary emotion to draw upon. They found that in countries in which women "actively participate in economic and political life" – that is, countries in which women have more equality – men are more than twice as likely than women to feel anger that has "no target". If anger has a target, it can be dealt with. Anger felt by a student towards a friend, teacher, or family member can be managed with a chat over lunch, a counselling session organised by the head of year, or a "restorative conversation" coordinated by a classroom teacher. Anger with no direct object is a little harder to deal with. The study also notes that men are a third times more likely to experience anger as a result of "small frustrations". This has huge implications for teachers, whose very job it is to throw "small frustrations" – or challenges – the way of the students in order to develop them as learners.

Self-harm

Although the majority of recorded incidences of self-harm are by females, a 2017 survey conducted by YouGov in conjunction with mental health charities, Young-Minds, The Mix, and selfharmUK found that 24% of boys aged 14–16 engage in self-harm.[13] Whilst girls are most likely to use "cutting"[14] as a form of self-harm, boys are most likely to "self-poison", most commonly through alcohol abuse. 21% of boys used this as a method of self-harm. Other methods include:

- Punching walls (19%)

- Controlling their eating (16%)

- Over-exercising (12%)

- Pulling hair (11%)

- Taking illegal drugs (10%).

Self-poison doesn't always mean taking illegal drugs. In 2016, 2,246 teenage boys were admitted to hospital after overdosing on prescription drugs like paracetamol or ibuprofen.[15]

The solutions

Even in times of increasing financial cuts, most schools will have dedicated, trained members of staff whose job it is to care for children experiencing emotional and mental health difficulties. If a child presents a mental health problem or an emotional disturbance, they should be referred to the designated person in your school. While the solutions below aren't offered as a panacea, they might be taken as the starting point for a reflective and open approach to mental health in your school.

Advice for school leaders and school teachers

A. Model emotional openness

If we ever want boys to discuss their emotions honestly and frankly, we need to normalise the process of doing so. This can be achieved by teacher modelling. I explained how I do this, in a blog post from 2018, entitled "Militant Tenderness":

> I try to be as honest as I can with students when it comes to my emotions. Whilst I would never discuss my personal life in any depth, I will openly discuss the feelings and emotions that arise in the context of what's being studied or discussed in the classroom. If a poem makes me very sad, I'll tell the class. If a kid makes me look at something in a new and exciting way, I'll express my childish delight. And, if a kid does a piece of work that's absolutely mind-blowing, to the point where it makes my heart swell with pride, and my eyes with tears, I'll acknowledge that fact, frankly and openly. In fact, I'll intentionally draw the class's attention to it. I'll say: "That's making me well up with pride, that", and face them, smiling and watery eyed.

> I'll be open about the way topics affect me and if appropriate, I'll attempt to explain *why* they affect me that way. A good exemplification of this is when I read the ending of 'Of Mice and Men.' Inevitably, as I read the final pages, my voice will falter and waiver with emotion. I don't try to hide this fact and when the kids notice it, and ask me why I am so affected by the ending of the book I'll explain to them that I see in Lennie and George the closeness I feel to my brothers and this informs my emotional response to the end of the novel.

Normalising frank and honest discussion of feelings does not require dedicated assemblies or afternoon visits from external agencies. It is best achieved by getting the people pupils would *normally* expect to find in a school – teachers and support staff – taking the opportunities to discuss male emotion in *normal* school environments: classrooms, corridors, and playgrounds. You don't need to be teachers of English (a subject some might think is more open to discussing emotions) to do this. Here are some suggestions how modelling emotional openness might be achieved in other school contexts:

- In history, the class are learning about the American civil rights movement. The teacher might say,

> As man I always feel there's a real pressure to be physically aggressive in threatening situations. I really respect Martin Luther King for his ability to keep it together during his peaceful protests, even when other men were literally spitting in his face. How do you think he managed that?

- In PE, the class are studying performance-enhancing drugs in sport. The teacher says, "I think that for men, there's a real pressure to always be the best at sport. I think that explains why so many men take to performance enhancing drugs. However, it's illegal. What might be a better way of dealing with the pressure to be the best at your particular sport?"

- During playground duty, a student asks a teacher, "How are you sir?" The teacher replies, "Actually, I'm having a bit of a down day today – I'm not feeling very positive. But that's okay; I'm going to see a friend later and talk things through – that usually helps".

B. Shoulder-to-shoulder talks

For some boys, the barrier to talking isn't so much that they don't want to talk but that they find talking incredibly awkward. Many educators advocate the effectiveness of shoulder-to-shoulder talks to get students talking about their problems. Ignore those that say this works with boys "because boys don't like eye contact". That's rubbish. A more accurate statement is "some children don't like eye contact". However, I do think that the way boys are discouraged from talking about their emotions may explain why *some* boys find it more difficult to talk face-to-face about their problems. The shoulder-to-shoulder method simply means having a conversation with a boy as you sit or stand or walk next to them. It feels quite unnatural to sit next to a child, rather than across from them, so "side-on-side" conversations, in my experience, are best conducted on a walk across the playground, around the school (so long as everyone else is in lessons), or on a walk from one lesson to another.

C. Talk about suicide appropriately

There might be occasions when suicide presents itself as a point of discussion in the classroom. The following advice, adapted from the Samaritans guidance on the media reporting of suicide,[16] provides useful guidance on how teachers might discuss suicide appropriately.

1. **Think about your audience:** remember that there are boys – and girls – in your class who may personally be affected by suicide and mental illness. School leaders should ensure that any scheme designed to normalise mental health discussion needs to run alongside a system of making staff aware of any significant mental health problems in students, or when a student has been personally affected by suicide

2. **When talking about suicide, never refer to methods or context:** details of suicide methods have been found to encourage vulnerable pupils to mimic suicidal behaviour. Because of this, teachers should never give any explicit details about suicide methods, if a suicide is being discussed.

If discussing a specific suicide – perhaps that of a celebrity, or someone in the local area – avoid, where possible, revealing too much about the person who has taken their own life. Overidentification with a victim of suicide can also prompt suicidal behaviours. Finally, refrain from saying that any particular method of suicide is "quick" or painless

3. **Don't oversimplify suicide:** suicide can rarely be put down to a single factor. Avoid any suggestions that it could be so, and never shy away from the complex reality of suicide and its impact on the family and friends of suicide victims

4. **Educate and offer support:** any discussion about suicide should end with an offer of support for those who might need it. Tell students that if they have been affected by the issue, there are people within the school they can talk to. Refer them also to The Samaritans

Whilst suicide may be discussed in a whole-class context, of course there may also be occasions when teachers find themselves talking face to face with an individual student about it, because either the teacher or pupil has initiated a conversation out of some concern. The first thing a teacher should do is refer this to the appropriate person, usually the designated safeguarding lead or the appropriate pastoral lead. This person should then take note of the advice provided by The Samaritans:

If you think somebody is suicidal, use the following questions:

- Ask directly "have you had thoughts of killing yourself?"
- Ask "have you thought about how?"
- Ask "have you thought about when and where?"

If the answer to all three of these questions is "yes", then the person is a suicide risk. An ambulance should be called and the student should not be left alone.

D. Talk with boys using their language

Anna Mullaney, from CALM, told me that, despite the dominant narrative of male emotional mutism, often men and boys *are* talking about mental health, but we're failing to notice that they are because they're not using the language we'd expect. She explained that men, encouraged to stifle any emotional outpourings from a young age, lack the vocabulary of mental health: so, whilst it wouldn't seem unusual for a female to say, *I've been feeling really anxious,* or *I'm worried I might be depressed*, the opposite is true for a male, who has been encouraged from birth to display stoic fortitude and strength at all times. Clinical words such as "anxious", and "depressed", which directly refer to mental health, are not part of the male lexicon because to speak those words would be to speak of weakness. There is a further issue, as Robertson and Baker[17] note, that even phrases like "I'm feeling unloved", or "I have butterflies in my stomach all the time", which avoid medical terminology, are feminised and therefore less likely to be used by men. An Australian study,[18] conducted by Fiona Shand et al., surveyed men on the language they used to express suicidal thoughts and depression. The top five words or phrases men used to describe feeling suicidal were:

Words	% (of men who used the term)
"Useless" or "Worthless"	74
I've had enough	69
Hopeless	68
Pointless	66
Over it	62

The top five words or phrases men used to describe feeling depressed were:

Words	% (of men who used the term)
Stressed	56
Not going down too well	56
Tired	52
Down in the dumps	52
Angry	42

Whilst you won't get many teenage boys using the phrase, "down in the dumps", what we do see here is acceptable male words ("stressed" and "tired" is what you should feel after a day of *all* that manly work) used euphemistically to express feelings associated with a serious mental health issue.

As teachers, we need to be mindful of the language boys use and the possibility that when a boy repeatedly tells us he's "tired", it might not be because he's had too much late night X-Box, but because he feels he's had too much life. When he tells us he's "stressed", it might not be that he's fed up with revision- it might be that he's fed up with living. As teachers, we need to ensure we take note of the frequency with which boys use these terms, and take note of the contexts in which they are used: *I'm tired because I stayed up late* is very different to *I keep falling out with my friends and I just feel tired of it all.*

Teachers should also ensure that when a serious concern presents itself, in the immediate instance, it may be useful to avoid using clinical terminology in our discussions with boys we are concerned about (although we should continue in our efforts to normalise these terms as explained above). Many mental health advocates recommend using the phrase "toolkit" rather than "coping strategies" to refer to the ways in which boys can deal with their depression or anger.

E. Provide men to talk to

Whilst students ascribe very little importance to a teacher's gender in terms of learning, a study in Australia found that where personal matters are concerned, students would prefer to talk to someone of their own gender.[19] In my previous school, the pastoral team – that is, the body of teachers responsible for helping and supporting students with issues not directly related to their subject learning – was largely female. Noticing that this was also the case with pastoral teams on a number of school-based television documentaries, I took to Twitter to see if this reflected a wider trend. Here are the results of a poll, in which 413 people responded:

At your school, does your pastoral team consist of:	
Mostly females	54%
Equal split	25%
Mostly males	12%

Overwhelmingly, the staff whose job it is to counsel and console children tend to be female. It's important that school leaders make a concerted effort to ensure boys know that in their schools, on their pastoral teams there is a man with a kind smile and a sympathetic ear. A boy who is anxious about his penis size, or confused with his sexuality, or fuming at the fact that Lucy in 9B told her friends about the love letter he wrote her, may be desperate for a man to discuss this with. If the shoulders to cry on are always female, we could be doing these boys a huge disservice and exacerbating any potential mental health problems.

F. Look for signs

Of course, not all men want to talk. In fact, Natasha Devon criticises male mental health campaigns that constantly reaffirm men's need to discuss their emotions. According to Devon, this is simply victim blaming, because if it were as simple as men and boys simply talking more, they would have done so already. Rather, for Devon, "what we should be doing is examining why men live in an environment that makes it nearly impossible for them to talk about their mental health, or to be understood when they do". As teachers, this is why we should do all we can to normalise mental health discussion (see above): we want to make talking about emotions the norm, rather than something that needs to be demanded by campaign posters and videos.

Whether they are willing to talk about their feelings or not, all boys contemplating suicide may present visual signs of being at risk. CALM recommends looking out for the following:

- Unexpected mood changes – including suddenly being calm and happy after being very depressed

- Social withdrawal

- Change in sleeping and eating patterns

- Lack of energy

- Neglect of personal appearance

- Reckless behaviour

- Increased drug or alcohol abuse

- Anger or irritability

- Talking about suicide or wanting to die – their statements may be vague or appear to be joking about it

- Giving away possessions

- Saying goodbye – to friends and family as if they won't be seeing them again.[20]

Of course, if every suicidal person were to show signs like these, there'd be less suicides. We'd spot the signs and we'd get help. The sad truth of the matter is that we can't always tell who might be experiencing suicidal thoughts. We've all heard somebody say, about a man who's killed himself: *I never would've believed it. He was the life and soul of the party.* Be aware that the life and soul of the party might be overcompensating. Never take anything for granted. Your "class clown" may be just that. Or he may be a boy desperate for someone to notice.

G. Provide care for male self-harmers

Punching walls, fighting, and even self-destructive behaviours such as fronting up to the teacher are all acceptable ways for boys to self-harm. Whilst any boys that display these behaviours need to be sanctioned firmly in accordance with the school's behaviour policy, schools also need to consider that these behaviours may be used as a method of self-harm. As a selfharmUK blog explains, often these behaviours are punished and nothing more:

> Punching walls or regularly getting into fights are also forms of self-harm that are missed in schools, because the behaviour is seen as

aggressive rather than emotional. Perhaps punching a wall until skin or even knuckles are broken is a way of releasing anger at self, others or feelings of failure. Regularly getting into fights shows signs of self-destructive behaviour. A young male might well know he will be hurt but will enter into an altercation recognising it will relieve the emotions he is feeling. [21]

It's important that school leaders and teachers ensure that these boys receive the same pastoral protection and support as a girl found to be cutting.

H.   Harness the benefits of physical exercise

A recent landmark study, the biggest of its kind, looking at data from 1.2 million participants, found a significant link between mental health and physical exercise.[22] The study found that over a period of 30 days, people who exercised reported 43.2% fewer days of poor mental health than those who had not exercised. Interestingly, certain types of exercise were found to be more beneficial than others: the largest associations between physical exercise and fewer reported days of poor mental health were in participants who took part in popular team sports, cycling, and aerobic and gym activities. Optimal timings for the effects were 45-minute stints, three to five times a week.

This study stands out because it's so huge, but there are countless other studies out there which suggest that people who are physically active live less stressful, happier lives. Because of this, school leaders need to work hard at engaging all students in exercise. "How do we engage all students in sport?" is a question whose answers prove as elusive as those to the question, "How do we get kids to read?" If there were a straight answer, we'd all be doing it and nearly a third of UK children wouldn't be overweight or obese.[23] When I asked on Twitter, "How do we get kids that hate physical education, doing physical education?" I received over a hundred responses, from experienced teachers all over the country. Suggestions included:

- Ensure students have positive experiences of PE. Positive experiences lead to students feeling more motivated to take part again

- Physical activity doesn't have to be sport – extracurricular clubs covering martial arts, yoga, dance are all things that can get kids moving

- In PE lessons, avoid gender stereotypes. Boys can play and enjoy netball, just as girls might prefer football

- Model a relentless love of sport and talk about the benefits to physical and mental health.

My favourite was this:

- Don't accept excuse notes that wouldn't be accepted in academic subjects.

Although being active may bolster the mental well-being of pupils in school, there is another factor of school sport that can improve student's mental health: tender coaching.

I.   Adopt tender coaching methods

Tender coaching: case study 1

Because gender stereotypes have led them to believe that they are "not academic", many boys arrive at secondary school preferring to direct all their efforts towards scoring tries on the sports field, rather than trying in English or science or maths. These are the boys who, although troublesome for teachers of geography, history, and business studies, are perfect and plimsolled saints for the (usually male) PE teachers whom they idolise. Because of their elevated position in these boys' esteem, PE teachers and school sports coaches may be the only adults in a school whose offers of emotional support to boys are accepted, rather than rejected. In the two case studies that follow, we can see how sports coaches – rather than falling into the trap of playing up to non-tender masculine stereotypes in order to engage boys (which as we saw in Chapter 3, could cause considerable long-term damage to a boy's academic career) – are using sport as a means of cultivating a tender-masculinity in the boys they're coaching.

David Sharkey, an English teacher and school rugby coach, recognises that as a sports coach, he has a unique opportunity to help boys develop their mental health as well as their physical health:

> I focus on how we feel as individuals and as a team. I like to tap into how players feel during moments in practice games and matches as a way into this. By focusing on how they felt in certain moments while playing or practising, it allows me the opportunity to segue into how they feel at other times during the week.

This seems a useful way in. Equally interesting is what Sharkey had to tell me about his proposed plans to introduce traffic light gates to his training sessions:

> There are three different gates to walk through before we start training: Green if you feel good and positive; Amber if you are ok; Red if you are not feeling good. The gates and labels are arbitrary but they can allow for a conversation to happen if their player is willing to engage with the process and the coach or players. If anything, it allows for a brief moment, prior to stepping onto the training pitch, of reflection and gives a chance for them to express how they feel. I'll ask coaches to take part too and to talk openly about their own feelings and how we might manage these emotional states rather than bottle them up.

I love this idea. Not only does it ensure the boys reflect on their own emotions, but it provides signals to others. A boy who has been encouraged by a competent coach to support his teammates may make a special effort to reach out to a troubled teammate who has entered training via the red gate; a student who enters training via the amber gate may receive a few more supportive pats on the shoulder than usual. The key to all of this is a respected coach who dares to eschew masculine stereotypes in favour of a more inclusive, tender approach to developing his or her players.

Tender coaching: case study 2

The Boxing Academy in Hackney is a school that takes on pupils at risk of exclusion in other schools. All of the pupils there undertake a programme of academic study alongside daily sessions in a boxing gym. The boxing gym ethos of the place has had an impressive impact on academic results, but the school's principal, Anna Cain, emphasised the importance of coaches in helping with her students' mental fitness, as well as their physical fitness:

> That relationship with an adult male is very helpful. What they're also doing in the boxing gym is building relationships with a competent, caring, responsible adult who is going to tell them the right and wrong way to think about things. Yes, the physical activity helps the mental health. That, alongside the feeling of family and support that a boxing gym provides – it all helps.

Cain says that boxing is unique in the way it provides emotional support to boys: "stepping into a boxing gym is like stepping into a second family", she tells me, "something that isn't replicated as strongly in other sporting environments". Of course, not all schools can provide students with boxing training. But I don't think boxing is necessarily the point; the boxing gym environment is what's crucial. As Cain explained to me, and as informed by my own limited personal experience, boxing gyms are places where egos are left at the door; where pros are willing to coach beginners; where lack of ability isn't laughed at or frowned upon, but seen as a starting point for improvement. Coaches and teachers of any sport would do well to create a similarly supportive training environment and ethos for their teams and students because often, students will only seek support in places they feel truly comfortable. This doesn't need to be in a sporting context. For some, it may be the cosy space of the school office, warmed by the strong smell of coffee and brightened by pictures of a friendly receptionist's recent holiday in the Dordogne. Yet for others, the cold confines of a dusty school gym, reeking of sweat and feet, is the place where they feel most relaxed and where support is most likely to be sought.

Fighting anger

Given the fact that boxing is often presented in the media as the saviour of many an angry young man, I asked Anna Cain if boxing really did have any impact on her students' anger:

> The problem is that some people think boxing is barbaric and shouldn't be allowed. These people tell angry children, 'You're not supposed to feel like that.' How does that help a child, a child that is so angry that they can't speak properly? Anger is part of mental health and the problem is everyone says that anger is a bad thing. But anger can be a good thing so long as you don't let it control you.
>
> If you lose your temper in a boxing ring you lose the fight. So be angry. But take it, and use it properly. Be in control of your anger.

As I mentioned earlier in this chapter, boys are often encouraged to externalise their anger. The problem is, when they do so, they are chastised for doing so, particularly in schools, where punching walls, shouting loudly, and swearing aren't desirable behaviours. Sport can provide opportunities for coaches to discuss with boys the ways in which anger can manifest itself in either positive or negative ways. If anger leads to a renewed, vigorous effort to get the ball further up the pitch, then anger has been harnessed for good. If anger leads to swearing at an umpire and being dismissed from the field of play, then that player has let their team down. If boys are given the chance to discuss anger, and reflect on the way they can use it positively in a sporting situation, it may help them to better distinguish between that and negative, destructive anger. In recognising the difference, it may be that the negative, destructive anger becomes easier to control.

J.   Take a proactive approach to homophobia

According to a study conducted by the Centre for Family Research at the University of Cambridge for Stonewall,[24] 61% of lesbian, gay, or bisexual students have self-harmed. Nearly a quarter of these (22%) have attempted to take their own life. For trans students, the percentages rise: 84% of students who identify as trans have self-harmed and nearly half (45%) have tried to kill themselves. Homophobic bullying is no doubt a significant factor in these heartbreaking statistics.

Where boys are concerned, they are more likely than girls to be the victims of homophobic bullying (57% compared to 35%). Given the value that traditional masculinity places on heterosexuality, this is of no surprise, and for this same reason, it is no surprise that boys are also more likely to be perpetrators of homophobic bullying (43% of bullying comes from boys compared to 31% from girls).[25] There are a number of pre-emptive approaches schools can take to ensure that their LGBT pupils do not have to endure homophobic bullying.

Role models

Daniel Gray is cofounder of #LGBTedUK, a network of LGBT educators working together to improve the educational welfare of LGBT pupils. When I interviewed him, he was keen to highlight the importance of role models in protecting the mental health of LGBT pupils:

> In schools, heterosexuality is everywhere. Straight students have visible role models all day, every day. Young gay people need role models too, either to help them figure out who they are, or to make them feel less isolated and alone.

Gray has personal experience of what it means to be a role model for LGBT students. He tells the following story of what happened after he revealed that he was gay to students during a school assembly:

> One student came up to me after the assembly who I didn't know. I have never taught him before. He looked very nervous and a little shy. But he had something to say.
> "Sir, your assembly has changed my life."[26]

The language we use

It's important to say that you needn't be an LGBT teacher to be a role model for LGBT students. Heterosexual teachers can still do their part in making LGBT students feel safe and supported at school. I have written before about my efforts to "normalise" homosexuality by considering the language I use in class:

> There was probably a time when the anecdotes and questions I used to illuminate a concept were heteronormative. For example, in a lesson on love poetry, I might have asked, "Why might a man write his girlfriend a sonnet?" Now, for every time I'll ask that question, I'll ask another that is homonormative. For example, "Why might a man write his boyfriend a sonnet?"

As I went on to explain in the same blog post, in embracing homonormative pronouns, and using them interchangeably with heteronormative pronouns, and without making a song and dance about it, I am telling students: *This is a safe space for you. Your sexuality is valued in this classroom.*

LGBT clubs

Clubs where LGBT people can go to discuss their sexuality openly, honestly, and safely are a really powerful statement of support for LGBT students, by the schools who run them, especially if these clubs are publicised by school teachers and school leaders in assemblies, form times, and school newsletters. Maria Vogler, a Personal, Social, Health and Economics (PSHE) teacher at Kings College in Guildford, started the school's first LGBT club, which meets one lunchtime a week, in May 2018:

> Each week there is a specific discussion topic, followed by 10 minutes in which students can just have a chat. The support students give each other is incredible. They advise each other about coming out, share their worries, reassure each other. These are kids from across the year groups from year seven to eleven. Every single student that enters into that room has a different experience, a different challenge, and a different story to share. They are each other's best assets. I am a straight teacher; my experience is not enough for these students. They need each other and that's why I believe every school should be running an LGBT club.

Of course, whilst these approaches work towards creating a school environment where homophobia is non-existent, when it does occur it should be dealt with severely. In their *School Report* document, Stonewall provide some excellent guidance on what can be done on a whole-school basis to ensure that LGBT students have a positive school experience that doesn't impact negatively on their mental health – I'd recommend that all school teachers and leaders read it.[27]

The final word

The topic of mental health is, by definition, very complex. Every mental health condition is different and every mental health condition affects different students in different ways. The suggested solutions presented here, whilst most definitely not a universal remedy, should at the very least form the basis of some reflection on what you and your school are doing to tackle the problem of boys' anger, self-harm, and inability to talk about their feelings. Hopefully, what's become most apparent, over the course of this chapter, is the need for a proactive approach that seeks to instill in boys a belief that talking about their feelings and emotions is the key to long lasting mental well-being that ensures they do not become, like so many others, one of the 75%.

Notes

1 Mental Health Foundation (2016) *Fundamental facts about mental health 2016.* Mental Health Foundation: London. Available at: file://kings-apps-02/staff$/Teaching%20Staff/MPinkett/Downloads/fundamental-facts-about-mental-health-2016%20(4).pdf (Accessed: 9th June 2018).

2 Office for National Statistics (2017) *Who is most at risk of suicide?* Available at: www.ons.gov.uk/peoplepopulationandcommunity/birthsdeathsandmarriages/deaths/articles/whoismostatriskofsuicide/2017-09-07 (Accessed: 6th August 2018).

3 Mental Health Foundation (2016).

4 Mental Health Foundation, *Mental health statistics: The most common mental health problems.* Available at: www.mentalhealth.org.uk/statistics/mental-health-statistics-most-common-mental-health-problems (Accessed: 8th August 2018).

5 Mental Health Foundation, *Mental health statistics: Children and young people.* Available at: www.mentalhealth.org.uk/statistics/mental-health-statistics-children-and-young-people (Accessed: 8th August 2018).

6 stem4, (2018) *One in three teachers fears harms for pupils waiting for mental health treatment.* Available at: https://stem4.org.uk/one-in-three-teachers-fears-harm-for-pupils-waiting-for-mental-health-treatment/ (Accessed: 7th August 2018).

7 Department of Health, Department for Education, (2017) *Transforming children's and young people's mental health provision*, DfE. Available at: https://assets.publishing. service.gov.uk/government/uploads/system/uploads/attachment_data/file/664855/ Transforming_children_and_young_people_s_mental_health_provision.pdf (Accessed: 7th August 2018).

8 Devon, N. (2017) 'The Government's promised £300 million for mental health won't fix our broken society', *TES Online.* Available at: www.tes.com/news/governments-promised-ps300-million-mental-health-wont-fix-our-broken-society (Accessed: 7th August 2018).

9 Krause, N. (2018) 'A comment on the Government's recently published Green paper on entitled "Transforming Children's and Young People's Mental Health Provision"', *stem4.* Available at: https://stem4.org.uk/a-comment-on-the-governments-recently-published-green-paper-on-transforming-children-and-young-peoples-mental-health-provision/ (Accessed: 7th August 2018).

10 Chaplin, T. (2015) 'Gender and emotion expression: A developmental contextual perspective', *Emotional Review*, 7:1, pp. 14–21.

11 Thornton, J. (2012) *Men and Suicide': Why It's a Social Issue*, Ewell: Samaritans.

12 Fischer, A., Mosquera, P., Vianen, A., & Manstead, A. (2004) Gender and culture differences in emotion, *Emotion*, 4:1, pp. 87–94.

13 YoungMinds (2017) *Young men and self-harm.* Available at: https://youngminds.org.uk/ blog/young-men-and-self-harm/ (Accessed: 12th September 2018).

14 'Cutting' refers to the act of deliberately inflicting physical pain on the body by creating incisions, with a knife, blade, or other sharp object, on the skin.

15 SelfharmUK, *Boys and self-harm*, Available at: www.selfharm.co.uk/get-information/ the-facts/boys-and-self-harm (Accessed: 12th September 2018).

16 Samaritans, *Best practice suicide reporting tips.* Available at: www.samaritans.org/ media-centre/media-guidelines-reporting-suicide/best-practice-suicide-reporting-tips (Accessed: 13th September 2018).

17 Robertson, S. & Baker, P. (2016) 'Men and health promotion in the United Kingdom: 20 years forward?' *Health Education Journal*, 76:1, pp. 102–113.

18 Shand, F.L., Proudfoot, J., Player, M.J., Fogarty, A., Whittle, E., Wilhelm, K., Hadzi-Pavlovic, D., McTigue, I., Spurrier, M., & Christensen, H. (2015) 'What might interrupt men's suicide? Results from an online survey of men'. *BMJ open.* Available at: https:// bmjopen.bmj.com/content/bmjopen/5/10/e008172.full.pdf (Accessed: 14th August 2018).

19 Martin, A. J. & Marsh, H. (2005) 'Motivating boys and motivating girls: Does teacher gender really make a difference?' *Australian Journal of Education*, 49:3, pp. 320–334.

20 CALM, *Worried about someone?* www.thecalmzone.net/help/worried-about-someone/ (Accessed: 13th September 2018).

21 SelfharmUK.

22 Chekroud, S.R., Gueorguieva, R., Zheutlin, A.B., et al. (2018) 'Association between physical exercise and mental health in 1.2 million individuals in the USA between 2011 and 2015: a cross-sectional study', *Lancet Psychiatry*, 5:9, 739–746. doi: 10.1016/S2215-0366(18)30227-X. (Accessed: 13th September 2018).

23 Health and Social Care Information Centre (2015) and Health Survey for England (2014).

24 Bradlow, J., Bartram, F., Stonewall, A.G., & Jadva, V. (2017) *The experiences of lesbian, gay, bi and trans young people in Britain's schools in 2017*. School Report. Available at: www.stonewall.org.uk/sites/default/files/the_school_report_2017.pdf (Accessed: 18th September 2018).

25 Statham, H., Jadva, V., & Daly, I. (2012) *The experiences of gay young people in Britain's schools in 2012*. School Report.

26 'Teacher Daniel Gray: the day I told students I was gay', *BBC*, 16th February 2017. Available at: www.bbc.co.uk/news/uk-38958873 (Accessed: 18th September 2018).

27 Bradlow (2017).

5 Expectations

Mark Roberts

The story

Let's imagine a head of department in a school with a sizeable gender achievement gap. Boys are generally doing ok in his subject but, when it comes to results, the girls are still miles ahead. He decides, therefore, to set pupils on *potential* rather than current ability. He sits down and discusses this with the teachers in the faculty. After a passionate and stimulating debate, they all agree that there is a moral consideration to this strategy: in the interests of pupils' future educational and career paths, it's the right thing to do. They also agree that there is a pragmatic dimension to the decision: in order to boost results, it's the right thing to do.

That settled it. They started by giving boys who are going into their GCSE groups – especially higher prior attaining free school meals (FSM)[1] boys – more of a chance by putting them in the top set based on their Key Stage 2 (KS2) score, not what they got at the end of Year 9. Something strange happened. That rarest of things occurred in a departmental meeting: an amicable consensus was reached.

The top set mindset

Six weeks later, the head of department fires out a regulation, nonchalant email, asking for any suggested set changes. Are there any pupils who aren't working hard enough? Are any kids clearly in the wrong group? Are there any students who need taking down a peg or two, by taking them down a set or two?

What happens next? Yes, you've guessed it. In an unprecedented move, he is inundated with urgent requests for downward movement. He usually gets one or occasionally two responses to this kind of email. But now there are ten requests to move down pupils who are "not top set material", who are "being a pain", who "don't have the right work ethic" and therefore "don't deserve to be there". Seven of them are FSM. Nine are boys.

The research

Do teacher's expectations of their pupils affect their outcomes? A classic study by Rosenthal and Jacobson[2] involved telling teachers in American public elementary schools that a number of their pupils had scored highly on an important test and could be expected to achieve at a high level over the coming year. In reality, the test – Harvard Test of Inflected Acquisition – was fictional and the children were chosen at random. The randomly selected pupils proved more likely to make larger academic gains than their peers, especially those of a younger age. Both "lower" and "higher ability" pupils who were selected benefited, with boys making particular gains to verbal intelligence.

The power of expectations

According to Rosenthal and Jacobson, starting the year with high expectations of pupil achievement resulted in ... higher levels of pupil achievement. The idea that high expectations have a highly beneficial influence on outcomes is known as the **Pygmalion Effect**:

> **Pygmalion:** In ancient Greek mythology, Ovid's *Metamorphoses* tells the story of how Pygmalion, king of Cyprus, fell in love with one of his own sculptures, which was then brought to life (Figure 5.1).

The opposite of the Pygmalion Effect is the **Golem Effect**, a type of self-fulfilling prophecy whereby negative attitudes about a pupil's academic ability or potential leads inevitably to poor outcomes.

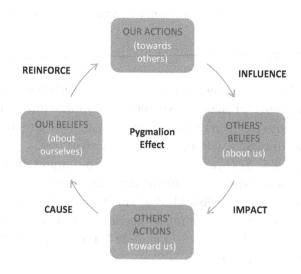

Figure 5.1 The Pygmalion Effect

In Jewish mythology, **the golem** was a clay creature brought to life by a Rabbi to defend the Jews of Prague. But over time the golem became corrupt and dangerous and had to be destroyed.

Babad et al.,[3] who coined the term in a 1982 study, contended that – when it comes to outcomes – Golem beats Pygmalion every time. Negative self-fulfilling prophecies have a more powerful hold over a pupil's self-efficacy than positive ones.

Teachers' expectations of boys

In an important piece of research published in 2004,[4] Susan Jones and Debra Myhill of Exeter University investigated whether teachers' perceptions of gender influenced their expectations of a pupil's likelihood of being educationally successful. Following interviews with 40 teachers and 144 children from primary, middle, and secondary schools, Jones and Myhill found that teachers held preconceived notions about the likelihood and typicality of high-achieving and underachieving pupils from both genders. In other words, girls who excelled academically were seen as typical girls, while underachieving boys were viewed as typical of their gender. Boys who were academic high-flyers were seen as anomalous, a challenge to gender norms, while underachieving girls were generally ignored. As Jones and Myhill put it, among these teachers there was a "tendency to associate boys with underachievement and girls with high achievement".

So, how do these gendered expectations of achievement manifest themselves? Are teachers openly prejudicial about boys' chances of success in the academic sphere? Not for a large majority. 80% of the teachers agreed in principal that there is no reason why boys and girls shouldn't be able to achieve the same results, which seems reassuring, until you consider the other 1/5th of teachers interviewed; this 20% had presumably, and very worryingly, written off boys from the outset.

At least the rest believed in the equality of opportunity for both genders. Alas in reality, according to the findings, there was a major problem for the 80% who opined that boys had as much chance of achieving as did girls. Once they got into the classroom, there proved to be a disconnect between what they said they believed in and their actions:

> 80% of the teachers expected that boys and girls should get same results. This commitment to equal achievement, however, was not reflected in teachers' perceptions...about classroom attitude and behaviour and ability within different areas of the curriculum.

Outside of the classroom, teachers were keen to express beliefs about equal chances of good outcomes. When discussing their positive experiences in the classroom, however, the teachers largely reverted to stereotypical generalisations such as "girls are better writers", "girls settle and get on with it", "girls are quieter", and "girls have better English skills". When it came to positives about boys, stereotypes again abounded: "boys are better at mathematics", "boys have better oral skills", "boys are leaders", and "when you capture their imagination, boys can be keen".

Negative statements about girls' achievement were few and tended to focus on a lack of self-belief and resilience, while negative statements about behaviour focussed on the emotional consequences of friendship breakdowns and the supposedly greater likelihood that girls will hold grudges. Boys attracted a much larger list of negative comments. In academic terms, lots of teachers felt that they have a disinclination towards reading and don't like writing, which are both fundamental bedrocks of academic success. In behaviour terms, there were a plethora of pejorative comments, describing boys' inability to sit still, their noisy and disruptive natures, their lazy or apathetic attitudes, and their lack of maturity.

Teachers' gender-biased judgements of ability and attainment

Longitudinal research by Camille Terrier[5] of MIT from 2016 found that middle school teachers favour girls when grading. Analysis of data of nearly 5,000 French pupils – taking into account variables such as social background and boys' "more disruptive behaviour" – led Terrier to conclude that "teachers' gender biases have a high and significant effect on boys' progress relative to girls in both mathematics and literacy".

The study from Tammy Campbell,[6] which we looked at in Chapter 2, also found evidence that gender stereotypes lead to biased judgements that affect pupil outcomes. Campbell notes that boys are systematically given lower scores than their ability warrants in English and reading. And this isn't just a KS2 phenomenon. Looking back to the beginning of primary school, Campbell cites a 2011 study by Hansen and Jones[7] which observed that

> Teacher assessments pronouncedly favour girls to a greater extent than cognitive test performance, indicating that gender disproportionality at the foundation stage may, like at KS2, be attributable to biased judgements.

A deficit model of male achievement

The findings that teachers are (a) biased against boys when assessing, (b) believe that boys are less likely to be academically successful, and (c) believe boys are more likely to misbehave are very concerning for a variety of reasons. First, we know from the Pygmalion Effect that high expectations of pupils often lead to improved outcomes. In the classroom at least, these teachers show evidence of the opposite: a Golem Effect whereby lower expectations of boys are witnessed, often before they even walk through the classroom door. Second, because of the "contradictory set of attitudes" where they "speak of boys and girls having equal academic potential, yet give voice to a deficit model of male achievement", 80% of the teachers involved in Jones and Myhill's study weren't aware of (or weren't able to admit to) their lower expectations of boys. In other words, most of them are happy to say that boys should do just as well, but when confronted with male behaviours in the classroom, they lower their expectations of boys' outcomes. Boys frustrate teachers. They are viewed in terms of the things they "cannot, will not and do not do".

By stark contrast, girls are celebrated for their apparent obedience and passive natures. *Wouldn't school be easier if boys were more like girls?* is the unspoken assumption. These conflicting internal attitudes mean that without training, teachers are unlikely to recognise their part in the problem of boys' underachievement. If we believe we treat our pupils equally, we are unlikely to recognise our culpability. We cannot help solve a problem that we have yet to acknowledge. Third, these kinds of comments do girls no good either. Seeing girls as successful but delicate, driven but risk averse contributes to unequal treatment of females at later stages of their education and careers, when masculine qualities appear to result in greater societal and financial recognition.

The early years: playful boys and the "class clown" label

Lynn A. Barnett's recent longitudinal study[8] into first, second, and third grade (Years 2, 3, and 4 in the UK) teachers' perceptions of playful children concluded that "playful boys were stigmatised by their teachers" in sharp contrast to playful girls, where confident, impulsive and mischievous behaviour wasn't taken into account during teacher ratings of pupils. Playful boys were seen as an increasing nuisance by primary age teachers, leaving them likely to be labelled "class clown" by teachers, unlike playful girls. Intriguingly, these attitudes showed a huge disconnect between teacher's views of playful boys, the pupils' initial views of themselves, and the perceptions of their peers at the start of Grade 1. Over time, however, with the accumulative impact of public reprimands, the Golem Effect had taken hold: "these negative perceptions were likely transferred by teachers to peers and to the children themselves, whereupon they changed their positive perceptions to be increasingly negative by the third grade".[9] Predictably, the playful boys' self-esteem and self-efficacy levels plummeted, to the extent that they now viewed themselves as "unpopular" with their peers and their behaviours as "problematic", unlike the playful girls who behaved in a similar manner but escaped the class clown tag.

"Laddy lads" or "absolute pains"

Further research into teachers' perceptions of boys' behaviour, and attitudes to work and school, was conducted in 2010 by Carolyn Jackson.[10] Using a similar interview sample size as Jones and Myhill, Jackson found similar attitudes from teachers towards boys. These included complaints about peer-influenced group behaviours (playing up to mates and showing a "pack mentality"), anti-academic attitudes, a lack of respect for authority, attention-seeking, competitive arrogance, and a particular focus on the pre-eminence of sport as a key indicator of "laddish popularity". Some teachers were more sympathetic towards certain boys, showing an awareness of the inner conflict faced by those who wanted to display their traditional masculinity and do well in class. These teachers still, however, argued it was inevitable in these cases that the laddish side would win out.

"Degrees of laddishness"

Jackson's research does uncover a fascinating, subtle difference from Jones and Myhill's clear cut findings about "troublesome boys". It would appear that some teachers' expectations of boys are influenced by a "blurred and highly subjective" pigeonholing, where they individually classify boys on a sliding scale that recognises *degrees of "laddishness"*:

> It depends on whether they're prepared to be laddish with you or laddish against you...there are some lads...who you quite like teaching because they're fun and entertaining, but they know when to stop...And then there are the lads who seem to come in dead set that they're not going to do anything academic at all...I like my laddy lads...But the ones who are set against you, even though you like them, they're just an absolute pain to teach. (Ms Cornish – Elmwood School)[11]

As a teacher who has had to cope with occasional lessons ruined by disruption over the years, I'm full of sympathy for Ms Cornish. But the laddishness spectrum – and teachers' expectations of academic outcomes based on these classifications – raises interesting questions. First, how quickly does a teacher decide whether a boy is going to be a "laddy lad" or "an absolute pain"? As teachers often compare class lists and pass on advice to their colleagues about pupils they've taught previously, could these reputations follow certain "absolute pains" throughout their school career? Second, how might it feel for a boy who has decided to turn over a new leaf to be treated with suspicion by a new teacher? It would seem that for many teachers in the study, expectations for boys were inextricably linked to matters of discipline and behaviour management.

How do pupils think teachers treat boys?

In a later study,[12] Myhill and Jones sought to discover pupils' perceptions of whether male and female pupils were treated equitably by their teachers in the classroom. During interviews, pupils – of primary, middle, and secondary school age – were asked to respond to a single question: *do you think boys and girls are treated the same?* The results were pretty clear. A sizeable majority of pupils *of both sexes* felt that teachers treat boys more negatively than girls. The researchers found that this perception increases with age, with secondary school pupils most likely to notice a discrepancy in teachers' attitudes toward boys and girls. Of the 136 pupils who made comments about teachers' conduct with boys and girls "84 (62%) claimed that boys were unfavourably treated by teachers, whilst only 8% felt the reverse was true. The remaining 30% believed they were treated the same". Some of the points made by the boys and girls who took part in the research included:

- Girls get away with poor behaviour because teachers don't expect them to be naughty

- Teachers think girls are more sensitive so are worried they'll cry if disciplined

- Teachers – especially male ones – are gentler with girls

- Teachers are less likely to shout at girls

- Girls are treated more like adults because teachers think they are more mature than boys

- Boys are told off more and punished more for similar behaviour

- Female teachers are kinder and seem more human

- Male teachers can be gullible and manipulated by girls

These are only perceptions, of course. Whether these attitudes occur in reality is a separate question. But the evidence from this study shows that a significant percentage of pupils believe that they witness unfair treatment of boys in their daily lessons. As a teacher or leader, if these damaging feelings were widespread in my lesson or school, I'd want to know about them. Leaving perceptions about the importance of the teacher's gender to one side (we'll return to this debate in Chapter 7), the comments made throw up other interesting perceptions.

While it appears on the surface that in certain instances girls get a better deal from teachers through the biased, favourable treatment that they receive, if we dig deeper, we can see that this behaviour still reinforces gender differences that harms them in other ways. Even seemingly kind gestures, such as the idea that girls are not to be reprimanded because of their "sensitive" natures, perpetuate stereotypical ideas that portray girls as fragile creatures lacking in emotional resilience. Boys, meanwhile, report feeling disproportionally slammed by teachers for behaviour that – in the eyes of their peers at least – is similar to that of girls (Figures 5.2 and 5.3).

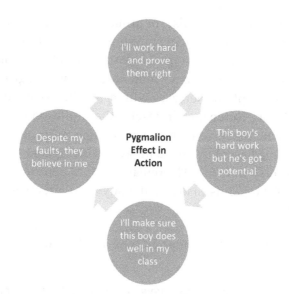

Figure 5.2 The Pygmalion Effect in action

Figure 5.3 The Golem Effect in action

Teachers' expectations of gender and specific subjects

According to Jones and Myhill, pupils also commonly believe that teachers have expectations about whether boys or girls will be able to do well in certain subjects.

A study by Tiedemann[13] supported this perception, finding that teachers of sixth grade (Year 7) pupils felt that boys were significantly better at maths than girls, despite identical test scores. A further study by Newall et al. found teachers "rated girls as less academically capable than boys in physics", "delivered less scientific information" to girls and "perceived stereotypically 'girly girls' as being the least likely to enjoy science".[14]

Now, if this perception of teacher attitudes is true, let's just ponder what gendered perceptions might look like in practice. A 13-year-old girl walks into a Physics lab, and before even reading her work, the teacher has already made assumptions about her GCSE forecast grade. A primary school teacher, who is about to start teaching rudimentary French to a group of seven-year-olds, worries about how well they'll pick it up as there are a lot of boys in his class. A food technology teacher looks at her option choice list and is anxious because 60% of her GCSE class are boys and she's concerned they will struggle with the new extended writing questions on the exam.

At least these (nonetheless damaging) gender stereotypes have so far remained unspoken. But when these feelings find a voice in the staff room, views about gender and ability in certain subjects become widespread and entrenched. Think back to the question Kate Myers asked of school curricula in Chapter 3:

> Do all subject areas, particularly those traditionally associated with one gender, offer learning environments that feel safe and attractive for both boys and girls?[15]

And by "safe", Myers isn't just referring to goggles that would fit a girl in a construction class. In this instance, safety implies an area where a boy can discuss his love of designing clothing during a textile class without mockery, or a girl will feel confident discussing the functions of cache memory in a computing class without being made to feel awkward because this is something that most of the boys in the class already know.

Pupils' views of gender and subject performance

What do pupils make of expectations about which gender might perform better in some subjects? During Becky Francis's research[16] into boys' underachievement, she interviewed boys and girls about gender and ability in subjects. She found that 66% of girls and 84% of boys believed that boys and girls "have the same ability at all subjects". What's more, she discovered a noticeable attitude shift, compared to previous research, by a greater percentage of girls responding positively towards subjects, like science and maths, which they have previously disliked in greater numbers. Could it be the case that the negative stereotyping about gender and subjects is more likely to come from teachers than from pupils? Society in general – and parents in particular – obviously plays a role in shaping attitudes towards which subjects students should apply themselves. Yet, one would hope that teachers and leaders at the frontline, most able to tackle these stereotypes, would be challenging not reinforcing these insidious ideas.

Because, things get more damaging still when (often well-meaning) teachers share their beliefs about gender and school subjects with their pupils. Francis found that

Six girls and two boys said that boys and girls tend to be better at different subjects. Of these eight pupils, six came from the same class, and one girl told me that her teacher had told this class that boys tend to be better at maths problems, and girls better at English and languages. This opinion certainly appeared to be reflected in the young people's responses, as four of the six pupils from this teacher's class claimed that boys tend to be better at maths, and girls better at languages.[17]

How many of us have unwittingly given 50% of our pupils a subliminal message that a specific subject (or type of subject) isn't for the likes of them? If I'm honest, off the top of my head, at various stages of my career, I have committed the following mistakes:

- Talking about not being good at maths at school (which wasn't actually true – I was pretty good at it but avoided work as I didn't enjoy it)

- Using the idea of doing maths as a punishment

- Using the idea of doing extended writing as a punishment

- When discussing my love of poetry with male pupils, feeling I have to counter it with something more stereotypically masculine, such as my love of sport

- In options interviews, occasionally nudging some pupils towards certain subjects based on their gender

- Showing signs of surprise at a male pupil who told me they would be missing my next lesson due to taking part in a dance event.

The bottom set mindset

It's the first day of the academic year. You've just started working at the school and have been given two shiny new Year 10 classes. You haven't looked at their prior data (you never do) or their previous behaviour logs. All you've got is a couple of lists of names, some basic data about micro cohorts that they belong to (FSM/SEND, etc.), and the knowledge that they have been placed into sets based on their ability. Let's call the groups 10P1 and 10Q4. You're not used to this: your eight years of experience so far has been entirely mixed ability, including scenarios like A* kids sitting next to pupils who have just arrived in the country and can't speak much English. Without even setting eyes on the pupils, you notice the following differences between the two groups:

10P1	10Q4
A large group (29 pupils)	A small group (14 pupils)
Only one FSM pupil	Nearly all FSM pupils
Majority are female	Majority are male

Then you meet them. 10P1 first. They enter quietly, immaculate uniform, sit where you ask them to without complaint, and start writing immediately when you ask them to complete a brief vocabulary-based starter. After a while, a meek hand is raised. *Sir, what set is this?* For some strange reason, you decide to paraphrase Viper, the ace flight instructor from the film *Top Gun*:

Ladies and gentlemen, I'm told you are the top English students that [name of school] has to offer. The elite, the BEST of the best. You may well be top set but I'm gonna make you better.

A couple of sniggers. Some raised eyebrows. But I can tell that they're impressed by (a) the initial flattery and (b) my arrogance. The rest of the lesson passes without incident. They produce some high-quality work. Straight after comes 10Q4. Or rather some of them. Noisy, tardy uniform, a few grumbles about the seating plan, even more grumbles about the writing task. Five minutes later, three of the lads burst into the class; one of them is literally thrown through the door by the other two. I seat them (more complaints) and settle the class. Not long after, one of the girls, mischievous look on her face, raises a hand. *Sir, what set is this?* This time you adopt a different approach, channelling Michelle Pfeiffer in the movie *Dangerous Minds*:

I don't care what it says on the timetable. I don't care what number it has next to our class name. I don't care what happened in English last year. I don't care how you behaved or what score you got in your end-of-Year 9 assessment. I don't care what other teachers have told you and I really don't care what your friends in other groups might say. Somebody has decided you aren't very good at this subject. I think they've got that wrong. I think you're going to surprise a few people. I think some of you are going to surprise yourselves. I think if you work hard and you listen to me, you're going to get really good results. Maybe better results than some of the students in the so-called top sets...

A shift in mindset

Over time, the bottom set begin to think less like a bottom set. 10Q4 talk to their friends in 10P1 (amazing isn't it, that pupils often ignore "ability" as a determining factor in selecting friends). When they chat about the work they're doing, they discover that I'm not misleading them: they really are covering the same stuff, being taught how to explain the effect of the same sophisticated terms, and are using the same complex contextual sources. After they get their first lot of assessments back, some of them start to believe me when I say they're good at English. Some of them have indeed scored higher marks than their esteemed top set counterparts. Some ask to move up a set. *Why would you want to when you're doing so well here*, I ask? Fair enough, they respond. When it gets to the start of Year 11, I start talking to 10Q4 about A level English. A few of them laugh, but a couple – one boy, one girl – linger behind at the end to ask me if I'm serious. Fast forward a few years and both of them sit in my Year 13 literature class, discussing liminality and hybridity in postcolonial discourse.

Who goes in the bottom sets?

In a study that investigated the impact of teachers' expectations on achievement gaps between different ethnic groups in New Zealand, Rubie-Davies, Hattie and Hamilton[18] argue that low teacher expectations of certain groups led to them being deprived of opportunities to encounter high-quality teaching and an atmosphere of academic excellence:

> As researchers have shown, minority students are simply not given the opportunities to enhance their learning that could decrease the achievement gap (Nichols & Good, 2004; Weinstein, 2002). Furthermore, by being frequently placed in low academic groupings where they are publicly labelled and categorized minority students have few opportunities to redress their racial, social and economic disadvantage (Weinstein et al., 2004).

Given the media panics about the "crisis of masculinity" and the well-documented fact that boys generally underachieve compared to girls, it is possible to see this Golem effect occurring for boys as well as the "minority students" that the researchers describe. What might this culture of low expectations for pupils perceived to perform badly look like?

> For example, teachers may slow the pace of lessons for particular student groups (Good & Weinstein, 1986)...students are given little independence, few cognitively demanding tasks, and little opportunity to interact with their peers.[19]

The link between the set that pupils are placed in and their self-efficacy has been established in a study by Ireson and Hallam.[20] They found that lower expectations of lower sets lead to a watered down curriculum, less homework, and less feedback. But surely, advocates of setting argue, pupils are allocated their groups based on ability, and putting them in a group where they are out of their depth will lead to them struggling, resulting in poor progress and feelings of inadequacy.

Not so. You'll recall from Chapter 2 the research of Hallam and Parsons[21] into streaming in primary schools, which revealed that being a boy led to a far greater likelihood of being placed in the bottom set at school.

Consciously or not, boys are often placed in lower sets for even more iniquitous reasons. With the "deficit model" of male achievement being a prevalent factor in education, higher prior attaining boys whose conduct does not meet the expectations of "top set" behaviour often find themselves demoted to bottom sets as a punishment for their non-compliance, reinforcing a vicious cycle of male underachievement and worsening rather than counteracting anti-school attitudes.

Mary-Claire Travers from UCL's Institute of Education has recently written about the relationship between setting and the academic underachievement of white working class boys.[22] During a 2016 study in which she interviewed a group of white working class boys who had been academically successful, she found that setting was frequently mentioned as an aspect of education that often held the academic aspirations of boys like them in check. Travers found that being in a lower set meant white working class boys:

> ...did not have any expectation of experiencing academic success and, from what the participants said, the teachers had little expectation that those children in the lower set would experience academic success.

The solutions

Advice for school leaders

Schools should avoid the allure of short-term miracle gains. Most courses, books, and CPD sessions about engaging boys, or improving their outcomes, are based on what Jones and Myhill call the "deficit model" belief that when it comes to learning most boys – especially the "laddish" ones – can't, won't or do not do the things that make girls, in the eyes of their teachers, more successful. As Chapter 1 demonstrated, pandering to supposed differences between boys and girls is a strategy doomed to failure. But just as damaging, if not more, in my opinion, are the low expectations that many teachers hold about the achievement of boys, while making contrasting noises about equality of opportunity.

A. Provide CPD on gender issues

This is not, of course, to blame teachers. Research suggests that the vast majority of teachers feel as if their initial teacher training didn't properly prepare them for dealing with issues of gender in the classroom.[23] Perhaps for this reason, teachers have also told researchers they feel awkward and unskilled when it comes to dealing with damaging gender stereotypes that emerge in classroom resources, discussions and pupil behaviour.[24] Ideally, Initial Teacher Training – whether as part of a university PGCE, or in school-based training schemes – would dedicate a greater amount of time to issues of gender in the classroom, going beyond generalised notions of gender achievement gaps.

Either way, gender issues should be high on the list of priorities for in-school CPD. As Gray and Leith[25] note, the Swedish curriculum insists that "all teachers should be taught in the areas of gender [and] equality". In order to address damaging stereotypical notions, other countries need to follow suit. Where government fails to set the lead, individual schools, as usual, need to fill the gap. You might want to consider using the following questionnaire as a starting point:

Questionnaire – Teacher expectations of female and male pupils

Age:

Gender:

Role:

Department/Key stage:

Statement 1: Boys are as capable as girls and should achieve the same academic results

5 Strongly Agree	4 Agree	3 Neither or N/A	2 Disagree	1 Strongly Disagree

Statement 2: Boys are more frustrating to teach than girls

5 Strongly Agree	4 Agree	3 Neither or N/A	2 Disagree	1 Strongly Disagree

Statement 3: When it comes to achievement, boys are often their own worst enemy

5 Strongly Agree	4 Agree	3 Neither or N/A	2 Disagree	1 Strongly Disagree

Statement 4: Girls lack confidence in the classroom

5 Strongly Agree	4 Agree	3 Neither or N/A	2 Disagree	1 Strongly Disagree

Statement 5: Boys and girls are naturally better at certain academic subjects

5 Strongly Agree	4 Agree	3 Neither or N/A	2 Disagree	1 Strongly Disagree

Statement 6: Boys and girls are treated the same in my classroom

5 Strongly Agree	4 Agree	3 Neither or N/A	2 Disagree	1 Strongly Disagree

Statement 7: Girls take more care with the presentation of their work

5 Strongly Agree	4 Agree	3 Neither or N/A	2 Disagree	1 Strongly Disagree

Statement 8: Girls are more likely to challenge authority than boys

5 Strongly Agree	4 Agree	3 Neither or N/A	2 Disagree	1 Strongly Disagree

Statement 9: I feel comfortable tackling sexist language or attitudes in my classroom and around the school

5 Strongly Agree	4 Agree	3 Neither or N/A	2 Disagree	1 Strongly Disagree

Statement 10: I feel comfortable discussing gender issues in my classroom

5 Strongly Agree	4 Agree	3 Neither or N/A	2 Disagree	1 Strongly Disagree

B.   Raise expectations

When it comes to expectations of what boys can achieve, difficult conversations need to be had. Teachers need to be trained (or retrained) to recognise the inherent preconceptions many of them hold about boys and achievement. Many teachers will happily tell you about their high expectations for boys. Yet, the evidence shows that there is a gap between what they say and what they do. Low expectations of boys is a self-destructive cycle. Saying boys can achieve is not enough. Believing boys can achieve is not enough. Actually doing it and showing it day-in, day-out in every single lesson is what will make the real difference. Because, believe me, boys are pretty good at quickly sussing out how much teachers and schools really believe in them.

There is, therefore, a delicate balance to be struck trying to tackle non-tender masculinity in schools while at the same time avoiding, alienating, and prejudicially labelling boys with low expectations. As we've seen in this chapter, boys feel that they are unfairly treated by teachers compared to girls. Many girls also feel that this is the case. Yet we've also seen in Chapter 3 that some boys will disrupt lessons and, fuelled by an anti-work or anti-school attitude, will frustrate the efforts of their teachers to educate them.

C.   Reconsider setting

As Chapter 2 illustrated, many of the issues around expectations of boys are exacerbated by setting. In *Cleverlands: The Secrets Behind the Success of the World's Education Superpowers*,[26] Lucy Crehan reveals that the majority of the countries with the highest performing education systems – such as Canada, Japan, and the ubiquitous Finland – are home to mixed ability classrooms.

It is hard to disagree with Mary Myatt, who has argued in *High Challenge, Low Threat*[27] that we should do away with the word "ability" altogether, in favour of the more neutral, and more accurate, "attaining".

Many school leaders remain unconvinced. But if you must stick with the damaging "ability" label and must stick to hierarchical sets, at least do something to mitigate the biggest, most pervasive, problems with setting, which we outlined in Chapter 2: the common practice of (a) dumping bright but challenging boys in bottom sets and then (b) allocating the least skilled teachers to bottom sets.

Advice for teachers

A.   Be self-reflective

Be honest with yourself. Are you sometimes guilty (hopefully subconsciously) of holding different expectations about what boys and girls can achieve? Do you teach to stereotypical beliefs about gender? A typical self-reflection table might look something like this:

Things I value in a student	Do the stereotypically "masculine" boys I teach fit this criterion?
Good presentation	X
Neat handwriting	X
Good sense of humour	☑
Completes homework on time	X
Obedient/follows instructions first time	X
Contributes to class debates	☑
Revises for tests/exams	☑ – say they don't but test scores suggest otherwise

B.   Increase the level of challenge

If, by accident or design, you end up with a class with lots of boys in it, make sure your expectations of what they can achieve start and remain high. This will include:

- Pitching the work to the top and providing support for those who require it. I'm not talking about making five different worksheets for every lesson here, merely offering extra scaffolds or simpler modelled examples to the same tasks that the rest of the class are doing

- Ditching extension tasks. I once spoke to a group of boys from another school about these additional "challenge activities". They told me they loved the opportunity to complete extra work if they found the main task too simple or had finished early. Do you usually do most of them, then? I asked. No, not very often, they replied. To many boys, extension tasks seem like optional work. Optional work, as we've seen in Chapter 3, is to be avoided

C.   Respond carefully to classroom behaviour

In a perfect world, pupils would just behave. The classroom is an imperfect world in microcosm. Pupils of both genders come with baggage. As well as all the usual issues that pupils bring into your lesson – unstable home life, parental neglect or abuse, low literacy levels, and so on – male pupils may also be burdened with the oppressive weight of trying to live up to the destructive peer group expectations of how traditionally masculine boys act.

In Chapter 9, we'll consider in detail how you might develop effective relationships with boys who fall into the trap of displaying poor behaviour while trying to impress their male peers. Stage one of dealing with classroom behaviour however, as this chapter has hopefully shown, is to avoid the knee-jerk response of anticipating that boys will be a problem *per se*. Of course some boys will mess around. And you'll need to be able to deal with their disruption. But so will some girls. And you'll need to make sure that you're being fair and even handed when dealing with poor attitudes from both genders.

D. Use paired observations

In the cut and thrust of the classroom, teachers often struggle to notice how they interact with pupils. Why not ask a trusted colleague to observe your teaching and ask them to feedback on your approach to gender in the classroom?

They might look at the following categories, some of which are based on the work by Becky Francis[28]:

- Voice – does your tone and volume change when you speak to boys and girls? What language do you use to communicate with different pupils?

- Attention – which groups of pupils get more of your time? Do you direct equal amounts *and types* of questions at boys and girls?

- Body language – do you smile more at certain pupils? Is it clear from your gestures that you like some pupils more than others? What clues does your body language give about the ways in which you react to disruptive behaviour?

- Behaviour management – do you escalate sanctions more quickly for boys? Are you more likely to apply sanctions for certain types of disruptive behaviour but ignore others? Is it obvious that certain behaviours "push your buttons" more than others? Are these aligned with gender stereotypes? Do boys get punished more for the same behaviour as girls?

- Interaction between pupils – how do you tackle relationships within the classroom? Do you tolerate male pupils talking over female pupils? Do you allow boys to take a back seat during group work? Are boys always given "leadership" roles in the classroom? Do boys get to go first? Do you tackle sexist attitudes?

E. Watch your language

Think about the language you use. Have you ever found yourself using the following expressions (or similar)? What impact might they have on the boys and girls in your classroom? What impact might they have on the way other teachers, especially trainees, think about gender?

- "It's a boy heavy class"

- "I need a couple of big strong boys to help me move the table"

- "He's a typical lad"

- "Good morning guys"

- "She's not top set material"

- "The boys won't be able to cope with that much reading"

- "A group of bitchy girls"

- "Drama Queen"

- "He's got girly handwriting"

- "A group of feral boys"

- "man up"

- "man flu"

The final word

The words you use may seem trivial, but potentially they reveal much about your attitudes towards pupils and expectations of how they might behave and whether they will achieve. Being more careful about the language you use, reflecting on your own beliefs and preconceptions, and adjusting your approach if necessary, will all go some way in helping you become a teacher who teaches children, not troublesome boys and compliant girls.

Notes

1 Pupils who are eligible for free school meals – used as an indicator of deprivation in the UK education system.
2 Rosenthal, R. & Jacobson, L. (1968) 'Pygmalion in the classroom', *Urban Review*, 3:1, pp. 16–20.
3 Babad, E.Y., Inbar, J., & Rosenthal, R. (1982) 'Pygmalion, Galatea, and the Golem: Investigations of biased and unbiased teachers', *Journal of Educational Psychology*, 74, pp. 459–474.
4 Myhill, D. & Jones, S. (2004) '"Troublesome boys" and "compliant girls": Gender identity and perceptions of achievement and underachievement', *British Journal of Sociology of Education*, 25:5, pp. 547–561.
5 Terrier, C. (2016) Boys Lag Behind: How Teachers' Gender Biases Affect Student Achievement, IZA – Institute of Labor Economics, Bonn, Discussion Paper No. 10343.
6 Campbell, T. (2015) 'Stereotyped at seven? Biases in teacher judgement of pupils' ability and attainment', *Journal of Social Policy*, 44:3, pp. 517–547.
7 Hansen, K. & Jones, E. (2011) 'Ethnicity and gender gaps in early childhood', *British Educational Research Journal*, 37:6, pp. 973–991.
8 Barnett, L.A. (2018) 'The education of playful boys: Class clowns in the classroom', *Frontiers in Psychology*, 9, p. 232.
9 Ibid.
10 Jackson, C. (2010) '"I've been sort of laddish with them…one of the gang": Teachers' perceptions of "laddish" boys and how to deal with them', *Gender and Education*, 22:5, pp. 505–519.
11 Ibid. – n.b. name of teacher and school are pseudonyms.

12 Myhill, D. & Jones, S. (2006) '"She doesn't shout at no girls": Pupils' perceptions of gender equity in the classroom', *Cambridge Journal of Education*, 36:1, pp. 99–113.

13 Tiedemann, J. (2000) 'Parents' gender stereotypes and teachers' beliefs as predictors of children's concept of their mathematical ability in elementary school', *Journal of Educational Psychology*, 92:1, pp. 144–151.

14 Newall, C., Gonsalkorale, K., Walker, E., Forbes, G.A., Highfield, K., & Sweller, N. (2018) 'Science education: Adult biases because of the child's gender and gender stereotypicality', *Contemporary Educational Psychology*, 55, pp. 30–41.

15 Myers, K., et al. (2007) *Genderwatch: Still Watching*, Stoke on Trent: Trentham, p. 23.

16 Francis, B. (2000) *Boys, Girls and Achievement: Addressing the Classroom Issues*, London: Routledge/Falmer.

17 Ibid., p. 69.

18 Rubie-Davies, C., Hattie, J. & Hamilton, R. (2006) 'Expecting the best for students: Teacher expectations and academic outcomes', *British Journal of Educational Psychology*, 76, p. 431.

19 Ibid., p. 431.

20 Ireson, J. & Hallam, S. (2009) 'Academic self-concepts in adolescence: Relations with achievement and ability grouping in schools', *Learning and Instruction*, 19:3, pp. 201–213.

21 Hallam, S. & Parsons, S. (2013) 'Prevalence of streaming in UK primary schools: Evidence from the Millennium Cohort Study', *British Educational Research Journal*, 39:3, pp. 514–544.

22 Travers, M.-C. (2017) British Educational Research Association website. Available at: https://www.bera.ac.uk/blog/setting-and-the-academic-underachievement-of-white-working-class-boys (Accessed: 28th November 2017).

23 Gray, C. & Leith, H. (2004) 'Perpetuating gender stereotypes in the classroom: A teacher perspective', *Educational Studies*, 30:1, pp. 3–17.

24 Commeyras, A.D., et al. (1997) Educators' stances towards gender issues in literacy, Paper presented at the Annual Meeting of the American Educational Research Association, Chicago, IL, 24–28 March, quoted in Gray, C. & Leith H. (2004).

25 Ibid.

26 Crehan, L. (2016) *Cleverlands: The Secrets behind the Success of the World's Education Superpowers*, London: Unbound.

27 Myatt, M. (2016) *High Challenge, Low Threat*, London: John Catt.

28 See Myers, K., et al. (2007), pp. 131–132.

Sex and sexism

Matt Pinkett

The story

A Year 9 pupil in my lesson asked another pupil, within my hearing, "Do you think Miss has ever given a blow job?"...He got a one-day exclusion.

Georgia, Maidstone

I had a student lean into the doorway whilst I was teaching and say, "You're lookin' fit today Miss."

Aafiya, Plymouth

A year 5 pupil once told me I had 'massive tits'.

Louisa, Penzance

In my first year of teaching, a student told me I had a 'gammy gash'. I felt very vulnerable and disgusted...He was excluded for a couple of days and then rejoined the class.

Jules, Bradford

One boy threw a condom at me – I had my hand on a table and it landed across it. When the condom incident happened I called for SLT support – the Head came but later told me I had wasted his time and should have turned it into a joke.

Abebi, Nottingham

I had a year 8 class. One lesson a boy in the class stuck a pencil up my skirt and called me a 'slut' whilst I was working with the student in front of him. I called a member of the behaviour team who went and found him and then brought him back to my lesson.

Ellie, Chobham

In my NQT year I had repeated comments about my appearance, which were reported but no sanctions were given apart from detentions set by me. A boy asked me if I sucked sausages and finally threw a pair of girl's knickers across the room! I was told by management that they wouldn't sanction as it could 'blow up'.

Danielle, Ottershaw

I've had a male pupil ask me if I can 'deep-throat'.

Laura, Frome

I taught a year 11 boy who used to pretend to have an erection in my lesson. He would request help, but then sit there using his eyes to try and encourage me to look at his crotch. He also made sexualised comments and would turn things I said into innuendo.

Felicity, Wigan

A Year 10 boy said he'd like to 'f**k me up the arse' in my previous school. He got very little punishment.

Charlotte, Lincoln

I had a Year 11 boy shout across a crowded corridor, "Miss, I'd love to f**k you."

Kate, Bramley

A female colleague of mine was asked by a Year 8 pupil if she would 'give him a gobble', whilst simulating some kind of blow job gesture.

Abi, Edinburgh

The stories above are just a small selection of a far greater number, related to me by female teachers (names have been changed) about their own experiences of sexual harassment, abuse, and intimidation at the hands of male pupils. Generally, all the anecdotes I hear tend to centre on a few common themes:

- Intimidation of female members of staff, particularly those who are less experienced or younger

- Frequent references to sexual acts, particularly those which can be referenced using hand gestures

- Casual, confident, and regular use of inappropriate sexual language

- Leadership teams who are either reluctant – or who simply refuse – to take the appropriate measures needed to deal with all of the above.

The stories above paint a depressing – and very real – picture about the sexual harassment that many female teachers face daily. But they also invite another question: if this is the kind of abuse that pubescent boys are inflicting upon the adults whose job it is to nurture them, what are they inflicting upon the girls with whom they share classrooms, playgrounds, and assembly halls?

The research

A recent report[1] by the Women's and Equalities Committee found that

- Almost a third (29%) of 16- to 18-year-old girls say they have experienced unwanted sexual touching at school

- Nearly three-quarters (71%) of all 16- to 18-year-old boys and girls say they hear terms such as "slut" or "slag" used towards girls at schools on a regular basis

- 59% of girls and young women aged 13–21 said in 2014 that they had faced some form of sexual harassment at school or college in the past year

Another report,[2] published in 2017 by the National Education Union and UK Feminista, found that

- Over a third (37%) of female students at mixed-sex schools have personally experienced some form of sexual harassment at school

- Almost a quarter (24%) of female students at mixed-sex schools have been subjected to unwanted physical touching of a sexual nature

Sexual harassment in schools isn't just a problem; it's a catastrophe. Inappropriate sexual behaviour and sexual language are the toxic foundations of a rape culture which towers dangerously above us. Today, in schools up and down the country, wolf-whistles, rape jokes, and gropes were heard and felt and seen, but not reported.

Marshall University's Women's Center defines a rape culture as:

> ...an environment in which rape is prevalent and in which sexual violence against women is normalised and excused in the media and popular culture. Rape culture is perpetuated through the use of misogynistic language, the objectification of women's bodies, and the glamorisation of sexual violence, thereby creating a society that disregards women's rights and safety.[3]

Britain's rape culture

Britain has a rape culture. According to Rapecrisis, 85,000 women in Britain are raped every year.[4] Sadly, of those women who experience sexual violence, only 15% will report it to the police. What's more, whilst charities such as Rapecrisis are doing everything they can to help rape victims, the feelings of shame, guilt, fear, and helplessness that many rape victims feel, means that they simply don't seek out the help or justice they deserve. As teachers we need to recognise the very real truth that one in five of the girls we teach – that's six girls in your Year

7 class – will experience sexual violence at some point in their life and we need to do more to ensure that we contribute to the eradication of a rape culture we may be unknowingly helping to sustain.

A list on the Marshall University Woman's Centre details the features of a society in which a rape culture exists. A rape cultured society:

- Trivialises sexual assault or inappropriate sexual behaviours ("Boys will be boys!")

- Tells sexually explicit jokes

- Tolerates sexual harassment

- Defines "manhood" as dominant and sexually aggressive

- Defines "womanhood" as submissive and sexually passive

- Puts pressure on males to be sexually experienced

- Puts pressure on women to not appear "frigid"

- Teaches women to avoid getting raped instead of teaching men not to rape.

All of these things can occur within the school environment: students tell sexually explicit jokes; boys compete with hyperbolic tales of their sexual prowess; girls and boys are grabbed inappropriately. Many schools are a microcosm of rape cultured Britain. As teachers, we need to do more.

In this chapter, we will focus on the areas of concern that schools and teachers can most easily address in their efforts to destroy the foundations of a rape culture that has been building for centuries. I will begin by discussing pornography, its impact on boys, and also the ways in which schools could harness pornography for good. Then, I will consider the approaches school leaders and classroom teachers can take to deal with the very real problem of normalised sexual language and sexist behaviour in schools.

The solutions

Advice for school leaders and teachers

A. Ensure your school provides pornography education

Before we can attempt to seek solutions to the rape culture problem, it is important that we try to account for why boys exhibit the sexualised behaviours observed in the stories that open this chapter. In the 21st century, heterosexuality is still a vital component of the hegemonic masculinity many boys have been pushed towards, consciously or unconsciously, from birth. Boys must prove themselves to be sexually experienced, sexually knowledgeable, and sexually confident, preferably in the heterosexual sense. For adolescents, the triumvirate of sexual experience, knowledge, and confidence are (thankfully) hard to come by but there is an easily accessible substitute which can provide the sexual experience that real life seems so damned reluctant to yield: this substitute is pornography.

Pornography and non-tender masculinity

Pornography is inextricably linked to non-tender masculinity. Its focus on dominant men achieving sexual gratification from submissive women is reflective of the patriarchal need for male assertions of power. Just as this power must be upheld in offices, schools, and television studios, so too must it be upheld in the bedroom. For the adolescent boy, pornography serves a dual purpose: first, it is sexually arousing and provides him with the physical gratification he needs, albeit on a superficial level. Equally as important though, is the role it plays in imbuing him with the heterosexuality he believes he needs to be a "proper" man. From Anal to Zentai,[5] pornography provides boys with the vocabulary and vicariously experienced scenarios, positions and sexual partners, needed to display the full depth and breadth of their sexual learnedness, and helps them to access a vital slice of the all-important masculinity pie.

A review study by the Children's Commissioner states that the rate of exposure to pornography in young people varies hugely from study to study. Some Swedish studies suggest that 99% of adolescents have watched pornography, whilst studies from other parts of the globe put the figure as low as 43%. One thing in which the research on adolescent porn habits agrees is that boys watch considerably more porn than girls. According to the report by the Children's Commissioner, "exposure and access rates for male children and young people range from 83 per cent to 100 per cent", whilst "reported rates for females are from 45 per cent to 80 per cent".[6] Of course, these statistics can't be taken at face value; girls could well watch as much pornography as boys. However, it is more socially acceptable for boys to admit to it, which is a problem in itself of course. Perhaps unsurprisingly, the report also showed that boys have a more positive attitude towards pornography than their female counterparts.

Does porn lead to sexual violence?

To put it bluntly, one of the major concerns about exposure to pornography is that it encourages boys to be sexually violent. This concern is justified. A recent analysis into 50 of the top-selling pornography titles in the USA found that of these films, "88.2% contained physical aggression, principally spanking, gagging, and slapping, while 48.7% of scenes contained verbal aggression, primarily name calling".[7] The majority of these aggressive acts were by males against females. As Michael Flood, of Queensland University, notes in a report into the effects of pornography on children: "if an individual watched the top 50 pornography titles in the US, they would see 3,375 aggressive acts." They would see that women were "gagged 756 times, experienced an open hand slap 361 times, had their hair pulled or yanked on 267 separate occasions, and were choked 180 times".[8]

And yet, despite the prevalence of violence in pornography, there is no reliable evidence to suggest that exposure to violent pornography alone turns those that watch it into people who will commit acts of sexual aggression, including rape. Neil Malamuth, a leading expert on porn and its links to violence, explains that "exposure to pornography does not have negative effects on attitudes supporting violence against women, or sexually aggressive tendencies for the majority of men".[9] For the minority of men who have watched violent porn and gone on to commit acts of sexual violence, the act of sexual violence itself cannot be reliably attributed solely to having watched violent pornography. As with all studies into porn and its effects on our behaviours, the link is correlational rather than causal. Furthermore, for men who do watch violent pornography and commit acts of sexual violence, there are "other risk factors for committing sexual aggression", such as narcissism and a violent upbringing, at play. Malamuth likens the effects of violent pornography on behaviour to the effects of alcohol. For some people, with certain pre-existing dispositions, alcoholic intoxication can cause them to commit frenzied acts of brutality. Others, on the other hand, can enjoy a bottle (or two) of wine and end the night in a blissful state of catatonia on the sofa, rather than in a prison cell. The difference between those that drink and commit violence, and those that drink and sleep, isn't the alcohol, but other facets of their personality and lived experience.

Does porn change the way people think?

What is concerning, however, is the effect of pornography on watchers' attitudes, particularly in relation to attitudes regarding gender. Evidence from experimental studies, rather than correlational studies, suggests that watching pornography perpetuates the idea that women are sex objects and also that women must play a submissive role to male dominance. This is significant. Correlational studies simply highlight links between two variables. For example, they may identify a link between the tendency to commit violent sexual acts and a tendency to watch violent pornography. Whilst there may be a link between the two variables, there's no suggestion that one causes the other. An experimental study, however, takes place in a laboratory setting and is systematically designed to test the impact of a stimulus on something else. For example, an experimental study may seek to assess the impact of exposure to pornography on participants' attitudes and behaviour. In his report, Flood references a number of these experimental studies, which show that "pornography consumption was shown to increase notions of women as sex objects".[10] It is feasible then that whilst pornography is not directly turning our boys into rapists, it is turning them into young men with sexist beliefs, which could then manifest themselves in the unpleasant ways mentioned in the stories at the beginning of this chapter and which legitimise sexual violence against women. Excessive pornography consumption could be what is causing *some* of our boys to routinely abuse, subjugate, and intimidate female teachers and female peers in classrooms, corridors, and canteens of schools all over the land.

Pornography and sex education

Pauline Oosterhoff, a specialist in gender and sexuality at the Institute of Development Studies, believes that UK schools could combat the negative attitudes that pornography watching seems to cause, by incorporating pornography into their sex education programmes. "Most young people are learning about sex by watching porn. This is a problem", says Oosterhoff, "because it's giving young people an unrealistic idea of what sex should look and feel like". According to Oosterhoff, schools have a duty to mediate the sex education that children are giving themselves through watching pornography. Michael Flood agrees: "Given that boys and young men are likely to continue to consume pornography, an important strategy is to teach them the skills with which to read it more critically". Flood states that experiments into pornography education among adults "did find that individuals shown violent pornography can be 'inoculated' against its negative effects through pre-briefing or 'cured' afterwards through debriefing".[11] Another study, with school age participants, found that students who underwent a "media literacy" curriculum (in which porn was discussed) were

> less likely to overestimate sexual activity among teens, more likely to think they could delay sexual activity, less likely to expect social benefits from sexual activity, more aware of myths about sex, and less likely to consider sexual media imagery desirable.[12]

Clearly, pornography education could be crucial in negating against the negative impact pornography has on watchers' attitudes towards sex.

Whilst incorporating pornography study into the curriculum goes some way to improving attitudes to sex and gender, it also has other benefits, such as making students realise that sex is an act which should be pleasurable. Oosterhoff believes that the British sex education system is too focused on reproduction, restraint, and biomechanics, and students might be better served by entering into discussions about the pleasures that sex can provide. According to Oosterhoff, focusing on the pleasure that sex can bring could make it easier for adolescents to say no to sexual acts that could be painful or uncomfortable. "In order to say no, you need to say yes", explains Oosterhoff. Students need to be told that the impossible sexual positions employed by contortionist porn stars are not only often demeaning, but physically painful. In a society in which some sex studies show that half of young porn consumers have engaged in anal sex, one cannot help but feel that if students learnt about sexual experiences, positions, and scenarios which may cause discomfort or pain it would become easier for them, one day, to enjoy a healthy sex life. A deconstruction of the positions employed by porn stars could be a useful and engaging way to educate students about how sex should feel.

Revenge porn

A final concern about pornography is the rise of "revenge porn". As Oosterhoff explains,

> Online porn companies like PornHub[13] have monopolised the industry. The industry is in decline and there's no money for porn actors anymore. Because of this, we are now seeing increasing amounts of amateur pornography posted on free porn sites like PornHub. The danger here is that this can turn into revenge porn.

A study by the NSPCC found that "Some 44% of males, compared to 29% of females, reported that the online pornography they had seen had given them ideas about the types of sex they wanted to try out".[14] In amateur pornography, the camera is as much a part of the sexual experience as is the penis, the vagina, or the sex toy. Many young people are filming their sexual exploits and it could be because they are trying to replicate the amateur pornographic experience that they are accessing, for free, on their smart phones. There are over 3,000 revenge porn sites on the internet. Many of these videos were filmed as part of a consensual sexual experience between people in apparently loving relationships, but when these relationships break down, angry people post these videos on the internet as a form of "revenge". My discussion with Oosterhoff has left me absolutely convinced that schools need to discuss this type of pornography head on, rather than using the euphemistic and fuzzy language of "sexting" if we are to protect our boys and girls from falling victim to this kind of thing.

Many students aren't aware that they are breaking the law if they:

- Take an explicit video or photo of themselves or someone they consider to be a friend or intimate

- Share an explicit image or video of a child (even if it's of themselves), even if it's shared with children of the same age

- Possess, download or store explicit images or videos of a child, even if the child in the image gave permission for it to be created.

On January 15th, 2018, it was revealed that "over 1,000 Danish children and youngsters have been charged by the police with sharing a sex video involving a 15-year-old girl and several boys".[15] Whilst the UK has not yet gone as far as charging children for these offences, the fact is the Crown Prosecution Service is well within its right to do so, should they deem it appropriate. Children should know this.

Clearly, pornography is something that needs to be discussed in the classroom. Ed Davis, a curriculum leader of PSHE and Citizenship at Callington Community

College in Cornwall with years of experience in teaching sex education to pupils, believes fervently that pornography should be a focus of the curriculum and cites reasons on top of the ones we've already discussed:

> An issue that concerns me is how the brain's capacity and desire to learn can lead to porn searches becoming more and more extreme. Also, the nature of quick searches from video to video is so removed from the intimacy of one sexual partner, that issues with erectile dysfunction in young men are on the rise.

What does a lesson in pornography look like?

"The best lesson I teach on the topic uses the Planet Porn resources from Bish Training", says Davis. The resources available from http://bishtraining.com/planet-porn/ are excellent. Described on the website as a resource which "enables conversations around self-esteem, body image, boundaries, pleasure, consent, communication, safer sex, sexual safety, the law, emotions, relationships, gender and sexual diversity and oppression", the stylish graphics and the game element combine to make a classroom experience which is informative. Here is a sample of Ed's lesson that draws upon the *Porn Planet* resources.

Lesson

Preamble

Having considered the importance and significance of topics including consent and contraception, today we will explore pornography which can have implications on both previous topics and beyond.

Stage 1 (15 minutes)

Display the following statements in response to pornography:

■ An educational resource that teaches teenagers about sex

■ Harmless fun

■ OK, if you're careful what you watch and how often

■ Causes serious harm to society and attitudes towards sex and gender.

Students should record which one is closest to their current view of pornography and why.

Display the PPT slide for the "pornography quiz" and have students pair/share whether each is true or false.

Teacher shares answers and explains why they are all false. Students are given time to respond if they wish.

Stage 2 (60 minutes)

In accordance to their gut reaction to each of the statements on "porn statements", get the group to stand in a continuum of agree to disagree. Alternatively have two areas of the room labelled agree and disagree or four areas labelled strongly agree, agree, disagree, and strongly disagree. Encourage them to constructively challenge each other if there are different perspectives in the group.

Another way to do this activity would be to distribute copies of the statements. Students place an "X" on the continuum in relation to their personal attitude, which they then stick in their exercise book.

Planet Porn card game

- Divide class into groups of 4/5
- Give each group a set of planet porn cards
- Students should divide the cards equally amongst themselves and take it in turns to read one out and decide whether the statement on the card is most likely to be true on "Planet Earth" or "Planet Porn" and place them in the relevant pile
- If anybody in the group disagrees with where a statement has been placed, they can challenge it and justify why. The whole group should then vote on which pile it should go into.

Once the game is completed, students should do one of the following activities in their exercise book:

- Record three examples of statements from planet porn and planet earth
- Identify a statement which members of the group disagreed on and explain why there was a disagreement
- Pick the statement from the planet porn pile that would be **most harmful** if it was true on planet earth and explain why it would be so harmful.

Stage 3 (10 minutes)

Display the following statements in response to pornography:

- An educational resource that teaches teenagers about sex
- Harmless fun
- OK, if you're careful what you watch and how often
- Causes serious harm to society and attitudes towards sex and gender.

Students return to this and reflect on whether their view has changed or not and how their learning today has influenced this.

B.   Be clear on what constitutes sexism and sexist behaviour

It's hard to disagree with UK Feminista when they say, "The use of sexist, misogynist language – which denigrates girls and femaleness – is commonplace in schools". According to their report,

> Over half (54%) of female students and a third of male students (34%) say they have witnessed someone using sexist language at school.[16]

Of these, "Just 6% of students who have experienced or witnessed the use of sexist language in school reported it to a teacher".[17] Teachers aren't completely blind (or deaf) to what's going on though. The report goes on to state that

> 64% of teachers in mixed-sex secondary schools hear sexist language in school on at least a weekly basis. Over a quarter of teachers (29%) report sexist language is a daily occurrence.[18]

The language of sexism

I have taught many boys for whom inappropriate sexualised language is a part of the in-group vernacular. Whilst use of the words "slut" or "slag" to describe females is a deep and valid concern, even more worrying are the casual references to paedophilia and rape. In 2016, I wrote the following blogpost:

> The language I'm hearing in some classrooms is appalling. The focus on paedophilia and rape is a real worry. Some boys jocularly dismiss each other as 'paedos' or 'nonces', when the recipient of these insults has done nothing even vaguely related to the act of forcing sex upon a minor. "You fancy whatsherface in Year 9? Paedo." I was recently reading *The Yellow Wallpaper* and one boy, upon learning that the nursery in which the main character resides has chains on the wall, exclaimed, "Ugh! They've bought a paedo house! They're all paedos!" And of course, some of the others found this hilarious.

Whilst some boys use the word "rape" with the intended violence of its original meaning, at other times the word is used quite casually, and in full ignorance of its real meaning. A few years back, I remember walking across the playground only to see two Year 8 boys, both friendly, well-behaved, and pleasant, play-fighting. One of the boys, as the other jumped on his back, shouted to me, "Sir! Help! Sir! He's raping me! Rape! Rape!" No offence was intended. "Rape" was simply the term he ascribed to his friend's rambunctious clambering.

The use of the word "rape" is also often used to mean "defeat severely". As in: "I am going to absolutely rape you when we play Call of Duty on the X-Box later" or "Spurs are going to rape Arsenal this Saturday". This usage is commonplace in the social dialects of many boys. For them, the use of the word in this way is an easy means of displaying both a rebellious disregard for what the adult word considers taboo and macho bravery in the face of something which is incredibly terrifying. In fact, all of the sexualised language boys use – derogatory words such as "slut", "slag" and "bitch" to describe women; jokes about celebrity sexual deviants from the 1980s; casual references to serious sex crimes – are used in order to enter the world of an outdated but still desirable masculinity, where sex–in all its forms can be discussed openly, with bravado, and without fear.

There are a number of ways in which classroom teachers and school leaders can help to combat the problem of sexualised language which normalises sexual violence against women.

Absolute clarity

First, there needs to be absolute clarity from school leaders on the issue of sexism and sexist behaviour. As Hannah Wilson, Head of Aureus School and co-founder of the Women-Ed movement says,

> We need a sexist log to sit alongside the racist log and the homophobia log. If we have a national agenda for diversity and equalities then we need to ensure that we are addressing and challenging schools' interpretation and application of it.

A lack of clarity regarding exactly what constitutes sexist behaviour means that teachers would probably welcome such a change. According to UK Feminista's report, "over half (64%) of secondary school teachers are unsure or not aware of the existence of any policies and practices in their school related to preventing sexism".[19] Schools need to have a clear and concise policy on sexism made publicly available to staff, students, and parents. This policy should outline exactly what isn't acceptable and clearly indicate what sanctions will be put in place should rules be broken. As it currently stands,

> Teachers report being unclear about what constitutes sexism or how to explain to students why it is harmful. This perpetuates a lack of awareness and understanding of the issue, as well as the perception that it is not taken seriously by the school.[20]

In December 2017, the Department for Education published guidance on how school leadership teams can combat sexual violence and harassment (of which sexualised language is a part) in schools. The advice is unequivocal:

> It is more likely that girls will be the victims of sexual violence and more likely that sexual harassment will be perpetrated by boys. Schools and colleges should place emphasis on:
>
> - making clear that sexual violence and sexual harassment is not acceptable, will never be tolerated and is not an inevitable part of growing up;

- not tolerating or dismissing sexual violence or sexual harassment as "banter", "part of growing up", "just having a laugh" or "boys being boys"; and

- challenging behaviours (which are potentially criminal in nature), such as grabbing bottoms, breasts, and genitalia. Dismissing or tolerating such behaviours risks normalising them.[21]

What's happening in the majority of schools is that inappropriate sexual behaviour and sexualised language is covered by a wider, more generic policy on bullying. This isn't good enough. As Hannah Wilson pointed out, many schools have dedicated policies on racism and homophobia, but not on sexual inappropriateness. This is because sexual inappropriateness is normalised. In many schools, it is an everyday part of school life and therefore it's not considered an issue. To combat this normalisation, school policies need to outline to staff, students, and parents, exactly what constitutes sexual harassment. The guidance from the Department for Education provides a useful summary of what can be considered sexist or sexually inappropriate:

Sexist or sexualised language

- ■ Telling sexual stories
- ■ Making lewd comments
- ■ Making sexual remarks about clothes and appearance
- ■ Calling someone sexualised names;
- ■ Sexual "jokes" or taunting.

Physical behaviour

- ■ Deliberately brushing against someone
- ■ Interfering with someone's clothes (schools and colleges should be considering when any of this crosses a line into sexual violence – it is important to talk to and consider the experience of the victim)
- ■ Displaying pictures, photos, or drawings of a sexual nature.

Online sexual harassment

- ■ Non-consensual sharing of sexual images and videos and sharing sexual images and videos (both often referred to as sexting)
- ■ Inappropriate sexual comments on social media
- ■ Exploitation, coercion, and threats.[22]

C.   Sanction sexualised language and sexist behaviour

Sanctions need to be severe. Many female teachers have told me that members of Senior Leadership Teams (both male and female, but more often male) have undermined a teacher's right to feel comfortable and secure in their classrooms by removing offenders from classes in which they've been sexually inappropriate, only to return them five minutes later. Worse than this are the stories (yes, plural) of female teachers being told that they are simply being "oversensitive" in cases of student sexual misconduct; often, they are told that they have brought the harassment upon themselves because of how they dress or how they look. Some have even been told that they need to accept this sort of behaviour simply because that's what comes with being a young, female teacher. Students who commit these offences, and staff who trivialise or ignore them, must be dealt with.

D.   Educate students about gender

The current statutory sex and relationship guidance states that where sex education is concerned, "traditionally the focus has been on girls",[23] leaving many boys to believe sex education does not take into account their needs. This assertion ignores the fact that often talks about masturbation are usually focused solely on male masturbation, and there's a much greater emphasis on the male condom as a means of contraception. Perhaps it is this incongruity that explains why a government consultation was launched in July 2018, calling for a systematic review of the sex education system. This consultation found that sex education teaching needed to focus on "different types of abuse, grooming, and harassment, as well as where young people can seek support", and claimed that "teaching about gender and sexual identity was seen as important".[24]

Whilst this seems to be a more positive step forward for sex education, I think that there needs to be a more direct insistence that schools discuss gender as a social construct. As it currently stands, most schools tend to take a reactive approach to sexual harassment. An act is committed and sanctions are put in place in the hope that this will prevent reoffending in the future. But, clearly, as the data from UK Feminista shows, this lazy approach isn't working. Schools need to take a proactive response to preventing sexual harassment. One way that they might achieve this is by encouraging boys and girls to discuss the socially-constructed gender expectations that govern people's sexual attitudes and behaviours. Surely, if boys understood that the sexist jokes and the casual use of derogatory sexualised language were the products of a constructed masculinity that has been imposed upon them against their will, they'd be less likely to exhibit these behaviours in their daily lives.

Gender education: a case study

Recently, male Key Stage 4 (KS4) students at Kings College in Guildford underwent a Personal, Social, Health and Economics (PSHE) session that explored the way males use sexist language in school. The session began with students being asked to sort a number of words into male and female piles. The results were startling:

Male	Female
Rich	Confident
Confident	Shy
Rude	Frigid
Disruptive	Caring
Player	Poor
Strong	Clever
Provider	Weak
Stupid	Quiet
Angry	Emotional
Loud	Calm
Emotionless	

After the card sort, a discussion ensued that deconstructed the expectations of masculinity. Important questions were asked: *Who tells us we have to be these things? Is it possible to be all of these things, all of the time? Are there contradictions present?* After the discussion, students played a game of "Spot the Sexism", in which there were tasked with spotting examples of negative male stereotyping in a series of advertisements, songs, and images from shopping catalogues. Then followed a discussion on how male students try to assert the ideal of masculine power on a day to day basis in the school. Rebellious behaviour, swearing, and sporting prowess all featured, but soon the discussion led onto sexualised language. At this point, a list of unacceptable terms was created and students were educated on exactly what constitutes sexual harassment.

Evaluations of the session were positive. One student wrote that the session "made me think about women a lot more because I didn't know how much pressure they're under". Another said that the session changed the way he thought about women because there "are lots of people who wolf whistle around women but that can make them feel insecure", whilst somebody else simply said "I'm more polite [to women] now". A particularly amusing outcome of the session was to be found on the playground. A member of staff entered the staff room one morning feeling happily ashamed. During break duty, he had told a boy, rolling around the tarmac theatrically after a slight knock during a game of football, to "toughen up princess". The boy responded by getting up and telling him, "You can't say that. It suggests women are weak and that men have to be strong. That's sexist".

E. Challenge pupils' language

I'd like to think that were teachers to observe or learn of an act of inappropriate physical sexual behaviour, they'd act on it according to the school's behaviour policy. What I'm less sure of is the chances that they'd sanction the sexualised language employed by boys in the classroom. The reasons teachers are less likely to act on this are numerous:

1. **For many boys, the use of sexualised language is so regular, it has become normalised.** Some teachers may be "immune" to it.

2. **Many teachers are unsure about what exactly constitutes sexualised or inappropriately sexist language** and are therefore reluctant to deal with it.

3. **Many teachers fear a lack of support from their senior leadership team in this area.** Clive Rowett[25] is a senior leader and spoke to me about how he supports female staff at his school in Lancashire:

> As a male member of SLT, dealing with cases of sexual harassment against female teachers has been one of the most difficult but eye-opening experiences of my career.
>
> Initially, there were times when I struggled to know what to say or what to do. My clumsy efforts to empathise left my female colleagues feeling understandably frustrated and hurt. *You don't know what it feels like; you've not had this happen to you; they wouldn't dare do it to you*, they've said, through tears of hurt and exasperation. And they're right. I can only begin to imagine what it feels like; this kind of violation has never happened to me; they wouldn't dare do it to a tall, burly man with a booming voice and an imposing physical presence. So, I've learnt to cut out the platitudes, make sure I listen fully to the anxieties and fears of my female colleagues, and have become a person who acts decisively rather than trying to quickly smooth things over.
>
> I've learnt most from watching other male SLT colleagues mess things up even more spectacularly than me. I've watched in shock as they've downplayed the seriousness of very serious cases, complained that the teacher in question should have reported it earlier, totally failed to understand why female colleagues have been so devastated by these "pranks" in the first place.
>
> Instead I've focused on making sure the boys are punished, re-educated and removed from the teacher's classrooms (permanently, if the teacher wishes it). This has occasionally brought me into conflict with SLT colleagues, but I sleep better at night knowing I've made a stand. I continue to make strident points on the topic in SLT meetings, especially when female SLT members fail to offer adequate support to these traumatised (mainly young) female teachers. I'm still not getting everything right but I'll keep on doing my best to help.

4. **Students can be intimidating**. For any teacher, regardless of age or gender, challenging a male student, particularly those who are older, or belong to a "gang" of friends, on his use of inappropriate sexualised or sexist language can be really scary.

5. **Shock and embarrassment**. Female teachers have told me that direct sexualised language has almost left them paralysed with shock. They were rendered mute from a sense of shame at being associated with such sexualised language, to the point where they felt unable to tell anybody about it for a significant amount of time.

It goes without saying that a school policy on sexism and sexually inappropriate behaviour/language would go a long way to solving a lot of issues here. School leaders need to realise this. Of course, whole school policies don't always reflect our own belief systems. So, if a policy refuses to acknowledge this issue, what is it that teachers at the chalk face can do about this issue of sexualised language?

Challenging pupils' language: a case study

Jordan Whale (name has been changed), a teacher from Cardiff, takes a useful approach:

I was doing some grammar work with Year 11 and I asked the class to provide me with an example of a verb. One boy shouted out, "Rape! Rape is a verb! Or raping!" Worryingly, this provoked rapturous laughter from most of the other boys in the class. I immediately stopped the lesson.
"What did you say?"
No response.
"Justin. I'm asking you. What did you just say?"
Still no response. I sternly told the rest of the class to be silent. They could tell I was rattled and they did as I asked.
"Justin. Tell everybody. What was it you just said?"
Apparently Justin wasn't interested in discussing rape. But I was. I apologised to the class for having to stop the lesson, but I wanted to talk about something serious. I asked the class why they thought all the boys had laughed at Justin's comment. When they still looked clueless, I explained to them that society had made the boys believe that jokes about rape were a way of asserting one's masculinity. Every single boy who laughed at that comment, whether they were aware of it or not, were trying to show everyone else in the class that they were a 'proper man.' I explained that actually, rape was a deeply terrifying experience from which one never fully recovers. I explained that jokes about rape go some way to normalising it. I explained to the girls and the boys in the class that from now on, they are to tell me if they ever hear jokes of that nature again.
Two weeks later a student came to tell me that, off the back of that talk, she felt like she could talk to me. She told me she thought a friend of hers had been raped at a party. I duly reported it to the Child Protection Supervisor at the school.

Context is key. I think Jordan's approach here was valid in his context; his students were older, and he had a relationship with his class that enabled him to have such a frank and honest conversation. I take a similar approach. If I hear a boy (or girl, for that matter) use words such as "rape" or "paedophile" inappropriately, I pause the lesson and explain to that child the full and actual meaning of the word. It might look something like this:

> *Daniel:* Ugh. James is going out with Susan in the year below. He's such a paedo.
>
> *Teacher:* Daniel. Paedophilia is a psychiatric disorder where an adult, feels sexually attracted to children. A 15-year-old boy who is in a relationship with a 14-year-old in the year below is not a paedophile, Daniel. Do you get what I'm saying? Do you want me to go over that again?

Or

> *Ben:* Ah mate! I was playing FIFA last night. Got absolutely raped.
>
> *Teacher:* Ben, rape is when a man puts his penis into a person's vagina, anus, or mouth without consent. Being beaten on a computer game has nothing to do with rape. Rape can ruin lives and can have serious lifelong effects on the victim. Using the word casually, as you are doing, is insensitive and inappropriate. Do you understand that? Want me to explain further?

Such an approach may be controversial, but in my experience it has always had a twofold positive impact. First, it is educational. Second, the prosaic bluntness of the language used in the explanation forces students to engage with the true meaning of the words. In my experience, students whose inappropriate use of sexualised language or sexual terms has evoked these responses, have never, within my hearing anyway, repeated these terms again. Jessica Eaton, a speaker, writer, and Ph.D. researcher into victim blaming supports such an approach, particularly in dealing with erroneous use of the word "rape":

> When the youngest generation use phrases like "I got raped on FIFA last night!" they have reached a stage where they have completely trivialised and moved away from the real definition of that word. Some could argue that they understand the word at some level, that it is a 'bad' thing to happen to them. But, what's interesting here is the linguistic parallel to 'winning and losing'. "I got raped on FIFA last night!" means someone beat them in a game and they lost. Similarly, "Got raped!" or "I raped him on FIFA last night" means they won, usually by a lot. This arguably reframes rape as a competitive act, of winning and losing. We have to deconstruct this movement in language as soon as possible.

The final word

It's tempting to describe sexual harassment in schools as the elephant in the room. But elephants are too small and the room is too big to fully describe the problem some schools have with sexually inappropriate behaviour and language. In many schools, sexual harassment is a mammoth in a matchbox. Clumsy metaphors aside, the fact is the problem is huge and it is there and we are ignoring it. Ignoring it, not because we advocate routine humiliation, subjugation, and derision, but because, to some extent, male sexism has become normalised. Sexual harassment is a problem that manifests itself in the adult world in any number of unpleasant ways: a grope in the office kitchen, a leering stare in a nightclub, an obscenity screamed from a passing car. But all of these things begin at school. School leaders and teachers must do what they can to combat the beginnings of a toxic rape culture that can linger, like a noxious mist, over the classrooms and playgrounds of our schools.

Notes

1 Women and Equalities Commission (2016) *Sexual harassment and sexual violence in schools*. Available at: www.parliament.uk/business/committees/committees-a-z/commons-select/women-and-equalities-committee/news-parliament-2015/sexual-harassment-and-violence-in-schools-report-published-16-17/ (Accessed: 15th January 2018).

2 UK Feminista (2017) *"It's just everywhere": A study on sexism in schools*. Available at: http://ukfeminista.org.uk/wp-content/uploads/2017/12/Report-Its-just-everywhere.pdf (Accessed: 15th January 2018).

3 Marshall University Woman's Centre, *What is the rape culture?* Available at: www.marshall.edu/wcenter/sexual-assault/rape-culture/ (Accessed: 15th January 2018).

4 Rape Crisis, *Statistics*. Available at: https://rapecrisis.org.uk/statistics.php (Accessed: 15th January 2018).

5 Zentai, in this context, refers to a fetish for skin-tight garments that cover the whole body. Apparently.

6 Horvath, M.A.H., Alys, L., Massey, K., Pina, A., Scally, M., & Adler, J.R. (2013) *"Basically...Porn is Everywhere": A Rapid Evidence Assessment on the Effect that Access and Exposure to Pornography has on Children and Young People*, London: Children's Commissioner.

7 Bridges, A.J., Wosnitzer, R., Scharrer, E., Sun, C., & Liberman, R. (2010) 'Aggression and sexual behaviour in best-selling pornography videos: A content analysis update', *Violence Against Women*, 16:10, pp. 1065–1085. Cited in Flood, M. (2016) 'Inquiry into the harm being done to Australian children through access to pornography on the Internet', New South Wales: *University of Wollongong*.

8 Bridges, A.J., Wosnitzer, R., Scharrer, E., Sun, C., & Liberman, R. (2010). Cited in Flood, M. (2016).

9 Interview for *Analysis* (Pornography: What do we know?), Radio 4, 30th June 2013.

10 Flood, M. (2016).

11 Ibid.

12 Pinkleton, B.E., Austin, E.W., Cohen, M., Chen, Y.C.Y., & Fitzgerald, E. (2008). 'Effects of a peer-led media literacy curriculum on adolescents' knowledge and attitudes toward sexual behavior and media portrayals of sex', *Health Communication*, 23:5, pp. 462–472. Cited in Flood, M. (2016).

13 PornHub is a website that provides pornography, free of charge.

14 Martellozzo, E., Monaghan, A., Adler, J.R., Davidson, J., Leyva, R., & Horvath, M.A.H. (2017) *"I Wasn't Sure it was Normal to Watch it..." A Quantitative and Qualitative Examination of the Impact of Online Pornography on the Values, Attitudes, Beliefs and Behaviours of Children and Young People.* London: Middlesex University.

15 'Over a thousand Danish youths charged for sharing sex video', Christopher, W., *CPH Post Online*, 15th January 2018. Available at: http://cphpost.dk/news/over-a-thousand-danish-youths-charged-for-sharing-sex-video.html (Accessed: 15th January 2018).

16 UK Feminista (2017).

17 Ibid.

18 Ibid.

19 Ibid.

20 Ibid.

21 Department for Education (2016) *Sexual violence and sexual harassment between children in schools and colleges: Advice for governing bodies, proprietors, headteachers, principals, senior leadership teams and designated safeguarding leads*, DfE. Available at: www. gov.uk/government/uploads/system/uploads/attachment_data/file/667862/Sexual_Harassment_and_Sexual_Violence_-_Advice.pdf (Accessed: 16th January 2018).

22 Ibid.

23 Department for Education (2000) *Sex and relationship education guidance.* Available at: https://assets.publishing.service.gov.uk/government/uploads/system/uploads/attachment_data/file/283599/sex_and_relationship_education_guidance.pdf (Accessed: 25th September 2018).

24 Department for Education (2018) *Relationships education, relationships and sex education, and health education in England.* Available at: https://consult.education.gov.uk/pshe/relationships-education-rse-health-education/supporting_documents/180718%20Consultation_call%20for%20evidence%20response_policy%20statement.pdf (Accessed: 25th September 2018).

25 Name has been changed.

7 In the classroom

Mark Roberts

PART A: Representations of gender in texts

The story

A design editor sits behind a chrome and glass desk, flicking through prospective covers for a new textbook on the BTEC Child Development course. Putting a large red X across the sample green cover, she instead opts for a pastel cover with a picture of a girl in a magenta cagoule pouring an imaginary cup of tea.

A school librarian decides to refresh the displays in a bid to get more boys reading. Ripping down the classic literature timeline, he replaces this tired-looking wall with sport-themed posters, including images of Premier League stars holding a novel featuring a young boy who dreams of becoming a professional footballer.

A grandmother, looking for Christmas present ideas online, ends up searching "gifts for five-year-old boys" and "gifts for seven-year-old girls". Having researched the recommendations, she ends up buying Star Wars Lego for James and a copy of *Charlotte's Web* for Jemima.

A primary school teacher, listening to a boy read during a lesson, shows surprise at his choice of a non-fiction book, *My First Little Book of Sewing*, asking him whether he hadn't seen the books on space and dinosaurs.

The research

As we shall see in Chapter 8, the socialisation of children to accept stereotypical gender norms begins early, with the use of toys, costumes, and discussion of feelings. It would be reassuring to think then that when it comes to the serious business of early years education – such as learning how to read – young children are exposed to texts that avoid such stereotypes. Sadly, this is far from the case.

This is not due to a lack of awareness on the part of publishers. Publishers are aware that they have propagated gender stereotypes. Macmillan, one of the world's leading textbook publishers, as far back as 1975, conceded that

Children are not simply being taught mathematics and reading; they are also learning, sometimes subliminally, how society regards certain groups of people.[1]

Macmillan recognised that educational resources contribute towards the "hidden curriculum" and therefore teach children as much about attitudes towards gender, ethnicity, and social class as they do about fractions, commas, and volcanoes. In their study, which begins by reviewing 25 years of research into the representation of masculinity in textbooks for young children, Lorraine Evans and Kimberley Davies[2] found the following negative stereotypes of males and females from the 1970s:

- Woman very rarely featuring in occupational roles

- Men very rarely portrayed in "fathering or caregiving" roles

- Boys never involved with dolls, flowers, etc.

But haven't things changed?

Such one-dimensional sexist portrayals are to be expected from a less progressive era, of course. Surely if we were to look at studies of more recent reading material, the situation would be different? Sadly not. In their 2000 study that analysed characters stories from a wide range of elementary textbooks, Evans and Davies found that

- Males were shown as "significantly more aggressive, argumentative, and competitive than females"

- Males were "significantly less likely to be described as affectionate, emotionally expressive, passive, or tender"

Indeed, the status quo holds, with the authors concluding that "male characters are being portrayed in the same way that they were 20 years [before]".

Other researchers have shown that illustrations from textbooks for young children also contribute to the early formation of gender stereotypes. Narahara[3] argues that illustrations in books act as a visual definition of expected standards of feminine and masculine behaviour.

Traditionally, female characters are depicted as passive and obedient, occupying roles within the domestic/private sphere, while male characters are portrayed as dominant and active, making decisions within the public sphere. Incidentally, it's worth noting that Narahara cites studies which found that children who were given non-sexist literature experienced positive effects including improvements to "self-concept, attitudes and behaviour".[4]

Books for boys; books for girls

So what happens when authors go out of their way to create non-stereotypical characters, which are designed to appeal equally to both genders? Gabrielle Kent, author of the Alfie Bloom series of children's books, believes that all too often, it is the adults who "stop boys from reading books with female protagonists". Kent explained, in a recent series of tweets,[5] that during her time spent in bookshops, signing copies of her latest novel *Knights and Bikes*, she noticed that boys asking for a copy of her novel – and other books featuring the word "witch" in the title – are often told no by their parents, because "that's for girls". She poses the question: "why are parents who are happy for girls to read *Harry Potter* scared of their sons reading about witches?".

Kent feels that some publishers are complicit in this gendered targeting of books:

> I've witnessed publishers making covers far too dark and creepy in relation to the content in order to trick boys into reading them, and girls tell me they enjoyed them but nearly didn't read them because they thought they were spooky books.

In particular, Kent argues young boys would benefit from reading about female protagonists who are depicted in a way that is at odds with the way girls are portrayed in the media:

> Reading about kick ass girls having awesome adventures, solving mysteries, and saving the world teaches boys to see girls in a different light to the ones they see screaming at rubber spiders in toy adverts. Let boys read the stories they want to read.

There's a (male) monster in your book

No wonder Kent is frustrated with the depiction of gender in the books children read. As recently as January 2018, research carried out by *The Observer*[6] newspaper found that anthropomorphised male characters in the most popular children's books of 2017 still portrayed harmful gender stereotypes. Male characters are usually presented as "powerful, wild, and potentially dangerous beasts such as dragons, bears, and tigers", in contrast to female characters who were more likely to be presented as "vulnerable creatures such as birds, cats, and insects". As with the texts from 50 years earlier, male adults are far less likely to be portrayed in nurturing and caring roles.

It would appear, then, that at a particularly influential period in their development, young children are being fed an unchanging diet of traditional gender roles in their learning materials.

Gender representations in college textbooks

But what of textbooks aimed at older students? Might these offer a more nuanced reading of gender expectations?

In an overview of research into textbooks aimed at college level educational psychology students, Yanowitz and Weathers[7] note that "photographs illustrating mental illness and therapy situations depicted women disproportionately more often than men". For this reason, it could be argued that certain content in textbooks contributes to the social stigma and resulting silence around male mental health issues. In addition, the fictional classroom management scenarios that are commonplace in these textbooks for trainee teachers also contain situations that reinforce beliefs about stereotypical male and female behaviour. For example, a scenario "where one child is bullying another and makes the target child cry" will usually feature a male perpetrator, perpetuating the aspiring teacher's negative view of boys' behaviour in the classroom. As Yanowitz and Weathers put it,

> As students progress through a teacher preparation program, they gradually form a schema or expectation of how a typical classroom functions, including beliefs about appropriate behaviour for boys and girls in the classroom.

The solutions

Advice for teachers

Unless you want to organise a boycott of gender stereotypical texts, or fancy a mass bonfire outside the science block, you might have to put up with the textbooks that are out there on the market. After all, over the past half century, few studies have found many texts that depict gender in an unbiased and neutral manner. Here's what you could do instead:

- Ensure your own resources don't fall into the (easy) trap of stereotyping gender. What subliminal message, for example, does a seemingly innocent bit of clip art, depicting a "nerdy" boy wearing a lab coat and glasses, slapped on to the bottom of a science revision timetable give?

- During lessons, confront gender stereotypes from textbooks as you come across them. What might you say to the class when confronted with these extracts?

---

1. Claire's mum uses kitchen spray when she is doing the housework each day. She wants to buy some refills. There are two deals on offer:

    A. Three bottles for £4.50

    B. One bottle for £1.99.

    Which is the better deal?

2. Listed below are five of the most important authors of the Victorian era. Choose one to research as part of your homework, summarising their life and major achievements on one side of A4 paper:

A. Charles Dickens

B. Robert Louis Stevenson

C. Thomas Hardy

D. Lewis Carroll

E. Anthony Trollope.

3. Being able to tackle is a vital skill in rugby. It helps you win the ball back or stop a man from the opposing team scoring. Timing and technique are essential to prevent injury.

Step A

For safety reasons, position your body on his right-hand side.

Next, put your right shoulder into his right-sided thigh.

It may seem pedantic to pick apart the language in these apparently innocent examples but I'd suggest that if we are to avoid teaching a harmful hidden curriculum, a quick discussion of the effects of gender stereotyping is necessary.

Suggested reading list

The Gender Equality Charter's website[8] has an excellent list of non-stereotypical texts, as well as further links.

Here are some suggestions for younger readers from their list, with a few others that I like:

- *Stories for Boys Who Dare to be Different* by Ben Brooks

- *Good Night Stories for Rebel Girls* by Elena Favilli

- *Women in Science: 50 Fearless Pioneers Who Changed the World* by Rachel Ignotofksy

- *Fantastically Great Women Who Changed The World* by Kate Pankhurst

- *The Wolf Wilder* by Katherine Rundell

- *The Last Wild* by Piers Torday.

And a few recommended reads for older students:

- *Everyday Sexism* by Laura Bates

- *How Not To Be A Boy* by Robert Webb

- *The Left Hand of Darkness* by Ursula Le Guin

- *The Power* by Naomi Alderman

- *Days Without End* by Sebastian Barry

- *The Perks of Being a Wallflower* by Stephen Chbosky.

PART B: Do boys need male teachers? Would single sex classrooms make a difference?

As Chapter 3 illustrated, many boys adopt anti-school work attitudes because striving for academic success is seen as effeminate. Additionally, some commentators[9] have argued that boys have suffered as a result of policies that have empowered girls and improved their educational outcomes and that the "feminisation" of teaching needs to be halted to bring about an upturn in outcomes for boys. The argument goes: schools are overly feminised, so let's appeal to boys by masculinising them, showing that real men can work hard and get good grades. One simple answer to boys' corrosive anti-work attitudes, the theory goes, would be to ensure that we match boy pupils with male teachers who will behave and teach differently to female teachers and will also act as positive male role models. This need for "matching" seems particularly relevant to subjects that are seen as stereotypically feminine (such as English), and in primary schools, which are stereotypically viewed as nurturing, caring – and therefore feminine – environments.

The big question is does this approach work?

The story

Recently, I visited a school in the south west of England. Despite a picture of general improvement, boys were doing poorly compared to girls. There was a hefty gender attainment gap. The English faculty, however, was more successful. Boys in English were still behind girls, but the gap was much smaller than in other subject areas. I wanted to find out what English were doing that the rest of the school weren't. Speaking to the subject lead, it became clear that one of the things English were doing differently was a boys-only class, paired with an experienced male teacher. This class was full of "disaffected and apathetic" boys. The boys, I was told, had previously messed around in lessons, shown little effort, and were likely to be distracted by the presence of girls. Having these boys confined to one class made sense: less disruption for girls (and boys who wanted to get on with their work), fewer problems in class for the other teachers, and a clear target group of hitherto underperforming but capable boys.

Was the strategy working?

Walking into the classroom, I was impressed by the purposeful, scholarly atmosphere. From the outset, the boys were tested by tricky questions on their knowledge of the literature texts they'd studied – including ones that they'd not focused on in class for a while. They got most of the questions correct. There was no hiding place. The work was challenging. The boys were responding. Soon, it was time to collect in the homework. Previously, these boys didn't do homework. But there had been a shift in attitudes towards home learning: only two of the large class hadn't done their homework that day. They were told they would be doing it at lunchtime. They accepted their punishment without fuss. I looked at the books. They showed signs of productivity and high quality analysis. Their predicted grades had gone up sharply from the previous year.

Later in the day, I had the opportunity to interview a group of the boys from the class. They adored their English teacher. He was funny. You could have a laugh with him. He understood them. He knew how to get the best out of them. You could tell he loved the books they were studying. He knew his subject inside out. You knew where you stood with him. He didn't stand for any nonsense.

Had I witnessed a key strategy to raise the attainment of boys? Do boys work better in all-boy groups? Do boys prefer male teachers? And do they attain better results when the teacher stood before them happens to have a Y chromosome?

The research

We'll return to our school and class full of superstar boys shortly. But before we do, let's look at what the research says about their success.

A large scale American survey, the National Educational Longitudinal Study of 1988,[10] focused "both on how teachers subjectively relate to and evaluate their students *and* on how much their students learn, as measured by standardised tests". Supported by large sample sizes, the researchers found "no evidence that, as compared to white male teachers, white female teachers increased, or decreased, the scores of either white male or white female students in any subject".[11] In other words, the gender of the teacher made *no difference* to academic attainment for boys or girls.

Further studies add weight to the theory that pupils aren't fussed about the gender of their educators. Becky Francis et al.[12] found that "an overwhelming majority of pupils surveyed felt that the gender of the teacher was insignificant, with many respondents articulating that male and female teachers are 'the same'". By this they meant that the nature of their professional role as teacher carries far more influence than their personal characteristics:

> Children overwhelmingly see the teacher's purpose or 'role' as to teach them – the children's concern is with the teachers' ability to do this effectively, rather than with what they consider to be irrelevant factors such as gender.[13]

Further studies in England,[14] Finland,[15] and Australia[16] have also shown that pupils of both sexes ascribe very little importance to their teacher's gender, although the latter study did find a notable exception: pupils who wish to speak about personal matters largely prefer to talk to a teacher of their own gender.

A typical male teacher?

Putting matters of personal privacy aside, why else might it be the case that students don't care about the gender of their teacher? In a separate piece of research into the classroom practices of male primary school teachers, Francis[17] notes the "absurdity in expecting that men teachers would teach, or relate to pupils, in predictable or uniform ways simply on the basis of their 'maleness'". Indeed, the teachers observed as part of Francis's work display "strongly contrasting pedagogic practices, disciplinary effectiveness, and approaches to pupils and to the teacher role". And, on reflection, this of course makes sense. After all, we've already seen in Chapter 1 that there is no such thing as a typical male pupil. Boys have as much differences with each other as they do with girls. So why would we assume that there is such a thing as a typical male teacher? And even if there were such a thing, we already know that the quest for relevancy is futile, that they wouldn't be able to meet the diverse interests, aspirations, and needs of pupils who happen to share the designation of "boy". Little wonder then that Francis's research found deeply contradictory statements, with different pupils labelling male teachers as both "stricter" and "kinder" than their female counterparts.

It is far from guaranteed, therefore, that male pupils will identify and look up to a teacher from the same gender. Indeed, it has been argued by certain researchers[18] that the way some male teachers attempt to form a rapport with their younger "brethren" may unintentionally play to notions of stereotypical masculinity, exacerbating existing anti-school work attitudes. It's quite easy for a male teacher to gain popularity with disruptive boys by poking fun at one of them. For example, he might easily get a laugh through a sarcastic comment on a pupil's pink bag ("That's a very manly accessory you've got there Josh?"), but at what cost? And with what unintentional message being conveyed? As such, Christine Skelton notes the self-contradictory logic of the drive to masculinise the primary school workforce:

> Governments have not been clear about what kinds of male primary teachers are required if boys are to be motivated to want to work harder at school. If the 'laddishness' of boys is equated with anti-school attitudes then presumably male teachers need to be the antithesis of such masculine constructions, but, if they do not draw on hegemonic forms of masculinity (such as 'having a laugh', being competitive, enjoying sport) then it is likely that boys will fail to relate to them.[19]

Single sex classrooms

So if male teachers as role models are not the answer, what about single sex classes? After all, single sex schools frequently make headline news[20] for topping the GCSE and A level league tables. Surely a bit of timetabled segregation will lead to similar positive results in coeducational settings?

For at least the last half a century or so, single-sex classes in mixed schools is a strategy that has been regularly recommended, at one time or other, by politicians, Ofsted, and educationalists. Frequently repeated reasons for keeping boys and girls apart include:

- Removing the distraction of flirtation with the opposite sex

- Girls feeling less self-aware and being more likely to contribute answers without boys around

- Targeting girls to succeed in subjects seen as "masculine", such as science, technology, engineering, and medicine (STEM) subjects, and targeting boys in "feminine" subjects, such as English and modern foreign languages (MFL)

- Boys messing around more than girls; girls-only classes stopping girls' learning being unfairly disrupted by boys

- Boys-only groups enabling teachers to focus on the strategies that most appeal to boys.

A much-cited study by Rowe et al. from 1986[21] concluded that boys and girls in single-sex classes became more confident and performed better than their equivalents in mixed-sex classes. Indeed, Rowe et al. claimed that "the most notable improvement between the two testing occasions occurred among girls in all-girl classes, followed by boys in all-boy classes". However, Marsh and Rowe revisited the data in 1996 and realised that the single class effect was less influential than first reported. This was because "the significant gains made by pupils in mixed-sex classes were largely ignored in the first analysis".[22]

Even had the impressive outcomes trumpeted in Rowe's original study been correct, there may well be other variables that cast doubt on the single-sex silver bullet for improving the results of boys and girls. Harker argues that because they are statistically far more likely to be selective, "single-sex schools end up with a more socially exclusive group of pupils, whose prior achievement levels are considerably higher than for pupils at coeducational schools".[23] For example, Harker cites a 1989 study by Bell which concluded that gains in science results were largely a result of the fact that in his sample "40% of the single-sex schools were either private or elite state 'grammar' schools while only 3% of the coeducational schools were in those categories".[24] Indeed, in studies where better results are found in single sex schools, Harker asserts that "when adequate control is exercised for the different ability levels and the social and ethnic mix of the two types of school, the initial significant differences between them disappear".

A 2004 Australian study[25] found that although results in mathematics showed no significant difference, results in English improved for pupils that were placed in single-sex classes. Girls-only groups made greater gains than boys, but boys-only groups still outperformed boys in mixed classes. The researchers admitted, however, that it is difficult to use the small study as evidence that single-sex classrooms improve results. As they make clear "other major factors such as quality and nature of curriculum, pedagogy, levels of psycho-sexual maturity in female/male relationships, peer group pressure ... are significant variables impacting on both boys' and girls' achievement of learning outcomes".[26]

A familiar pattern

This is the pattern found in many classic studies that have been used as evidence by proponents of single-sex education over mixed schools: impressive results that fail to show with any sort of certainty that the absence of the other gender has actually made the difference. Another problem associated with the studies is the focus purely on attainment as a measure of the worth of single-sex groupings. As Carolyn Jackson[27] noted in 2002, "there is an increasing tendency amongst educational researchers with an interest in gender to focus almost exclusively upon attainment, and to neglect classroom interaction issues". In other words, claims about whether single-sex grouping is effective more often than not focuses on results, without considering relationships.

Thankfully, a comprehensive 2014 meta-analysis of 184 studies, featuring data collected on over one and a half million students, carried out by Pahlke et al.[28] cleared up a lot of the contradictory claims and narrow scope of previous research. Focusing on a wide range of issues – including academic attainment, attitudes about school, relationships – they found that in methodologically dubious, uncontrolled studies (the ones often quoted by advocates of single-sex schooling), large effect sizes were found in favour of single-sex schooling. Crucially, however, in controlled studies (the ones that took into account other factors such as socio-economic background, selective admission policies, smaller class sizes), they found effect sizes "close to zero". This led Pahlke et al. to a clear conclusion: there is no decent evidence to suggest single-sex schools or classes confer any kind of educational advantage.

Are there further downsides to single-sex schooling?

Halpern et al.[29] argue that single-sex environments increase pupils' awareness of gender difference. This stereotyping arises, they claim, "because the contrast between the segregated classroom and the mixed-sex structure of the surrounding world provides evidence to children that sex is a core human characteristic along which adults organise education". In other words, by separating children educationally by gender, adults reinforce the notion of gender difference, limiting "children's opportunities to develop a broader range of behaviours and attitudes".[30] This is particularly true of single-sex classrooms where teachers attempt to appeal to supposed learning preferences of one gender. As Chapter 1 highlighted, teaching to stereotypes about "what boys want" (movement around the classroom, sport, competition, "boys' book boxes", and so on) is counterproductive in its reinforcement of gender stereotypes and has left some boys falling behind academically. An Australian study, conducted by Martino et al.,[31] documents worrying examples of what can happen when well-intentioned but misguided teachers appeal to typical notions of masculinity:

> [A male teacher of a boys-only class] had implemented an activities based curriculum for boys, which involved doing 'hands-on activities'…boys would be granted permission to leave the class for three to five minutes to jog around the oval. He referred to these as 'testosterone surge sessions' and claimed that this helped boys manage their high energy levels. He was also of the view that 'boys are very competitive' and 'love sport'. They were also considered to be more active than girls in their orientation to learning.

The boys certainly enjoyed these interludes from learning. Who wouldn't like a good old "testosterone surge" to break the monotony of the fusty, surge-less classroom? Unfortunately, as the researchers discovered, the boys-only class started to feel that despite the joy of their jogging jamborees, they were covering far less academic mileage:

> …the pedagogy and curriculum in the mixed-gender class were more intellectually demanding than in the single-sex classroom. While apparently appearing to be less fun, the boys in the mixed class felt that they were being prepared more adequately to cope with the future demands of high school.[32]

The atmosphere of boys-only classes

In addition to the dangers of teaching to perceived gender difference in segregated classes, Jackson[33] notes the longstanding historical argument that teaching pupils in mixed-gender classes is effective due to the positive effects on boys of having female peers in the classroom. As Jackson points out, "the notion that girls act as a civilising influence upon boys and therefore enhance boys' performance dates back to Dale (1969, 1971, 1974) and before".

Evidence from other studies supports the view that behaviour in classrooms can deteriorate in the absence of girls. A study by Gray and Wilson,[34] focusing on Year 8 pupils in a Northern Irish school in a large working-class catchment area, found that single-sex classes were very unpopular with the school's teachers. Four years into the single-sex grouping initiative, 77% of teachers felt that "single-sex classes [had] not had a positive effect on boys' behaviour", while 61% thought that it had not improved boys' academic performance. The reasons for this were clear: increasing competition and bullying, especially among boys; "highly stressful" bottom set boys-only classes; a decline in academic outcomes compared with previous years. Carolyn Jackson's study found similar concerns, this time from the perspective of students. Boys felt they were more heavily punished in boys-only groups. Other worries included "fighting and roughness", with around a third of boys listing violence or excessive physicality as "one of the worst features of boys' classes". Halpern et al. agree, citing research showing that boys who spend more time with other boys "become increasingly aggressive" and can "experience greater risk for behaviour problems", while girls who spend more time with other girls "become more sex-typed".[35]

The presence of girls and the "caretaking role"

Furthermore, a 2007 study[36] by Lavy and Shlosser found that an increase in the proportion of girls in the classroom in Israeli schools resulted in "significant improvement in students' cognitive outcomes". What's more, the authors found that an uplift in the female:male ratio reduced "the level of classroom disruption and violence", improved "inter-student and student-teacher relationships as well as students' overall satisfaction in school, and lessened teachers' fatigue". Interestingly, the behaviour of individual pupils didn't change. The reduction in disruption was instead a result of "compositional change". Simply put, having more girls in classes meant that poor behaviour was less likely to occur in the first place.

While putting more girls in a classroom won't act as a magic behaviour wand, having girls in a classroom with boys nonetheless contributes towards a reduction in disruption. And orderly classrooms with minimal disruption are good for improving the results of boys and girls. But the idea of using girls in this way, quite rightly, sits uncomfortably with many teachers. Yes the dilution of poor behaviour is a universally good thing, but employing girls in classes as a "civilising influence" – in what Jackson terms a "caretaking role" – risks maintaining an environment where girls, through their "better natures" are expected to sort boys out. As Chapter 6 showed, girls are often subject to sexual harassment from boys; deploying girls as a civilising influence isn't enough. Boys need to be educated in a way that their attitudes change, leaving girls free to sit near boys safe in the knowledge that they won't have their learning disrupted, nor will they be abused or groped during lessons.

The classroom relationships between boys and girls aren't, however, as straightforward as we might first imagine. Girls-only groups might well offer a sanctuary from distraction and abuse, but as Kenway and Willis[37] have shown, "girls want gender reform to change boys, for boys to try to see things from a girl's perspective, for boys to deal with feelings and to be more mature emotionally". It's time to state something that might seem obvious, but can be forgotten in the clamour to "protect" girls: despite the problematic behaviour from some boys, girls actually like learning alongside them. Boys need to change. Girls want them to change. Girls want to work alongside them. Segregation makes things worse.

What matters most: the teacher's gender or the teacher's expectations?

Let's go back to the school I mentioned earlier. The one with the highly promising group full of boys. So how come the boys-only class, that I witnessed first-hand, was flourishing? How come the grades had gone up? How come their attitudes had improved? How come they were doing better than many of the boys in mixed classes? Well, there are a plethora of variables that one might want to take into account. Class dynamics. Positive peer influences. Developing maturity levels. Better focus as they embarked upon their GCSEs. But, on reflection, from my perspective one thing was most responsible for their improved outcomes and behaviour: their teacher. The fact that he happened to be a he was irrelevant. He was funny, which helped build a rapport, but – and this really shouldn't need spelling out – a female teacher could quite easily have developed a similar humour-based relationship. As we've seen previously, the National Educational Longitudinal Study of 1988[38] found that "the gender of the teacher made *no difference* to academic attainment for boys or girls". Remember too that Francis et al.'s[39] research into pupil perceptions found that an overwhelming majority of pupils interviewed felt that the gender of their teacher was irrelevant. What was extremely relevant in this case, however, was the experience, knowledge, and pedagogical skill of the teacher. Dylan Wiliam[40] has argued that in the quest for better attainment "the only thing that really matters is the quality of the teacher". He explains:

> In the classrooms of the best teachers, students learn at twice the rate they do in the classrooms of average teachers…Moreover, in the classrooms of the most effective teachers, students from disadvantaged backgrounds learn just as much as those from advantaged backgrounds, and those with behavioural difficulties learn as much as those without.

The teacher I had seen with his class of boys had, skilfully, ensured his pupils were doing the following:

■ **Retrieval practice:** revisiting things they'd learnt before, to ensure they were becoming embedded in long-term memory

■ **Completing homework:** developing knowledge about the topics they were currently studying, as well as content they hadn't looked at for a while

■ **Putting full effort into their work:** sloppy writing with shoddy spelling and punctuation didn't receive feedback. If they couldn't be bothered to try, he wouldn't bother to mark it. The challenge was high, support was in place for some, and the class as a whole were rising to it

■ **Gaining appreciation for their subject:** this teacher knew his stuff and loved teaching English. His enthusiasm was rubbing off on the pupils

■ **Concentrating and listening to instructions:** amidst the jokes, the entertaining anecdotes and the clear care for his pupils, there was a tacit but palpable sense of authority. This was his classroom and disruption of any kind would not be tolerated

■ **Treating each other with respect:** the humour was affectionately daft but there was no "banter". Polite behaviour was modelled and celebrated. Pupils spoke respectfully to their peers

■ **Sexist attitudes were challenged:** the teacher is a role model. Not a male role model for boys, just a general role model for teenagers of either gender.

These pupils were thriving. But pretty much any pupils – female, male, black, white, middle class, working class – would have thrived in this environment. The effect of the individual teacher was very likely making all the difference.

The solutions

Advice for school leaders

Much of the research we've cited in previous chapters contends that mixed ability teaching is more likely than grouping by "ability" to lead to improved results for boys. Yet, many senior and middle leaders argue that the evidence on setting isn't definitive and prefer to continue with what they feel is most effective in their school's context. While we suggest that mixed ability groups across subjects is the most effective and equitable arrangement, you might feel more comfortable, say, using setting in subjects that are seen as hierarchical in content like mathematics, languages, and science. Whichever way you go, it's essential that, as leaders, you give very careful consideration to the groupings you use and think long and hard about your rationale for doing so. Things to ponder include:

■ What are the male/female ratios, especially in top/bottom sets (if you have them)?

■ How many boys are in the top, or higher, sets?

■ What proportion of disadvantaged pupils are in different groups?

■ Are you setting on current ability or *potential* ability? You need to be thorough and totally honest at this point of reflection: go back and look at the Key Stage 2 (KS2) levels, not just what they got in a test at the end of Year 8. Is their current "ability" reflective of their true ability or is it only indicative of their disaffection with the curriculum/set they've been dumped in/attitude of the teacher?

■ Is there an unintentional (I hope) bias against some boys which creates an atmosphere of low expectations and low challenge?

■ Are the "difficult boys" given to the teachers who you think can deal with them on their level? Male or female, are these teachers forced to revert to stereotypes and become "cultural accomplices", relying on their assertive, confrontational "masculine" traits to tackle behaviour? If so, what message does this send out to the other teachers and other pupils?

Advice for teachers

A.   Think carefully about seating plans

Regardless of the age range of your pupils, whether you teach in £10,000 a term public school, a primary school or a pupil referral unit,[41] you'll want to maximise learning by deciding where pupils sit. Here are some of the common mistakes I've seen when it comes to dealing with poorly-behaved boys (and girls):

1. **Attempting to contain the contagion**: this is my term for the tactic used by teachers who try to minimise bad behaviour in class by putting all the disruptive pupils together on one table/row. The theory goes that by locating a small group of difficult students in a confined area you can restrict poor behaviour, usually by "keeping an eye on them". In my experience, this very rarely works and instead amplifies poor conduct. When you dig a bit deeper you normally discover that this arrangement was actually suggested by the pupils themselves, often for an unspecified "trial period". Instead of trying to contain the contagion, you need to separate and tackle the individual poor behaviour. It sounds obvious, but you'd be amazed by the number of teachers who don't insist on "my classroom – I decide who sits where"

2. **Sticking to the seating plan come what may**: you've spent ages working out where they're being seated. Your plan is fool proof. The following calculations have been used to organise your class: gender, academic ability, socioeconomic status, average behaviour points in the previous academic year, sign of the zodiac, how sullen they look on their school mugshot ... But within minutes it's clear that Iqbal and Abdul don't get on. One of them politely explains that they've had issues in the past and putting them next to each other won't work. Or Sarah comes to see you at the end of the lesson, and explains that she's just broken up with Jake and it feels really weird. You, however, have spent ages on your plan – you've colour-coded and laminated it for Christ's sake – and will not be denied. There will be no flexibility: "It's my classroom – I decide who sits where" you repeat, several weeks later as Iqbal begins to cry and Sarah slaps Jake

3. **Assuming boy/girl seating plans are a panacea for preventing classroom problems**: According to a survey[42] by Teacher Tapp,[43] boy/girl seating plans are popular across the UK. 47% of a sample of over 2,298 teachers said they

used boy/girl seating plans, with a quarter of respondents saying they used them "frequently" or "almost always". In a subsequent poll,[44] only 3% of respondents said that their use of gendered seating plans was dictated by whole school policy. Therefore, teachers that use these plans presumably do so out of a personal belief that they contribute to a positive classroom climate.

Boy/girl plans are my preferred seating arrangement. Even prior to reading the research by Lavy and Shlosser[45] on the influence of girls in the classroom, I'd always felt that mixing genders led to less disruption and a better working environment. Yet, as a great deal of other work in this chapter shows, girls can sometimes suffer as a result of being used to "civilise" some of their male classmates.

A while back, I had a fascinating Twitter debate with a group of female teachers who told me how sick their daughters were of being asked to act as a calming influence by sitting next to the same difficult boys all day at primary school, or repeatedly across subjects – particularly due to what one termed the "tyranny of alphabetical seating" – at secondary school. These hard-working, eager-to-please girls hadn't complained, partly because they recognised that they were being asked to do something helpful, and they wanted to be helpful. The teachers assuming no-news-is-good-news maintained this arrangement for as long as possible. So, like I've started to do over the last year or so, think carefully about whether the girls in your class – and the polite and studious boys – you use as a fire blanket are genuinely happy to sit with certain pupils, regardless of what they say. It may be that some challenging pupils need to be seated on their own, for everyone's benefit

B.   Have high expectations for all

Think back to the exemplary practice of the teacher (who just happened to be male) with his "group of lads". His standards were sky high, irrespective of the fact that he'd been given a class of none-too-easy boys. These were working with "challenging, disaffected" boys, but –as Dylan Wiliam pointed out – would work with any child. Let's remind ourselves of his expectations:

- Complete work – including homework – to the best of your ability

- Act on the given feedback, striving for continual improvement

- Rise to the challenge of memorising knowledge and grasping difficult concepts

- Listen to the teacher and each other respectfully at all times.

The final word

Part A of this chapter looked at the way males and females are portrayed in the fiction and non-fiction books read by children at home and in school, and the textbooks we use to teach them in our classrooms. Through publically questioning the lazy assumptions about gender that can be seen in the pages of these tomes, teachers can go a long way towards combating the deafening stereotypical noise about gender elsewhere in young people's lives.

In Part B of this chapter, we considered the arguments for single-sex schooling, boys-only classes, and the idea that male teachers are the best role models for male pupils. The evidence suggests that these structures and strategies will not work in isolation. When pupils (of both genders) do well under these arrangements, it is probably the result of many other factors including, most significantly, the expertise, experience, and knowledge of the teachers the pupils come into contact with day in, day out in lessons.

The recipe for success with boys in the classroom is clear:

Take an orderly environment and don't forget to insert clear routines. Wait for behaviour to settle. Add a warm, knowledgeable, and demanding teacher, who understands how pupils learn best. Keep the levels of challenge high but include a scaffold when required. Put the gender of the pupils to one side. Discard stereotypical ideas, which appear harmless but can leave a bitter taste. Repeat until results begin to rise (Figure 7.1).

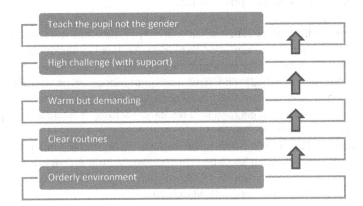

Figure 7.1 Teaching boys effectively

Notes

1 Quoted in Britton, G.E. & Lumpkin, M.C. (1977) 'For sale: Subliminal bias in textbooks', *Reading Teacher*, 31, pp. 40–45.
2 Evans, L. & Davies, K. (2000) 'No sissy boys here: A content analysis of the representation of masculinity in elementary school reading textbooks', *Sex Roles*, 42:3/4.
3 Narahara, M.M. (1998) *Gender Stereotypes in Children's Picture Books*, Long Beach: University of California.
4 Ibid.
5 Kent, G. Twitter Post. 1st September 2018, 1.41 p.m. Available at: https://twitter.com/GabrielleKent/status/1035991070620958721.

6 Ferguson, D. (2018) 'Must monsters always be male? Huge gender bias revealed in children's books', *The Guardian*, 21st January. Available at: www.theguardian.com/books/2018/jan/21/childrens-books-sexism-monster-in-your-kids-book-is-male (Accessed: 22nd January 2018).

7 Yanowitz, K.L. & Weathers, K.J. (2004) 'Do boys and girls act differently in the classroom? A content analysis of student characters in educational psychology textbooks', *Sex Roles*, 51:1/2.

8 Gender Equality Charter Website, *GEC Best Books List*. Available at: www.thegenderequalitycharter.com/gec-best-books/ (Accessed: 22nd July 2018).

9 See, for example, Biddulph, S. (1997) *Raising Boys*, London: Thorsons.

10 Ehrenberg, R., Goldhaber, D., & Brewer, D. (1995) 'Do teachers' race, gender and ethnicity matter? Evidence from the National Education Longitudinal Study of 1988', *Industrial and Labor Relations Review*, 48, pp. 547–561.

11 Ibid.

12 Francis, B., Skelton, C., Carrington, B., Hutchings, M., Read, B., & Hall, I. (2008) 'A perfect match? Pupils' and teachers' views of the impact of matching educators and learners by gender', *Research Papers in Education*, 23:1, pp. 21–36.

13 Ibid.

14 Carrington, B., Tymms, P., & Merrell, C. (2008) 'Role models, school improvement and the gender gap – Do men bring out the best in boys and women the best in girls?' *British Educational Research Journal*, 34:3, pp. 315–327.

15 Lahelma, E. (2000) 'Lack of male teachers: A problem for students or teachers?' *Pedagogy, Culture and Society*, 8:2, pp. 173–185.

16 Martin, A.J. & Marsh, H. (2005) 'Motivating boys and motivating girls: Does teacher gender really make a difference?', *Australian Journal of Education*, 49:3, pp. 320–334.

17 Francis, B. (2008) 'Teaching manfully? Exploring gendered subjectivities and power via analysis of men teachers' gender performance', *Gender and Education*, 20:2, pp. 109–122.

18 For instance Skelton, C. (2002) 'The 'feminisation of schooling' or 're-masculinising primary education?', *International Studies in Sociology of Education*, 12:1, pp. 77–96.

19 Skelton, C. (2009) 'Failing to get men into primary teaching: A feminist critique', *Journal of Education Policy*, 24:1, pp. 39–54.

20 See for example 'This year's exam results shows girls' schools are producing pupils who aim for the sky', Bernice McCabe, *The Telegraph*, 20th January 2017. Available at: www.telegraph.co.uk/education/2017/01/20/years-exam-results-shows-girls-schools-producing-pupils-aim/ (Accessed: 7th March 2018).

21 Rowe, K.J., Nix, P.J., & Tepper, G. (1986). Single-sex versus mixed-sex classes: The joint effects of gender and class type on student performance in and attitudes towards mathematics. Paper presented at the annual conference of the Australian Association for Research in Education, Melbourne.

22 Gray, C. & Wilson, J. (2006) 'Teachers' experiences of a single-sex initiative in a co-education school', *Educational Studies*, 32:3, pp. 285–298.

23 Harker, R. (2000) 'Achievement, gender and the single-sex/coed debate', *British Journal of Sociology of Education*, 21:2, pp. 203–218.

24 Ibid.

25 Mulholland, J., Hansen, P., & Kaminski, E. (2004) 'Do single-gender classrooms in coeducational settings address boys' underachievement? An Australian study', *Educational Studies*, 30:1.

26 Ibid.

27 Jackson, C. (2002) 'Can single-sex classes in co-educational schools enhance the learning experiences of girls and/or boys? An exploration of pupils' perceptions', *British Educational Research Journal*, 28:1.

28 Pahlke, E., Shibley Hyde, J., & Allison, C.M. (2014) 'The effects of single-sex compared with coeducational schooling on students' performance and attitudes: A meta-analysis', *Psychological Bulletin*, 140:4, pp. 1042–1072.

29 Halpern, D., Eliot, L., Bigler, R.S., Fabes, R.A., Hanish, L.D., Hyde, J., Liben, L.S., & Martin, C.L. (2011) 'The pseudoscience of single-sex schooling', *Science*, 333:6050, pp. 1706–1707.

30 Ibid.

31 Martino, W., Mills, M., & Lingard. B. (2005) 'Interrogating single-sex classes as a strategy for addressing boys' educational and social needs', *Oxford Review of Education*, 31:2, pp. 237–254.

32 Ibid.

33 Jackson, C. (2002).

34 Gray, C. & Wilson, J. (2006), pp. 285–298.

35 Halpern, D., Eliot, L., Bigler, R.S., Fabes, R.A., Hanish, L.D., Hyde, J., Liben, L.S., & Martin, C.L. (2011).

36 Lavy, V. & Shlosser, A. (2007) *Mechanisms and Impacts of Gender Peer Effects at School*, Cambridge, MA: National Bureau of Economic Research.

37 Kenway, J. & Willis, S. (1998) *Answering Back: Girls, Boys and Feminism in Schools*, London: Routledge, cited by Jackson, C. (2002).

38 Ehrenberg, R., Goldhaber, D., & Brewer, D. (1995).

39 Francis, B., Skelton, C., Carrington, B., Hutchings, M., Read, B., & Hall, I. (2008).

40 Wiliam, D. (2010) 'Teacher quality: Why it matters, and how to get more of it', Paper delivered at Spectator 'Schools Revolution' conference, March. Available at: www.dylan wiliam.org/Dylan_Wiliams_website/Papers.../Spectator%20talk.do (Accessed: 26th April 2018). Here he is citing evidence from Wiliam, D. (2009) *Assessment for Learning: Why, What and How?* London: Institute of Education, University of London; and Hamre, B.K. & Pianta, R.C. (2005) 'Academic and social advantages for at-risk students placed in high quality first grade classrooms', *Child Development*, 76:5, pp. 949–967.

41 In the UK, an establishment that provides education for pupils who have are unable to attend mainstream schools due to illness or exclusion.

42 TeacherTapp website. Available at: www.teachertapp.co.uk (Accessed: 16th July 2018).

43 An app that asks UK teachers three daily questions and then analyses the responses in a weekly blog.

44 TeacherTapp website. Available at: www.teachertapp.co.uk (Accessed: 26th July 2018).

45 Lavy, V. & Shlosser, A. (2007).

8 Violence

Matt Pinkett

The story

There's a certain poetry to be found in the memory of a half-eaten kebab, congealing on Formica. For over 15 years now, the flaccid remnants of what was spuriously sold to me as "meat", stuffed among a few wet threads of lettuce and encased in pitta, has remained a metaphor for a masculinity only partially realised: a symbolic reminder of my own failure to live up to expectations of a brand of masculinity thrust upon me since early childhood; the physical embodiment of my own impotence to truly prove my 15-year-old self as the man society had led me to believe I needed to be.

I was on my own when three older boys from the sixth form entered the kebab shop in which I was eating and took it upon themselves to savagely mock my clothes, hair, and overall appearance. As is often the case in these situations, nobody intervened. Bystanders watched as I was mocked to the point of tears and as soon as my tormentors received their chips and pitta, they left, one of them giving a quick flick to one of my (admittedly protruding) ears on his way out, just to ensure that the verbal demolishing they gave me was bolstered with some physical humiliation for good measure. When they had gone, I stopped eating, and waited for five minutes, staring through tears at the half-eaten kebab my mother had given me the money to buy as a treat. Then, I left.

At home, I wept as I looked at myself in the bathroom mirror. I felt so angry. So humiliated. I remember being grateful for the fact that my seven-year-old baby brother hadn't witnessed the moment his older brother had been bullied to the point tears. I remember feeling that I needed to do something; that an act of violent, bloody retribution would be the only thing to rebuild the masculinity that hours earlier had been left smeared amongst the grease of a kebab shop floor.

But I didn't do anything. I was too scared to do anything. And so, I went to bed a failure. A failure who wasn't brave, strong, or manly enough to get his violent revenge on the bad guys.

Of course, I realise now that finding a weapon that night, and committing an act of bloody retribution, as a means of making myself feel better about myself, would have not only been wrong, but futile too. Yet, years later, the memory of this event still makes me feel an acute pang of shame. I still feel angry at the injustice of it all. When I think of that half-eaten kebab, my skin prickles and my palms sweat. In spite of all the books I've read; in spite of all I know about the dangerous consequences of male violence; in spite of the fact that I was raised to "be the bigger man and walk away". In spite of all this, I'm still ashamed of the time I failed to act as society led me to believe a man should act in such circumstances: with violent and bloody vengeance.

The research

Violence: a male phenomenon

Of course, it's natural that I'd feel such shame when one considers the fact that I failed in an area where so many men before me have succeeded. In his excellent treatise on violence and its evolution, *The Better Angels of our Nature*, Steven Pinker explains that "in every society it is the males more than the females who play-fight, bully, fight for real, carry weapons, enjoy violent entertainment, fantasize about killing, kill for real, rape, start wars and fight in wars".[1] Men's association with violence is backed up by solid data: a huge meta-analysis on male aggression, conducted by John Archer, of the University of Lancashire in 2004, found that "men are vastly overrepresented in the most dangerous forms of physical aggression".[2] Data from the Crime Survey for England and Wales (CSEW) shows that in 2016, 76% of those who committed violent crimes were male.[3]

Violence in schools

A 2017 report on violence in schools, from the National Union of Teachers, reported that

> A survey by the Association of Teachers and Lecturers in 2016 found that 40% of teachers had experienced violence from pupils in the past year. Of those who had been subjected to violence, nearly 80% said they had been pushed and around half had been kicked or had an object thrown at them.[4]

Recent exclusion data backs this up and confirms the fact that violence is a very real threat in some schools: according to data from the Office for National Statistics, in 2016, 78% of students permanently excluded from education were male and of these exclusions, 43% were for physical violence.[5] In fact, in some areas of the UK, violence in schools is on the up. In Scotland in 2014/2015, 24% of exclusions were due to acts of physical violence. By 2016/2017, this figure had risen to 28%.[6]

On his blog, teacher Malcolm Wilson writes an excellent evocation of what it's like to be young and male and fighting in the playground[7]:

There, in the circle of boys, I was alone with him. His eyes stared intently at me, waiting for my reaction to the fist that had just smashed into my nose. A slight grin betrayed his excitement. Some six inches shorter than me, he was enjoying this fight. Taking down the lanky boy. Blooding himself.

I lunged back at him but missed my target. His smiling face dodged my fist. He was almost dancing now. The other boys cheered, jeered. There were only two ways out of this circle: tearful humiliation or a bloody, sweating fight to exhaustion.

Knowing my fists alone were of little use, I launched myself at him. We locked arms, knocked heads. My ear was suddenly hot as it rubbed against his scalp. With one arm, I grappled for a good grip, some way to keep him close enough and underneath me. With the other, I tried to jab punches at anything vulnerable: the side of his head, his groin, his stomach. He was doing to the same, though beneath me. His fist made contact, his shoulder pushed up at me; his fingers gripped at soft flesh somewhere. We were hardly standing, our legs locked in an effort to floor each other. Then we were on our bare knees, still in each other's arms as we fought for an advantage. Somehow we struggled back to our feet.

And then I found myself with a leg free and his body bent in front of me, held there by my free arm. Without a thought, I drove my knee into his face. Once, then again and again. He stopped fighting. I felt his arms loosen. I'd hurt him badly.

He was crying, his face a mess of blood and snot as we disengaged.

As Anthony Ellis mentions in his book, *Men, Masculinities and Violence*, "most 'real' violence [is] a desperate, painfully unskilled contest"[8] far from the tightly executed Kung-Fu duels contested by macho action heroes on the big screen. Wilson's piece encapsulates this "real violence" beautifully.

Read the opening lines again:

There, in the circle of boys, I was alone with him. His eyes stared intently at me, waiting for my reaction to the fist that had just smashed into my nose.

The schoolboy Malcolm has two choices here: walk away or offer the returning blow and invite the inevitable violence that will lead to the shedding of adolescent blood. We know that Malcolm takes the latter option, but what causes him to do so?

The testosterone fairy tale

Popular folklore will tell you that testosterone is what causes the schoolboy Malcolm to hurl himself at his opponent, just as it would explain my own initial reaction to the humiliation I endured in the kebab shop all those years ago. Testosterone, the so-called "male hormone" (men carry as much as 13 times more of it than women[9]) has long been the biological scapegoat of choice, explaining away male violence with the support that "scientific fact" provides:

- "Oh you know what they're like – they're so full of testosterone, these teenage boys."

- "Has Jack punched another wall? Bless him – must be hard though, y'know, with all that testosterone coursing through his veins."

- "Look at those two, madly bludgeoning each other to a bloody pulp. That's the ol' testosterone again!"

Let it be said now, unequivocally: male violence cannot be reliably attributed to the effects of testosterone. As Cordelia Fine explains in her controversial but enlightening book, *Testosterone Rex*, the role of testosterone in influencing male behaviour isn't so great as we have been led to believe.

The problem with risk studies

Fine calls into question the long-held assumption that testosterone is responsible for greater tendency towards risky behaviours such as violence. According to Fine, studies into risky behaviour are flawed at a fundamental level, because the majority of studies on risk are gender-biased themselves. The hypothetical risks posed to male and female participants in risk studies – *Would you do a sky dive?; How much would you be willing to bet on such and such a game?; Would you have unprotected sex?* – are biased in favour of men. That is, the risky situations posed relate to experiences more commonly experienced by men as a result of gender socialisation. For example, society encourages men to take part in elaborate displays of machismo such as jumping out of metal objects thousands of feet high in the air; men are also more likely to be found sweating in betting shops and, because men are not troubled with the burden of carrying an actual human being inside them for nine months, unprotected sex is far less risky for them.

Fine cites studies that show human tendency towards risk are context based. For example, in China, women are every bit as risky as men so long as they aren't aware of being observed. In the same study, men became *more* risky in the presence of an observer. Risk is a slippery and intangible topic and as such, it's very difficult to say that tendency towards risk is a masculine behaviour created by testosterone.

The complex biology of testosterone

Fine's most convincing argument in her debunking of the testosterone myth comes in her discussion of testosterone's role in guiding the body's biological and behavioural processes, which she says is simply the most easily measurable amongst a whole host of other, more difficult to measure processes such as:

> the conversion (of testosterone) to oestrogen, how much aromatise is around to make that happen, the amount of oestrogen produced by the brain itself, the number, and nature of androgen and oestrogen receptors, where they are located, their sensitivity...[10]

All this means that actually, "the absolute testosterone level in the blood or saliva is likely to be an extremely crude guide to testosterone's effect on the brain".[11]

Horny monkeys and crying dolls

As if this wasn't enough to cast some shade on the long-held belief that testosterone acts as a kind of hormonal tyrant, dragging men into all sorts of danger and criminality, there is increasing evidence to show that hormones don't actually *cause* behaviour; rather, they simply make a behavioural response to an external stimulus more or less likely depending on wider social context. A number of animal studies on testosterone, such as one in which male rhesus monkeys were given a testosterone suppressant, show that the sexual behaviour of the highest ranking males was not affected by testosterone suppression, whilst those of lower ranking males was.[12] All of which points to the fact that social context has greater impact than testosterone.

Although the widely held view is that testosterone influences social behaviour, some studies have actually shown the reverse: social behaviour influences testosterone levels. For example, in humans, becoming a father will lower testosterone in men. However, the extents to which levels of testosterone are lowered depend on context. Tribes where paternal care is the norm see a greater reduction in testosterone levels than in tribes where paternal care is minimal.[13]

Another fascinating study[14] gave male participants a fake baby to look after. For some men, the babies were programmed to cry persistently, irrespective of the care given to it by the participants. Participants who received the crying babies saw increased testosterone levels whilst those whose baby stopped crying when attended to saw a testosterone drop. Again, all this is to say that testosterone is controlled and influenced by external stimuli (in this case a crying baby), rather than, as one might expect, the testosterone having an impact on men's ability to care for a child.

The studies cited by Fine are supported by John Archer's previously mentioned meta-analysis into sex differences of aggression. Archer puts the matter of testosterone and male aggression, specifically male *adolescent* aggression, bluntly: "There [is] no increase in the size of the sex difference in physical aggression at puberty, as would be expected if testosterone facilitated aggression in males ... testosterone has no effect on human aggression".[15]

Sexual selection theory: men's greatest get-out?

Testosterone is a complicated beast and boys' aggression and tendency towards risky behaviours (such as violence) cannot be reliably attributed to the effects of testosterone alone. As teachers, we should take comfort in this fact: after all, it is easier to reverse social behaviours than it is to reverse the effects of thousands of years of biology.

If we can't blame male violence on testosterone, what can we blame it on? John Archer states that "observational studies showed a sex difference in physical aggression early in life, from 2 years of age or younger".[16] According to Archer, the fact that statistically significant differences in levels of aggression between males and females are observed so early on in life is supportive of what he calls *Sexual Selection Theory (SST)*: SST theory is best explained by beginning with the following from Steven Pinker:

> In most animal species, the female makes a greater investment in offspring than the male. This is especially true of mammals, where the mother gestates her offspring inside her body and nurses them after they are born. A male can multiply the number of his offspring by mating with several females – which will leave other males childless.[17]

In other words, men are able to produce millions of sperm in one ejaculation and are not tasked with the responsibility of carrying a child for nine months after that ejaculation. Because of this, they are free to copulate again and again with any women who consent to them doing so. And, according to the theory, *with all that sperm*, men are understandably dead keen on rising to this challenge. In effect, SST states that the world is full of horny men, in desperate competition with other horny men, to unleash all that sperm upon the female world. In our more primitive days – days before we had language with which to convey anything that may be feasibly defined as a personality – the only way to get one over on a rival was to smash his face in. Smash his face in and you get the girl. However, SST theory, as a way of explaining (or excusing) male violence, cannot be taken reliably. After all, if violence is something deep-rooted within men, why aren't all men spending their time beating the hell out of each other in order to gain the affections of those they want to have sex with? Why are speed-dating nights held in trendy nightclubs instead of gladiatorial arenas? Why do some of men waste their time penning poetry, when they should be perfecting their punches? Why are men taking women out to the cinema instead of taking rival suitors out with well-executed blows to the skull? The fact is most men are capable of following the rules, whether dictated by law or etiquette, that deem it wholly inappropriate to gain the affections of a partner through the destruction of another human being by violent means.

In an educational context, if teachers view SST theory as something to whole-heartedly believe in, why are they teachers at all? Isn't teaching about changing, for the better, the way students engage, interact with, and experience the world they live in? A solid belief in evolutionary theories of any behaviour, not just a propensity for violence, is as good as saying, "Well, there's nothing *I* can do about these brutish boys so why bother trying?"

The problem with us

If male violence can't be reliably credited to the effects of biology and evolution, what else can we blame? What is it that leads a schoolboy to use violence to turn another schoolboy into a bleeding knot of breathlessness and snot? The answer, I'm afraid, is us. Us and society's relentless adherence to the dominant view that men should be able to handle themselves in a fight.

Imagine a stone being thrown into a lake; the ripples from this stone stretch out further and further until a bird, on the opposite shore, is disturbed and flies off in a cacophonous explosion of feathers and squawks. That tiny stone is biological and evolutionary theories of masculine violence which are based on huge numbers of contradictory and often unreliable studies. The endless ripples that multiply in number and size as a result of the stone's impact are the social expectations of male violence provoked by these flimsy biological and evolutionary theories. The frenzied flapping of the bird on the other side of the lake represents the chaotic and damaging impact of the harmful social expectations of male violence.

Social expectations of male violence manifest themselves in a myriad of subtle and not-so-subtle ways. They reveal themselves in the toy soldiers and camouflage duvet sets found under the "Boys" section of the big department stores, in the plastic guns we give boys for Christmas and the super-hero chocolate eggs we give them at Easter, in the computer game shoot-'em-ups dominated by male "heroes" who shoot and stab and maim and kill, and in the Hollywood movies dominated by muscle-bound action men who solve all the world's problems with knuckles, rather than nous.

An awkward truth

As parents, we push our boys towards activities that depend on rough physicality, while we'd rather our girls stay indoors and play house. It's hard to imagine that there are many boys who haven't heard the advice, from well-intentioned parents or loved ones, *If he hits you, you hit him back.* Even the most peace-loving of parents worry about their boy, or boys, appearing weak in front of other boys. *If you don't deal with this weakness, you will be bullied your whole life.* As Anthony Ellis states, "Violence represents a distinctly masculine resource ... and a means with which to defend oneself is often relayed from father to sons".[18] The uncomfortable reality is that, whilst we may not want to admit it, sometimes violence *works.* For many boys, dealing with bullying using physical violence gets the job done. And, if you are one of the lucky ones for whom it did work, why would you not pass that on as advice to your own children? I spoke to John and Adam, two parents of primary age boys and asked them what advice they would give their sons, were they to learn that they had been pushed over by another boy, in the playground. "I'd tell him to lamp him one", says John, "because if he doesn't, he will be bullied again and again and again. It's the animal in us. Some of us only respond to being bashed about". Adam replied similarly: "I'd tell him to tell the teacher and if that didn't stop it, I'd tell him to belt him". I asked Adam, the father of two girls also, if he'd give the same advice to them: "Not at all. Never". John and Adam are both teachers.

Unfortunately, as teachers, we are part of the problem too. The study by Susan Jones and Debra Myhill, which we looked at in Chapter 5, found worrying trends in the way that teachers perceive boys' behaviour: "A simple tally of comments made about boys and girls, respectively, revealed 54 positive comments made about girls as compared with 22 negative comments, and 32 positive comments made about boys compared with 54 negative comments".[19]

These negative comments included, "Boys can be aggressive" and "Boys are more physical". As teachers, we need to be honest. Let's eschew this "look-how-liberal-and-open-minded" façade some of us seem so desperate to put on, particularly when discussing gender, and ask ourselves: *In what ways might we push boys towards violence?* Have you ever told a student to "man up"? Ever ribbed a male student, or a male colleague, for having "man flu"? Have you ever selected a poem or play that contains war and death simply because you have a "boy heavy" class? If you have done any of these things, you could be reinforcing society's appetite for male toughness, a thing best displayed through violence.

The solutions

Advice for school leaders and school teachers

A. Be realistic

It's important that as teachers, we realise that we're on a hiding to nowhere if we refuse to even try to understand that for many boys, fighting – whether the fight is won or lost – *will* make them feel good. Landing a well-aimed punch that immobilises an opponent might do more for their self-esteem than reading any book or solving any equation could ever do. We need to understand – no, we simply need to *accept* – that sometimes, fighting, whether the fight is lost or won, is ultimately what makes a boy feel like the man he's been led to believe he should be. Acceptance isn't tantamount to condoning or ignoring. Acceptance is, however, going some way towards empathising. And if we can empathise with our students, we can open up a dialogue based on trust and understanding, rather than sanctimonious preaching.

B. Take a proactive response

As it currently stands, violence in schools is dealt with reactively. In spite of the startling statistics that surround male violence, violence is something that is still only discussed *after* the fact. That is, a fight occurs and *then* it is dealt with. Punishments are dished out, "restorative" conversations are held, and then violence is forgotten until it inevitably occurs again. Schools could benefit from taking a proactive response to male violence. School leaders need to initiate a systematic programme of study, facilitated and led by teachers in a position of responsibility, which makes boys aware of the violence that they are being conditioned for.

Michael Flood, is one of the world's leading authorities on male violence. A report by Flood, on violence intervention programmes in schools states that "education programs that are intensive and lengthy, and use a variety of pedagogical approaches have been shown to produce positive and lasting change in attitudes and behaviours".[20] Flood goes on to outline the characteristics of an effective programme of study aimed at preventing violence in schools. These are:

1. **A whole school approach**

   Working as a school community ensures that *all* staff members within a school are invested in reducing incidences of violence within the school and outside of it. It is a shared mission of peace for which everybody has responsibility. For Flood, this whole school approach is more important than any of the other criterion for an effective programme.

2. **A programme framework and logic**

   Flood tells us that "violence prevention programs in schools must be based on a sound understanding of both the problem – the workings and causes of violence – and of how it can be changed".[21] The programme design and delivery must be underpinned by a solid understanding of why violence occurs and how it can be combatted. The programme must also be designed with an understanding of what the programme aims to achieve.

3. **Effective curriculum delivery**

   As with any curriculum, the violence intervention curriculum must be designed in a way that incorporates sound pedagogical principles. Exploration of violence must follow logical patterns and allow students to engage with the content in an interactive manner. Lecture style approaches have been proven to be ineffective. As with all learning, the curriculum must allow for the revisiting of previously learnt material. Students should have a firm understanding of *why* they are engaged in the programme and to what end. The most effective programmes ensure that discussion of violence is relevant for the students; there is no point focusing on gang violence if there are no gangs in your school community.

   An important question to consider in the area of effective curriculum delivery is the question of optimum target audience. Are single-sex or mixed-sex groups most conducive to an effective intervention? I believe single-sex groups are best used when discussing male violence and I for these reasons:

- Mixed-gender discussions on gender can often dissolve into chaotic argument and personal jibes between sexes
- Experiences of violence are different for males and females and as such, all-male groups will allow for a more tailored, beneficial experience
- Boys may be more open in all-male groups, and less likely to "show off in front of the girls"
- All-male groups lead to a less diluted discussion of gender. Boys are able to focus on masculinity and masculinity alone
- All-male groups allow students to use each other as trigger points for their own gendered experiences and ideas.

Of course, this does not mean in any way that boys should discount female experiences of violence. On the contrary, a concerted effort should be made to acquaint boys with female experiences and understanding of violence. Empathetic boys are less violent boys.

We must also consider the issue of who is best suited to lead such programmes of violence intervention? Without a doubt, the facilitators of this programme must have a solid understanding of male violence, its causes, effects, and how it might be prevented. As with any programme of learning, students learn more from skilled teachers. But what about the gender of the teachers? Flood points out the advantages of using female educators in such a programme. Using female teachers demonstrates an egalitarian approach and models a shared interest in defeating violence. Flood does, however, note that there are certain advantages to using male educators:

- Male educators and participants can act as role models for other men
- Male educators possess an insider's knowledge of the workings of masculinity and can use this to critical advantage with male audiences
- Male educators tend to be perceived as more credible and more persuasive by male participants
- The use of male educators embodies the recognition that men must take responsibility for helping to end men's violence against women.[22]

4. Relevant, inclusive, and culturally sensitive practice

Violence intervention programmes are most effective when they reflect the concerns of target audience. As Flood notes,

> Among males...there is significant diversity in the constructions of masculinity that are dominant in particular social contexts and

communities. This diversity certainly is shaped by ethnic differences, but also by many other forms of social differentiation. There are social groups, workplaces and social networks of boys and men in which violence against women is frequent and viewed as legitimate, and other contexts in which this violence is rare and seen as unacceptable.[23]

For example, students from a white, middle class background in London may have quite different issues relating to violence when compared to a group of white, disadvantaged boys from Sheffield. Equally, a group of mainly Afro-Caribbean boys in Year 7 may have a quite different experience and understanding of violence when compared to a group of mainly Polish boys in Year 11. The programme must be tailored to the specific needs of the school's community and the issues of violence that surround it.

5. Impact evaluation

For any violence intervention programme to be successful, it needs to undergo a process of constant review. This can be formative assessment of where the course needs to be adapted for future programmes. For example, it may be discovered that analysis of violence in Hollywood was found to be too distracting for pupils and something that detracted from the core issue. In which case, perhaps next year, this part of the course would have to be altered. The course also needs summative assessment of the measurable impact of the course. For example, has the course reduced the numbers of exclusions in the school? Has the school seen a decrease in playground fights?

Below, I include a suggested programme of violence intervention to be used in schools. Each session follows a model which I have termed explanation, reflection, and expression (ERE). The ERE model means that each session involves the following key components:

- EXPLANATION: A key aspect of violence is explained to students through the use of engaging talk and activities designed to facilitate deeper understanding

- REFLECTION: Reflection gives boys the opportunity to reflect on their own attitudes and experiences in light of what has been discussed in the explanation. This section of the model involves prompt questions to encourage deeper, more engaged, reflection

- EXPRESSION: A vital component of the model, the expression phase gives students free reign to express their own ideas and views on the content learned during the session. It begins with the teacher simply saying, "Please, begin a discussion on everything we've discussed today". This task requires a withdrawal of judgement from all involved, allowing boys to express any concerns they have without worry.

Session Number	Explanation	Reflection	Expression
1	Boys are provided with the statistics surrounding male violence. They are then told that the reason for this is **testosterone**. Support this with examples from the media which blames male violence on testosterone. Boys are presented with the idea that actually, the **testosterone argument** is likely to be a myth.	• What do you think about the belief that there's a hormone in you that makes you more likely to be violent than girls? • Are you stronger than your hormones? • Can you think of a time testosterone has made you feel violent? • If all men have lots of testosterone, why don't all men commit crime? • Why do you think people like to blame male violence on testosterone? • Does the idea of the testosterone argument being a myth reassure you or make you more concerned about male violence? • If testosterone isn't to blame for male violence, what is?	"Talk about … testosterone and male violence".
2	Boys are presented with the idea that gender is a social construct that begins at birth and that stereotypical expectations are perpetuated by the **mainstream media**. Ask boys to detail typically masculine / feminine behaviours. Examine toys in a catalogue and ask students to see how the toys we are given in childhood may contribute to the typically masculine or feminine behaviours mentioned earlier. You can do the same with the TV listings of cartoons – How many of them feature characters who contribute to gender stereotypes? Turn the focus to violence by asking students to note how many of the boys' toys feature weapons or have associations of violence. The same can be done with a list of children's cartoons, books, Hollywood movies, or computer games.	• Make a list of twenty cartoon characters. How many of them are male *and violent*? • What do you think about cartoon characters that aren't violent? • Would you buy a computer game featuring a man whose job it was to simply spread peace and understanding? Why or Why not? • Should we ban violence in cartoons? • Should we ban violent toys?	"Talk about … toys, television, and male violence".

(Continued)

Session Number	Explanation	Reflection	Expression
3	Boys are presented with the idea that some social expectations of gender are perpetuated by **families**. Students are to list "male jobs" vs "female jobs". Rate each job on a physicality scale. Can you rate them on a scale of aggression needed to perform them? What does this tell us? Ask students about advice given to them by their parents. Do these perpetuate expectations of gender based violence?	• Should boys look up to violent fathers? • What makes a **strong** father? • If your own son were to tell you he'd been pushed over in the playground, what advice would you give him? Is this the best advice? • Can anybody think about how female family members might encourage sons to be violent either explicitly or implicitly? *(Obviously, this session requires some careful planning and sensitivity)*	"Talk about … families and male violence".
4	Boys are presented with the idea that some social expectations of gender are perpetuated by **schools and teachers**. Ask students to consider how their primary, junior and then secondary schools push boys and girls towards gendered behaviours. Students could do a survey of "option subjects" and the boy to girl ratio within these. Are boys more likely to do "physical" or "practical" subjects? Explain to boys that some teachers choose to do war poetry, rather than love poetry, with boys. What do they think about this?	• Think of the texts you study in English Literature and make a list of the main characters. How many of them are violent and male? • Think of the violent figures you study in history. How many of these are males? • Do schools have a responsibility to include more "peaceful men" in the curriculum, even if it means ignoring some key content knowledge? • Do teachers "make" boys more violent? • Do teachers "make" girls less violent? • Does violence increase or decrease as you move from primary to secondary? Why do you think this might be? • Who has the greatest responsibility for male violence? Primary or Secondary schools?	"Talk about … schools and male violence".

			"Talk about"
5	Boys are to consider the **consequences of violence.** Present boys with footage of a Hollywood fight scene and ask them to compare with footage or an idea of real violence. What differences do they notice about the perpetrators of violence in these two scenarios and what about the victims? Present students with a newspaper article about a fight between two schoolboys that tragically results in one of the boys dying.	• Is the Hollywood version of violence real? • Who is affected by violence? Is it just the perpetrator and the victim? • What is the "effect chain" of violence? • What irreparable damage might violence do? • What happens to people who "get away" with violence?	"Talk about … the consequences of male violence".
6	Boys are to develop skills in non-violence and conflict resolution. This will need to take place over a number of sessions. Detailed suggestions for activities can be found in *Engaging Boys and Men in Gender Transformation:The Group Education Manual,* published by USAid, which can be accessed here: www.xyonline.net/sites/default/files/ EnGender,%20Engaging%20Men%20and%20 Boys%20-%20Group%20education%20manual.pdf.		"Talk about … how you can deal with your own anger". "Talk about … what bravery really is".

Note that with all these sessions, there is a risk of simply rehearsing and intensifying stereotypical ideas about gender. The educator will need to work hard to challenge these and will need good teaching materials to do so. Examples of these may be found here: www.xyonline.net/content/engaging-men-preventing-men%E2%80%99s-violence-against-women-practical-guides-and-manuals.

C. Provide support for those who fight

Boys self-harm in different ways to girls. Engaging in physical violence – like punching walls or faces – should be regarded as a form of self-harm and any boys who engage in violent behaviour should not just be sanctioned; follow-up conversations need to take place, with an appropriate member of the pastoral team, to check whether violent behaviour is actually a method of self-harm. If it is, the appropriate measures need to be taken in line with the school's policy on self-harm.[24]

We also need be mindful of the impact of peer pressure on reinforcing socialised attitudes towards violence. Society sets the parameters for male violence; peer groups enforce them. It's naïve to think that telling boys to "be the bigger man and walk away" will be of any use in preventing violence. For an in-depth discussion on the negative influence of peer pressure on boys' behaviours, refer to Chapter 3.

D. Provide support for those who walk away

There are boys in our schools who, when challenged to a fight by a fellow pupil, "do the right thing", "be the bigger man", and walk (run) away. Whilst it is nice for us, as teachers, to attribute the backing out of a playground fight to noble strength of character, for many of the boys who walk away from a schoolyard punch-up, the reason they do so is because they're simply terrified. They're absolutely petrified that they will be hurt or humiliated and so, like Paris faced with Menelaus, they listen to the self-serving, self-protecting thing inside of them that says, "sod this" and they take the coward's way out: they retreat. And unfortunately, in spite of what we realise as adults, for teenage boys, there is rarely anything heroic or noble about walking away from a fight.

I began this chapter with a story about my own experience of choosing the coward's way out. Do I feel good now about the fact that I did so? Clearly not. After all, I'm writing about it years later in a desperate attempt to put my demons to bed. I'm *still* bitter about the whole thing. I'm *still* embarrassed when I walk down the street holding my baby daughter and one of those boys, now an adult with children of his own, walks past me. We need to realise that for boys who have been led to believe, from birth, that the true measure of a man is his physical capacity for violence, walking away leads to acute feelings of shame, worthlessness, and embarrassment. Schools need to be aware of this and they need to provide pastoral support for the ones who walk away. Because if they don't, these boys may one day try to atone for the "failures" of their past by seeking out situations in which, this time, they don't walk away and in which they commit the violence they feel they should have enacted previously.[25]

The final word

Male violence is a social problem and it's a problem that schools should be doing more about. Student perpetrators of violence, however horrible, are victims themselves. They are victims of a society that teaches boys, from a very early age, that the ability to cause physical harm to others is a sign of strength of which one can be proud. As teachers, we need to change this by anticipating male violence and dealing with it directly and proactively.

Notes

1 Pinker, S. (2011) *The Better Angels of our Nature*, London: Penguin.
2 Archer, J. (2004) 'Sex differences in aggression in real-world settings: A meta-analytic review', *Review of General Psychology*, 8:4, p. 291.
3 Office for National Statistics (2016) *Overview of violent crime and sexual offences*, 2016. Available at: www.ons.gov.uk/peoplepopulationandcommunity/crimeandjustice/compendium/focusonviolentcrimeandsexualoffences/yearendingmarch2016/overviewofviolentcrimeandsexualoffences#things-you-need-to-know-about-this-release(Accessed: 11th October 2017).
4 NUT (2017) *Violence in schools*. Available at: www.teachers.org.uk/help-and-advice/health-and-safety/v/violence-and-assaults-against-staff-schools (Accessed: 19th September 2018).
5 Office for National Statistics (2016) *Permanent and fixed exclusions in England: 2015–2016*. Available at: www.gov.uk/government/statistics/permanent-and-fixed-period-exclusions-in-england-2015-to-2016 (Accessed: 11th October 2017).
6 Scottish Government, *Exclusions – historical datasets*. Available at: www.gov.scot/Topics/Statistics/Browse/School-Education/exclusiondatasets (Accessed: 19th September 2009).
7 Wilson, M. (2017) *For the benefit of Mr Pink*. Available at: https://chorleywoodsix.com/2017/08/28/for-the-benefit-of-mr-pink/ (Accessed: 18th October 2017).
8 Ellis, A.J. (2016). *Men, masculinities and violence: an ethnographic study*, London: Routledge Studies in Crime and Society, Routledge.
9 Kushnir, M.M., Blamires, T., Rockwood, A.L., Roberts, W.L., Yue, B., Erdogan, E., Bunker, A.M., & Meikle, A.W. (2010). 'Liquid chromatography: Tandem mass spectrometry assay for androstenedione, dehydroepiandrosterone, and testosterone with pediatric and adult reference intervals'. Available at: http://clinchem.aaccjnls.org/content/56/7/1138/tab-figures-data#abstract-1 (Accessed 13th October 2017).
10 Fine, C. (2017) *Testosterone Rex: Unmaking the Myths of our Gendered Minds*. London: Icon Books.
11 Ibid.
12 Wallen, K. (2001) 'Sex and context: Hormones and primate sexual motivation', *Hormones and Behaviour*, 40:2, pp. 339–357. Cited in Fine, C. (2017).
13 Muller, M., Marlow, F., Bugumba, R., & Ellison, P. (2008). 'Testosterone and paternal care in East African foragers and pastoralists', *Proceedings of the Royal Society B*, 276:1655, pp. 347–354. Cited in Fine, C. (2017).
14 Van Anders, S.M., Tolman, R.M., & Volling, B.L. (2012). 'Baby cries and nurturance affect testosterone in men', *Hormones and Behaviour*, 61:1, pp. 31–36. Cited in Fine, C. (2017).
15 Archer, J. (2004).
16 Ibid.
17 Pinker, S. (2011), p. 40.
18 Ellis, A. (2017), p. 72.
19 Jones, S. & Myhill, D. (2004) 'Troublesome boys and compliant girls: Gender identity and perceptions of achievement and underachievement', *British Journal of Sociology of Education*, 25:5, p. 552.
20 Flood, M., Fergus, L., & Heenan, M. (2009). *Respectful Relationships Education: Violence Prevention and Respectful Relationships Education in Victorian Secondary*

Schools, Melbourne: Department of Education and Early Childhood Development, State of Victoria.

21 Flood, M., Fergus, L., & Heenan, M. (2009), p. 33.

22 Ibid., p. 54.

23 Ibid., p. 56.

24 For a more detailed discussion on this issue, refer to Chapter 4.

25 Winlow, S. & Hall, S. (2009) 'Retaliate first: Memory, humiliation and male violence', *Crime, Media, Culture*, 5:3, pp. 285–304.

Relationships

Mark Roberts

The story

I left school at 16. Despite doing very little work during my GCSEs, and spending most of the last year of school truanting, I came out with a few decent grades. Noise about "staying on at sixth form" and "going to college" emitted from some of my teachers. But the tinnitus of apathy rang loudly through my ears. None of my mates were going to do A levels. One of them had already landed a job at a local factory that made motorised gearboxes. I didn't want to study. I just wanted to go out drinking with my mates. A job would give me money. Beer money. On a sunlit Friday afternoon, I went for a perfunctory interview and was offered a position starting on the Monday morning. At the end of my first week, I got a wage slip – tucked inside a beautiful beige envelope – informing me that £141 had been paid into my bank account. I was loaded. First round was on me.

Life in the factory was tough: a cyclical diet of dirty, hard, monotonous labour. Tougher still was the welcome from my co-workers – big, hard, heavy-drinking men. "Banter" was rife and any signs of vulnerability were pounced upon. Coming from a school where I could hold my own in battles of mockery, taunting, and physical violence, I felt assured I'd be able to deal with a few blokes in an industrial unit. And I could, but even I was taken aback by the ferocity of the jokes. People who had worked alongside each other for years and were apparently best mates would greet each other with an oddly affectionate form of vitriolic abuse, usually involving indiscriminate swearing. If they did this to their friends, you can imagine what they did to a cocky, fresh-faced, long-haired lad whose mum worked in the offices. Ah, the hair. Shoulder length and tucked behind my ears, the hair set me out as different, despite the matching blue uniform and steel-toed boots. From the moment one of them shouted "Oi, Gayboy, pass us a 1 inch bolt!", the name was destined to stick to me like the bearing grease on my trousers. A few months of temporary respite came from my fatal decision to quickly fill in a *Daily Star* quick crossword that someone was struggling with, which quickly gained me the (non-ironic) nickname "Wordsworth". But apart from that literary interlude, Gayboy I was. Scalping myself down to a grade 2 buzzcut and pointing out that I wasn't homosexual and had aspirations to sleep with actual girls made no difference. The doublethink of the factory dictated that if you had long hair you were "a poof", even if you weren't.

Exclusively male

Four years later, I left. After a short and satisfyingly disastrous spell in a call centre, the tinnitus had changed its persistent clang from apathy to tedium. Beyond bored, I went to college.

There were no male pupils in my English class and very few in my other classes. Two years later, with the kind of A level results that get you in the local paper, even if you're not a lithe, crop-top-wearing girl, I set off for university.

Looking back now, my relationships with male friends – and until college my friendships were almost exclusively male – were based on the four topics: sport, drinking, fighting, and sex (or, more accurately, thinking about having sex).

The intelligence curse

Until the age of 22, I wasn't taught English by a man. Until the age of 22, I'd never discussed literature with anybody male. Until the age of 22, I avoided using fancy sounding words in male company.

Until the age of 22, and often occasionally thereafter, I used to think that being intelligent was a curse. Not a blessing. Not a gift. Not something that made me feel fortunate or talented. No. Being clever, for the first two decades of my life, was an unpleasant joke, a recurrent pain, an unbearable burden. Being intelligent was a curse. This curse came not in the sense of *why won't anybody recognise my genius?* but rather *why should I have to hide the fact that I know most of the answers?* This soon became *wouldn't it be lovely to be thick? Wouldn't it be great to be stupid?* Then, I'd never have to hide the fact that I understood poetry or could remember chemical formulae. Thick people had easy lives, I reckoned. Clever people that I knew had to put up with more brutal banter. And banter made them stressed and left them living in fear of mockery, ridicule, and ostracism.

What impact does banter have on the way boys interact with each other? What implications might this have for boys' attitudes towards school and schoolwork? And should schools or individual teachers – as some have done[1] – attempt to banish banter completely?

PART A: Boys' relationships with each other

Scenario

   Boy A: "Nice shoes mate"
   Boy B: "Cheers man"

Boy A: "Did your mum pick 'em for you again? They're gay"
Boy B: "Oi!"
Boy A: "Banter mate".

The research

"Banter" can be defined[2] as follows:

1. Verb – Make fun of a person good humouredly; talk jestingly
2. Noun – Nonsense talked to ridicule a person; humorous ridicule; good-natured personal remarks.

Dating back around 300 years from origins unknown, "banter" began life as a verb, soon provoking the wrath of Jonathan Swift, who condemned the term he claimed was "first borrowed from the bullies in White Friars",[3] an area of 18th-century London renowned for its lawlessness. In recent years, usage of the term has exploded in popularity, perhaps on the back of the lads' mag movement of the 1990s. According to Google's Ngram Viewer – a flawed but interesting search engine that scours a large database of written sources to identify how often a particular word is used – "banter" was used twice as often in 2008 as it was in 1980. Alongside the increasing frequency of usage, there appears to be an accompanying shift in meaning: the gradual erosion of the "good-natured" element of the definition. Since the dawn of time, humans have enjoyed ribbing their friends. And British men have always considered themselves connoisseurs of mutually affectionate and mutually entertaining urine extraction. Yet lately, frequently but not exclusively in our schools, there is a sense that when the term is used, the emphasis is on ridicule. In simple terms, banter is now often employed as a catch-all euphemism that covers the full gamut of ways that teenagers – especially boys – can humiliate each other: name-calling, mockery, malicious "pranks", verbal and physical abuse.

Your mum

A question often asked in staffrooms in schools in most places around the world – rhetorically with a sigh of exasperation – is: *why are boys so horrible to each other?* And by this, teachers are not necessarily referring to animosity between boys who simply do not get on. No, the rhetorical interrogator is most likely pondering young men's propensity to be bloody horrible to other young men who they consider *friends.* In the 2018 Annual Bullying Survey, conducted by international anti-bullying charity Ditch the Label,[4] 29% of young people who had been bullied in the previous 12 months reported that the bully was "a close friend".

One classic example of such meanness is the puerile and perennial pejoratives about other boys' mums. On the surface, these maternal insults seem to be just a part of growing up; infantile but, when generic in nature, innocent enough. After all, Shakespeare, who was especially fond of a caustic retort, used "your mum" jokes as part of his humorous repertoire, most notably in *Titus Andronicus*:

> *Demetrius:* Villain, what hast thou done?
> *Aaron:* That which thou canst not undo
> *Chiron:* Thou hast undone our mother
> *Aaron:* Villain, I have done thy mother.

Yet juvenile jokes about sleeping with a friend's mother (or variants that depict her as fat, stupid, or lacking in any number of desirable refinements) perform a different purpose, which gets to the heart of what it means to be accepted or rejected by one's masculine peers. In their enlightening look at how boys use humour to reinforce status based on adherence to traditional masculine values, Mary Jane Kehily from the Institute of Education, University of London, and Anoop Nayak, from the University of Newcastle, explain how verbal abuse directed towards another boy's mother acts of a test of "masculine" resilience to humiliating barbs:

> The invocation of a boy's mother into the discourse of the male peer group taps into the contradictory 'private' emotions of maternal affection and the public disavowal of the 'feminine'...This produces heterosexual hierarchies between 'real' lads and those susceptible to 'feminine' sensibilities and capable of crying.[5]

When banter becomes highly sexualised, highly personalised and highly competitive, boys who show signs of vulnerability become targets for further examination by ridicule. At the same time, banter acts as an agent of gender conformity. In the Annual Bullying Survey, 20% of those who were bullied said they were "accused of being gay when they're not". Not being able to handle jokes about your mum might be seen as undermining a boy's heterosexual status.

Is there a place for banter in schools?

Ben Lovatt, Lead Facilitator at The Training Effect, an organisation that designs, develops, and delivers emotional health and resilience programmes in schools, tells me that he recognises the pressure for boys to join in with offensive banter:

> The risk of challenging behaviour such as the objectification of women outweighs the dangerous repercussions of not doing it [such as ostracism from the group]. Do boys understand that what they're doing is wrong? Yes. But the consequences are worse than standing up to their peer groups and saying this is wrong.

To some, concerns about banter might seem like political correctness gone mad, a few healthy boyish bouts of taboo-busting subjected to too much scrutiny. What could be so harmful about a few far-fetched insinuations that a mate has been sleeping with your mum, or that "your mum's a slut"? Well, as Kehily and Nayak show, these "jokes" often escalate to a level of nastiness that plays to formulaic but deeply disturbing misogynistic attitudes, with an example from their study including:

- "Your mum's been raped so many times she puts a padlock on her fanny"[6]

Regardless of how horrific the personal slights are, boys are expected to accept them without flinching. As Martha Evans, National Coordinator of the Anti-Bullying Alliance, explains to me, "boys have to show that it doesn't hurt them: *we're men and we don't feel it, whatever you say*". It appears then that boys tell mum jokes for a couple of reasons. First, mums are something they all have in common. As opposed to teasing each other about the football team they support, they tease each other about their mothers. Some boys don't care about football; they all care about their mothers. Therefore, mum jokes become a universal litmus test for "strong" masculinity. Second, if certain boys can't take the joke, it means – in the eyes of their peers – that they are soft and emotional like girls. There is, of course, a telling irony here: maternal insults are employed as a demonstration of your ruthless disavowal for feelings. And yet, the reason the mother is targeted is because there's a deep and genuine affection for her. As long as the façade of indifference is maintained, so is one's status as a "real lad".

Vindictive examples of personal jokes may well be passed down from generation to generation. But the current obsession with unpleasant laddish banter may well be amplified by media examples of brash and brutal masculinity. According to Martha Evans, expectations of masculinity and the need to be seen as a macho man pervade our television shows and social media:

> shows like *TOWIE*[7] where men constantly banter and say hurtful things to each other. Or media depictions of sportsmen, which often show men being horrible to each other and the men are supposed to brush it off.

Teachers and banter – when colleagues go rogue

During my chat with Evans, we discussed the blurred boundaries of banter and bullying, amusement and abuse, humour and harassment. One comment in particular left me considering whether some teachers might be contributing to a toxic banter culture. Evans told me that "adults can be their own worst enemies and are just as a capable of misusing banter". Does this happen in our schools, I wondered? Do teaching colleagues use inappropriate banter in front of their pupils? Using social media, I asked teachers for their personal experiences and received a large amount of responses in the affirmative. Here are just a few of the anecdotes:

- I was told by a male physical education (PE) teacher, in front of my Year 11 class, that my knickers were showing at the top of my trousers. When I ignored it (by saying something like, "anything I can help you with, sir?"), he followed up by telling the group that I was wearing them back to front. He was their Head of Year. *Carla, Birmingham*

▪ I was absent from school, to attend a funeral. A student in my tutor group asked where I was during registration. A teacher covering me – a young male teacher wanting to be liked – said I was caught doing something with a sheep. My family are Welsh. The student was shocked and told me about this comment the next day. I told management and they made him apologise, but they suggested the student had actually misheard. *Peter, Hull*

▪ I've been mildly sexually harassed by female colleagues in front of kids. Things like having female teachers telling me I'm handsome in the corridor while, say, rubbing my chest or bicep as the pupils transition from one lesson to another. A weird line between banter and harassment. *Toby, Margate*

▪ Once I was behaviour support in a science lesson and the (female) teacher said, in front of 30 Year 7s, "Miss doesn't really understand science so she can learn with us too". I have a degree in biology. Thankfully it backfired, as one kid said "she knows more than you so maybe she should teach us!" *Sally, Nottingham*

▪ A male colleague popped into my lesson and said, "So Miss is your English teacher? I always hated English. Not much better when you have a grumpy teacher (pointing at me), eh?" A pupil came to my rescue by saying that I "wasn't always grumpy". *Charlotte, Cornwall*

▪ Head of sixth form came in to my lesson and I told him how disappointed I was that some of the students had not read *Gatsby* over the holiday as instructed. He said he understood as reading novels was hard and asked, in front of them, if there was a film version I could recommend instead. *Jenny, Chichester*

These (anonymised) examples follow a familiar pattern of the anecdotes I was told. The misuse of public banter between teaching colleagues can be categorised as (a) unwanted sexualised attention or comments; (b) "jokey" personal insults, involving stereotypes based on background, a supposed lack of intelligence or lack of humour; and (c) negative remarks about subjects taught by colleagues. These incidents were, one hopes, intended as humorous, but each example acts as an unwelcome and possibly dangerous model for impressionable youngsters. The unspoken messages here range from the seemingly trivial to the obviously nasty. First, the highly damaging (as we saw in Chapter 5) idea that certain subjects are only suitable for one gender. Second, that hard work and application is best avoided. Third, that it is ok to touch or grope another person without consent. Lastly, that crass sexualised language that demeans or objectifies another person is an appropriate form of humour. All of the professionals, male and female, who deployed banter in these examples, were seemingly attempting to adopt the role of what Jeffrey Smith terms the "cultural accomplice".[8] In other words, they were attempting to curry favour or popularity with the pupils in their school by undermining, mocking, or humiliating a colleague in a stereotypically masculine way.

The solutions

Advice for school leaders

Dealing with banter

Given the iniquitous effects of nasty banter, and the corrosive role it plays in encouraging young men to adhere to damaging notions of masculinity, it's tempting to ban banter outright. Martha Evans sees this as a mistake. "Some schools", she informs me, "have a zero tolerance approach policy to banter. But it's impractical". If you're not careful, she explains, it can be counterproductive and by banning something "you cast more of a light on it", creating a perverse incentive to join in with taboo behaviour. "If it's a word that's in widespread use you will need to address it but certainly don't introduce it as a word if pupils don't already use it. You need to get to the reasons behind it and do some work in the curriculum about where the lines are". Ben Lovatt concurs, telling me "I don't think you can ban banter. It's so subjective. Also, schools already have too much put on them". Additionally, as Evan makes clear, banter doesn't have to be a negative experience; in the right spirit, it can be fun and mutually entertaining. The focus needs to be on explaining the difference between banter, teasing, and out-and-out bullying. Lovatt agrees: "Most children involved in bullying don't see what they do as bullying. It's about education. You can't ask pupils to stop doing things they don't know they're doing".

Challenging banter

So what can school leaders do to tackle banter gone bad? "We need to be smarter about how we deal with this", Lovatt advises. "Bullying never exists in isolation. Punitive approaches just add stress on to the perpetrator" who is usually doing this due to problems in their own life. "There needs to be a shift in ethos and culture within schools, rather than standalone sessions. Restorative approaches certainly help those that bully to see the impact of their words".

Duncan Byrne, Headmaster of Loughborough Grammar School, agrees that an outright ban on banter is futile. In his blog,[9] he argues that trying to persuade boys to eliminate banter from their lives is a mistake. Instead he recommends teaching boys about the fine line between learning how to laugh at ourselves and recognising when attempts at humour upset and hurt our peers.

> We know, as teachers of boys, that we are not going to stop boys wanting to take the mickey out of one another. What we need them to understand is that banter is only banter if both people find it funny and that "it was just banter" is not an acceptable excuse for bullying. With any form of bullying, boys are always told to

speak up and to inform an adult if they are being bullied. Of course, this is good advice. However, I believe that most of the boys who go too far with their banter would be mortified to be accused of bullying. We need to remind them that everyone has a different tolerance to banter, and that their antennae must be alert to signs of discomfort in their friends and classmates. In a recent assembly, I advised boys that the appropriate response to banter that has gone too far is to say "that's enough; I don't find that funny", and that everyone must respect this boundary. To continue with banter once you know that your victim is uncomfortable is to move into the realm of bullying.

Dealing with inappropriate staff banter

Senior leaders must, however, take a firm stance on the use of "banter" among teachers that causes hurt, embarrassment or reinforces negative stereotypes about learning. It's telling that not many of the cases I was made aware of were brought to the attention of senior management. It's even more telling that in the examples I heard, when complaints were made to senior leadership team (SLT), they were largely downplayed or hushed up. Intended or otherwise, where a professional blatantly and publicly ridicules or sabotages a fellow professional, then words of advice must be given. In serious incidents, disciplinary proceedings should follow. Only when an ethos of openness and approachability is created will staff feel comfortable about discussing their feelings about inappropriate banter. If you fail to tackle it, don't be surprised when such attitudes are normalised and cascaded down to your pupils.

Banter: other things to consider

Here are further suggestions from my conversations with Evans and Lovatt:

1. **Let pupils set the tone of the discussion and use the language they want to use.** Evans says, "they know what they think banter is. But when you break it down into how teasing can become bullying, they start to realise that banter can be used as an umbrella term to cover any humour".

2. **Begin by focusing on the impact and consequences of what they say and how they say it.** As Lovatt advises, you need to get them to consider whether it matters how banter is intended.

3. **Be supportive but take young people out of their comfort zones.** Lovatt gives me an example of a simple yet effective task from his team's sessions: "we do an exercise where we challenge young people to give each other a compliment other than one based on appearance. It's a very difficult thing for young people – especially young men – to do".

Advice for teachers

Evans recommends the following practical strategies to help pupils be able to discern the difference between bullying and banter:

1. **Use examples from the media:** "Age appropriate real life examples that they can relate to are far more helpful than talking about banter and bullying in abstract terms."

2. **Don't take a condescending or censorious tone:** "You need to have an open conversation without being patronising. In some ways, they understand banter better than we do. They just don't have the skills to unpick examples and need help from teachers to do so".

3. **Adopt a patient, long-term approach**

Lovatt encourages teachers to focus on a positive mindset:

Be nice. Persevere. It's about creating a purposeful learning environment. If pupils are involved in learning they're less likely to get distracted and become involved in banter.

PART B: Boys' relationships with their teachers

As I made clear in Chapter 1, I've made plenty of mistakes when it comes to dealing with problematic behaviour from some boys, particularly trying to "engage" them, in a futile effort to avoid behaviour issues in the first place. In well-ordered schools with efficient centralised behaviour systems, complete with excellent, wide-ranging pastoral support, behaviour shouldn't be the primary focus of your teaching. Yet, I would argue that even when schools prioritise – or have the funds to prioritise – the provision of outstanding behaviour support to their teachers, many teachers still benefit from being aware of certain behaviour management tools that can help improve relationships with their pupils to develop a more purposeful classroom environment.

But wait, I hear some of you say, *why should teachers need to work on their behaviour management skills? Shouldn't pupils all be held to the same expectations: here are the rules, break them and you're out? It's our job to educate – they should just behave.*

I'm sympathetic to these feelings of frustration. Ultimately though, I still believe that the role of teachers is to find ways to run a tight, orderly classroom while acknowledging that some pupils just need a huge proverbial stick, while others will need more work, care and sensitively-thought-through discipline. Many of these will be boys. But guess what? Many of them will also be girls...

The research and the solutions

Advice for teachers

I believe that certain approaches to behaviour help to develop positive relationships with boys while still holding them to the highest of expectations. They also work well, I think, with girls and other human beings. But does the research support my anecdotal experience? Here are my Five Behaviour Principles for teachers of boys:

A.   Avoid confrontation and public reprimands

Boys tend to be impressed if you can keep your cool. This doesn't mean ignoring challenging behaviour. But giving boys thinking time, cooling off time, and the opportunity for them to back down without losing too much face is very important. A phrase I like that describes this approach is the teacher as a "warm demander". For example, when asking a misbehaving pupil to do something, thank you, with its polite expectation of compliance, is perhaps more powerful than please, which suggests that you are making a request.

Be aware of your body language and posture. It is easy, especially for male teachers, to use your physical size or the act of speaking down on someone to intimidate a pupil into doing as told. As you'll recall from Chapter 3, however, adopting the role of "cultural accomplice",[10] through displays of dominant traditional masculinity, might work in the short term but ultimately reinforce the often aggressive behaviour you've had to tackle in the first place. I tend to restrict my instinct to control confrontational boys through physical presence and raising my voice to situations where pupils are otherwise in danger: playground fights, running down the corridor, silly behaviour during fire alarms. Because regular shouting simply doesn't work. Staying calm not only helps your stress levels, it gives you the moral high ground when they shout. One of my stock phrases is "I'm not raising my voice at you; why are you raising your voice at me?" I find this invariably leads to the volume going down to two or three, not going up to 11. Taking this approach also means that when you do have a blast they are genuinely shocked. *We must really have done something wrong if Miss Clark is angry!*

Reid et al.,[11] who studied Key Stage 2 pupils, found that being shouted at was viewed by pupils as not just ineffective but also harmful to longer-term relationships between teachers and pupils. As professionals, I think it's our job, however riled, to try and model courtesy, dignity, and respect.

B.   Depersonalise behaviour and deal with it as discreetly as possible

A fascinating Australian study by Josephine Infantino and Emma Little[12] into pupils' perceptions of classroom behaviour found that 78% of the 350 pupils sampled felt that a private telling off was most effective in dealing with inappropriate behaviour. Only 12% felt that a public rebuke was the most effective. This supports the findings of previous studies[13] which found that pupils are least incentivised to improve their behaviour when discipline involves some form of public embarrassment.

Non-verbal instructions are powerful. They (a) prevent stopping the flow of the lesson and (b) don't draw attention to problematic behaviour. This is an important and often overlooked point. Often, the miscreant male's intention is to have their disruptive behaviour noticed, in an effort to display their traditionally masculine anti-schoolwork ethos.

As Infantino and Little observe "male [students] are more likely to act inappropriately and engage in troublesome behaviour if they know that they are going to receive social rewards from peers when they are reprimanded loudly".[14] Creating a scene or stand-off adds to the distractions. Bringing names into it – unless all other attempts to get the pupil's attention have failed – adds to the sense of picking a pupil out. An earlier study[15] found that over half of the 99 teachers surveyed confessed to using public reprimands, despite being aware that such reprimands are usually counterproductive. Are you one of those teachers who can't help themselves? If so, try "I'm waiting for some of you at the back to follow my instructions", even if it's just one pupil. This removes the "I wasn't doing anything!" retort and eliminates the possible perception that a child is being picked on.

Strategies that attempt to snuff out behaviour issues before they become a real distraction – such as a non-verbal signal for a pupil to put down a pen – have an additional benefit for teachers. An Australian study[16] into the relationship between behaviour and teacher stress found that a "significant predictor of teacher stress was the use of reactive behaviour management strategies" which are "used in response to disruptive behaviour". By contrast "proactive studies [which] prevent troublesome behaviour from occurring or escalating" appeared to be far more likely to improve the teacher's well-being.

C.   Involve parents and find quick wins

With difficult boys, particularly those exhibiting (or attempting to disguise) low self-esteem, I think it's vital to find an early opportunity to phone home with positive feedback. This may well be time-consuming but research has consistently found that positive contact with home is "universally effective"[17]in promoting good behaviour, unlike negative contact with home. I don't think you can underestimate the power of parental support.

I remember once calling home to speak to the mother of a troubled boy who I'd taught for a couple of weeks. "What's he done now?" she shouted at me. "Nothing", I said. "I just wanted to tell you how impressed I am with his efforts in English so far". After apologising, she explained through tears that she'd had enough of the constant stream of calls about fights, detentions, and missed homework. I called regularly after that. Sometimes the message wasn't good, but through the occasional frustrations that followed, the relationship remained one of mutual support.

One reason why parental calls – or postcards if you're pushed for time – might be so successful is that pupils, and I would suggest especially male pupils, are often wary of being praised publicly. As well as highlighting the dangers of public bollockings, Infantino and Little also found that students "prefer being praised quietly for good work and good behaviour". This research supports the findings of Houghton et al.[18] who noted that private praise was "less embarrassing" than public accolades as it didn't "single out the student and make their behaviour noticeable to others". When we think back to Chapter 3 and remind ourselves of the very real pressures boys face to conform to an anti-schoolwork ethos, it makes perfect sense that they would be reluctant to be thrust into the harsh limelight of "geekdom" by a well-intentioned teacher.

Now, of course we need to change the culture of our schools so that boys are free to soak up the glory of hard-earned academic success, and to enable them to enjoy being rewarded with a kind word for a classroom task well done. But in the meantime, lavishing loud praise on boys during lessons may well be counterproductive.

Teachers often assume that motivation leads to success in education. Numerous studies have, however, shown that although the relationship can go both ways, it is more likely to be the case that success leads to motivation. Research from 2016 into motivation and achievement in mathematics in elementary age pupils by Garon-Carrier et al.[19] found a directional link between prior achievement and subsequent intrinsic motivation. They argued that this increase in intrinsic motivation could possibly be explained by the fact that "achievement in mathematics is self-reinforcing".

Intrinsic motivation comes from within the individual, when they find something naturally satisfying.

Extrinsic motivation is inspired by some kind of external reward or demand.

To put it in simplified terms, doing well at something makes you enjoy it more and makes you want to do it more. With this in mind, finding quick wins with seemingly switched off boys becomes even more important. Looking for early opportunities to make positive contact with home can generate newfound levels of effort.

Furthermore, a recent article by Bugler et al.[20] cites studies which have shown that the motivation of boys to succeed academically is "more closely related to their attainment compared to girls" because boys "to a greater extent than girls, need to be successful academically in order to be motivated".[21] In other words, an improved test score is more likely to do more to encourage boys to work harder than a hundred growth mindset assemblies. Indeed, as teacher and author Andy Tharby has explained, psychological interventions that exhort underperforming pupils to work harder can often have the opposite effect:

> One of the most common mistakes is to encourage pupils to make more effort when, in actual fact, they require a better strategy. In this scenario, students quickly become disheartened when they realise that putting in more effort does not always lead to more success.[22]

So what might you do instead? Well, appeals for pupils to up their effort should always be specific and linked to clear targets. For example, rather than saying "You need to make sure you revise before your geography assessments, Jack", you are more likely to spur Jack on if you say "you need to go over erosional processes at home, Jack. From looking at your book, I can see this is an area that you struggled with in lessons".

D. Focus on productivity

Once you've enabled your male pupils to taste the honey jar of academic achievement, it's important to maintain very high expectations to ensure that complacency doesn't take hold. Apart from showing respect by listening when you, and their peers, are talking, I would argue that the most important thing you need to instil into apparently troublesome boys is the need to be productive in lessons.

An interesting question to ask yourself is: do you sometimes allow certain boys to get away with withdrawing their labour as long as they keep quiet and don't disrupt others? While this appears to be a pragmatic decision when dealing with a difficult class, particularly if you're an newly qualified teacher (NQT) who is still finding your feet with classroom management, I'd argue that you're sending out a subliminal signal that not working is ok. And it will be difficult to reverse that attitude once the rest of the class settle.

Education writer David Didau has coined a satisfying and succinct phrase to sum up this kind of egregious error: "what you permit you promote".[23] By ignoring laziness you are saying it is sometimes acceptable. And it really isn't. But, deep down, you knew that, of course. Because refusing to work – as opposed to not being able to do the work – is an act of defiance that, in its own way, is just as serious as truancy or telling you to shut up. Teachers might well avoid tackling this issue because a quiet but determined refusal to work can be hard to deal with. After all, you can't physically make Tyrone pick up a pen if he really doesn't want to, can you? No, you can't, but there are other weapons in your arsenal for the most reluctant of workers.

First, find out whether this pupil works in other lessons but not in yours. If so, are they taking advantage of your unwillingness to sanction them for it? The most effective teachers of boys (and girls) don't accept incomplete, inadequate, or generally half-arsed efforts. What might this look like in practice?

A simple little trick that lets pupils know you're on their case is *the dot*. When confronted with a case of malingering, all you need to do is silently draw a dot in the margin next to the miniscule amount of work the pupil has produced. What may appear to just be a dot is actually all-powerful. It's omniscient. It says to the pupil

> I've got my eye on you. There may be 29 of you, but I know exactly where you're up to on this task. When I get back in five minutes, my friend Dot will tell me exactly what you've achieved.

Invariably, after a bit of time you'll get to the stage where just mentioning "the dot" will provoke a frenzy of work. If that fails, insist on working in silence until the slackers adopt better work habits.

And if that doesn't have the desired effect? The next step is to make them complete work in their own time, either in a centralised detention or, if your school doesn't do those, as extra homework. If that's not completed, use the beginning of the next lesson, while the other pupils do a retrieval starter. And if all else fails? Isolate them during lesson time. Make them finish missed work in a different classroom, outside the head of department's office – wherever they feel particularly uncomfortable. Allow them to work their way back into your classroom. Only then will they truly grasp that you will never tolerate a lack of productivity in your classroom.

E.   Display confidence, knowledge, and humility

When it comes to improving the academic outcomes of boys (and girls), it really makes a difference if you know your subject, or subjects in primary, really well. Researchers have consistently found a positive link between strong subject knowledge and student gains.[24] As Rob Coe[25] has argued, a key strategy for improving outcomes is "targeting support for teachers at particular areas where their understanding or knowledge of student misconceptions is weak". This means that as a teacher of boys, you should not only be able to provide effective instruction and explanations, but you should also be able to anticipate likely errors that they might make in the application of this knowledge.

For example, a PE teacher might be an expert on the subtle variations of the fartlek training method, but even more important is having a solid awareness of how pupils might misunderstand, and incorrectly evaluate, these different elements. In my experience, occasionally you have to show off your passion and expertise to impress a difficult group. Telling them you are an expert – "You should listen to what I'm saying: I've got a masters in Russian history" – isn't enough in itself.

This is why live modelling – as well as being an excellent teaching tool[26] – is important. By displaying your mastery of a topic before their eyes, you are illustrating your knowledge and helping them improve. A combination of self-deprecation and self-assurance is a potent combination.

Indeed, humour is often cited as a key determiner in the building of a positive rapport with pupils. Research conducted by *TES* magazine[27] in 2017 asked more than 3,000 pupils in the UK to rank the characteristics those most valued in their teachers. Among both primary and secondary schoolchildren "'funny' won by a landslide". Anecdotally, I can confirm that well-judged humour is very effective at getting boys on side and can lead to memorable ways of ensuring knowledge is instilled. A 2006 American study by R.L. Garner[28] argued that humour can have a positive effect on retention and recall of information. Significantly, though, Garner agrees with other researchers[29] that humour must be linked to the content of the curriculum:

> For humour to be most effective in an academic setting, it must be specific, targeted, and appropriate to the subject matter.

If we remind ourselves of Daniel Willingham's explanation of learning – "memory is the residue of thought"[30] – then we can see how, if teachers are not careful, pupils might remember the jokes and forget the content unless the jokes are relevant to the content, in which case they are far more likely to stick.

As well as improving memory, humour can also work well to alleviate boys' concerns about their ability to succeed. We know from Chapter 3 that boys are more likely to withdraw their academic labour if they feel that they are unlikely to be successful. Banas et al.,[31] reviewing four decades of research into the effect of humour in the classroom, assert that "the use of instructional humour to relieve tension may be especially useful for teaching topics that are generally perceived by students to be anxiety-provoking".

For example, if I'm teaching boys poetry based on love and relationships, I might decide to share a deliberately awful love poem that I've written, to encourage them to laugh at the standard of my work (encouraging them to take risks with their own creative writing), and to give them a reference point for the genuine quality of the poetry that they will be studying.

The trouble with sarcasm

Nonetheless, experienced teachers will have seen countless situations where poorly-judged attempts at humour have caused conflict, resentment, and a loss of trust. For example, the use of sarcasm – an understandable temptation when dealing with a frustrating class – can backfire badly. I would argue that it should be avoided unless you know a group really well and have developed a safe space for some gentle teasing. Yet, even when it doesn't offend or upset pupils, sarcasm can have other pernicious effects. I once heard a teacher, who was stood in his doorway waiting for a group of dawdling Year 10 boys, say "come on lads, I know you're just dying to get into your history lesson. I know you love the subject so much that you're virtually sprinting to get here". In my view, this seemingly benign sarcasm was badly-aimed for the following reasons:

1) **It wasn't funny.** If you must use sardonic jokes, at least think of something that will get a laugh
2) **It assumes all the pupils don't like your lesson.** Maybe some of them do but they feel the need to turn up late *en masse* to avoid being labelled as swots?
3) **It reinforces stereotypes about boys being anti-learning.** What if they were late because they had been late getting changed in PE? The teacher didn't bother to ask, preferring to assume the reason was anti-academic in nature
4) **It carries with it a subtext that history – a subject grounded on reading and writing – is boring.** Would a teacher of a "practical" subject like design technology or drama be as likely to run down their subject?
5) **It creates a negative start to the lesson.** Deal with the lateness at the end, for sure, but don't waste further lesson time
6) **Pupils generally don't like sarcasm.** Wanzer et al.[32] found that students usually don't like humour that targets individual students, whether intended to cause upset or not. Boys have enough banter to deal with in the playground. Surely relationships with adults should offer a respite from teasing?
7) **Are the boys allowed to use sarcasm with you?** Banas et al.[33] argue that "the power difference between teachers and students inhibits reciprocal teasing". As a teacher, you may have the authority to target pupils and raise your status at the expense of others, but using it in this way will harm relationships in the long run.

The final word

At the beginning of this chapter, we looked at the malign nature of much of what passes for banter in schools. Many boys have a tendency to denigrate and belittle each other in an attempt to display their manly credentials. Not only do these seemingly light-hearted barbs cause suffering and embarrassment, they also perpetuate the damaging notion that to express heartfelt emotion is to display weakness that could be seen as effeminate. We've also learnt that teachers, often but not exclusively men, can also undermine colleagues and reinforce non-tender masculine values.

We've also seen that the key to successful relationships between teachers and male pupils lies in an approach that motivates boys through achieving success and takes careful consideration of boys' feelings. At the same time, we've also found that teachers who do well with boys are subject experts who have very high expectations of what they can achieve, using "tough love" to ensure that they aren't allowed to adopt a self-defeating anti-work stance. Finally, we saw how humour can be a powerful tool that must be used with caution.

There is always room for fun in our schools. It's an essential component of the human existence. Yet, schools and individual teachers need to ensure – when it comes to interactions between boys, between teachers, and between boys and teachers – that humour isn't malicious or misogynistic in nature (Figure 9.1).

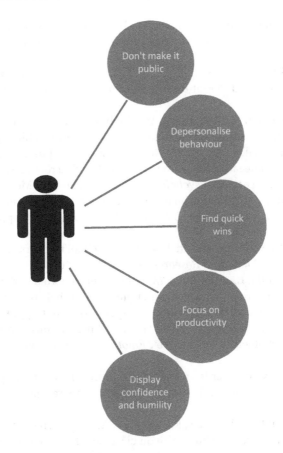

Figure 9.1 Developing positive relationships with boys

Notes

1 See for example TES online, 10th November 2014. Available at: www.tes.com/news/ why-im-banning-banter-my-classroom (Accessed: 14th March 2018).

2 Brown, L., ed. (1993) *The New Shorter Oxford English Dictionary*, Oxford: Oxford University Press.

3 Green, J. (2008) *Chambers Slang Dictionary*, Edinburgh: Chambers.

4 Ditch the Label (2018) *The annual bullying survey 2018*. Available at: www.ditchthelabel. org/wp-content/uploads/2018/06/The-Annual-Bullying-Survey-2018-2.pdf (Accessed: 13th September 2018).

5 Kehily, M.J. & Nayak, A. (1997) '"Lads and laughter": Humour and the production of heterosexual hierarchies', *Gender and Education*, 9:1, pp. 69–88.

6 In the UK, 'fanny' denotes the vagina, see Green, J. (2008).

7 *The Only Way is Essex*, a tacky and inexplicably popular British reality television series.

8 Smith, J. (2007) '"Ye've got to 'ave balls to play this game sir!" Boys, peers and fears: The negative influence of school-based "cultural accomplices" in constructing hegemonic masculinities', *Gender and Education*, 19:2, pp. 179–198.

9 Loughborough Grammar School website (2017) *Banter and bullying*. Available at: www.les grammar.org/news/headmasters-blog/banter-and-bullying/ (Accessed: 18th March 2018).

10 Smith, J. (2007), pp. 179–198.

11 Reid, K., Challoner, C., Lancet, A., Jones, G., Rhysiart, G.A., & Challoner, S. (2010) 'The views of primary school pupils at key stage 2 on school behaviour in Wales', *Educational Review*, 62:1, pp. 97–113.

12 Infantino, J. & Little, E. (2005) 'Students' perceptions of classroom behaviour problems and the effectiveness of different disciplinary methods', *Educational Psychology*, 25:5, pp. 491–508.

13 For example Houghton, S., Merratt, F. & Wheldall, K. (1988) 'Classroom behaviour problems which secondary school teachers say they find most troublesome', *British Educational Research* Journal, 14: 3, pp. 297–312.; Leach, D.J. & Tan, R. (1996) 'The effects of sending positive and negative letters to parents on the classroom behaviour of secondary school students', *Educational Psychology*, 16: 2, pp. 141–154; Merratt, F. & Tang, W.M. (1994) 'The attitudes of British primary school pupils to praise, rewards, punishments and reprimands', *British Journal of Educational Psychology*, 64: 1, pp. 91–103.

14 Infantino, J. & Little, E. (2005).

15 Caffyn, R.E. (1989) 'Attitudes of British secondary school teachers and pupils to rewards and punishments', *Educational Research*, 31, pp. 210–220.

16 Clunies-Ross, P., Little, E. & Kienhuis, M. (2008) 'Self-reported and actual use of proactive and reactive classroom management strategies and their relationship with teacher stress and student behaviour', *Educational Psychology*, 28: 6, pp. 693–710., quoted in Nash, P., Schlösser, A. & Scarr, T. (2016) 'Teachers' perceptions of disruptive behaviour in schools: A psychological perspective', *Emotional and Behavioural Difficulties*, 21:2, pp. 167–180.

17 Payne, R. (2015) 'Using rewards and sanctions in the classroom: Pupils' perceptions of their own responses to current behaviour management strategies', *Educational Review*, 67:4, pp. 483–504.

18 Houghton, S., Wheldhall, K., Jukes, R., & Sharpe, A. (1990) 'The effects of limited private reprimands and increased private praise on classroom behaviour in four British secondary school classes', *British Journal of Educational Psychology*, 60, pp. 255–265.

19 Garon-Carrier, G., Boivin, M., Guay, F., Kovas, Y., Dionne, G., Lemelin, J.P., Séguin, J.R., Vitaro, F., & Tremblay, R.E. (2016) Intrinsic motivation and achievement in mathematics in elementary school: A longitudinal investigation of their association, *Child Development*, 87:1, pp. 165–175.

20 Bugler, M., McGeown, S.P., & St Clair-Thompson, H. (2015) 'Gender differences in adolescents academic motivation and classroom behaviour', *Educational Psychology*, 35:5, pp. 541–556.

21 For example Logan, S. & Medford, E. (2011) 'Gender differences in strength of association between motivation, competency beliefs and reading skill', *Educational Research*, 53, pp. 85–94.

22 Durrington Research School website (2018) *Stealthy psychological interventions.* Available at: https://durrington.researchschool.org.uk/2018/04/25/stealthy-psychological-interventions/ (Accessed: 13th August 2018).

23 David Didau website (2016). Available at: www.learningspy.co.uk/behaviour/five-things-every-new-teacher-needs-know-behaviour-management/ (Accessed: 14th August 2018).

24 For example Timperley, H., Wilson, A., Barrar, H. & Fung, I. (2007) 'Teacher professional learning and development: Best evidence synthesis iteration', Ministry of Education, Wellington, New Zealand; Blank, R.K. & de las Alas, N. (2009) 'The effects of teacher professional development on gains in student achievement: How meta analysis provides scientific evidence useful to education leaders', Council of Chief State School Officers, Washington, DC; Rockoff, J.E., Jacob, B.A., Kane, T.J. & Staiger, D.O. (2011) Can you recognize an effective teacher when you recruit one?', *Education Finance and Policy*, 6: 1,

pp. 43–74; Agathangelou, E., Nigmatullin, I.A. & Simonova, G.I. (2016), 'The content of pedagogical support of students' social adaptation', *International Electronic Journal of Mathematics Education*, 11: 1, pp. 243–254.

25 Coe, R., Aloisi, C., Higgins, S., & Elliot Major, L. (2014) *What Makes Great Teaching? Review of the Underpinning Research*, Durham: Durham University, Sutton Trust.

26 Coe, R., Aloisi, C., Higgins, S., & Elliot Major, L. (2014) 'Classify modelling as having a "strong evidence of impact on student outcomes"'.

27 Ziebart, G. (2017) '25 traits that make a perfect teacher...', *TES Online*, 21st July. Available at: www.tes.com/news/25- traits-make-perfect-teacher (Accessed 27th August 2018).

28 Garner, R.L. (2006) 'Humor in pedagogy: How ha-ha can lead to aha!', *College Teaching*, 54:1, pp. 177–180.

29 For example Kaplan, R.M. & Pascoe, G.C. (1977) 'Humorous lectures and humorous examples: Some effects upon comprehension and retention', *Journal of Educational Psychology*, 69, pp. 61–66.

30 Willingham, D.T. (2009) *Why Don't Students Like School?* San Francisco, CA: Jossey Bass.

31 Banas, J.A., Dunbar, N., Rodriguez, D., & Liu, S.J. (2011) 'A review of humor in educational settings: Four decades of research', *Communication Education*, 60:1, pp. 115–144.

32 Wanzer, M.B., Frymier, A.B., Wojtaszczyk, A.M., & Smith, T. (2006) 'Appropriate and inappropriate uses of humor by teachers', *Communication Education*, 55, pp. 178–196.

33 Banas, J.A., Dunbar, N., Rodriguez, D., & Liu, S.J. (2011).

Other voices

Masculinity in primary schools, by Ben King

Ben King is a Year 5 teacher in a primary school in West Sussex. Having spent time teaching in Hampshire and United Arab Emirates, Ben now focuses on promoting a love of reading and ensuring quality children's literature is at the centre of teaching and learning. Ben's MA thesis examines the link between parental academic achievement and its impact on their engagement with their child's education. As well as writing a weekly column for HWRK magazine, Ben has also recently started The Teacher Book Awards, the first online book award that uses nominations and voting from teachers alone.

Miss Trunchbull

At Primary school in the 1990s, I had the displeasure of being taught by a teacher who I'm sure must have had a shrine to Roald Dahl's Miss Trunchbull inside her cave-like teacher cupboard. She didn't like me – not in a *he can be such hard work sometimes* kind of way – but in an actual bullying, intimidating, pushing-other-children-to-shun-me type way. I wasn't the easiest boy to teach but the treatment that was levelled at me was undeserved and, to this day, sticks to me like PVA glue. I can't peel away the memories of her abject rudeness, her favour-itism, and the fact that she treated me, and the other boys, entirely differently to the girls. Us boys were expected to behave like men. We were expected to re-spond to her daily criticism like soldiers in a drill hall, as opposed to seven-year-olds in a classroom. *Don't be such a sissy*, she said to me whilst my long-suffering father dragged me back to school. *Pull yourself together.* I sobbed, I wailed, I ran away and she shrugged it off, firm in the knowledge that she knew what was best for me.

When I became a teacher, I swore to myself that high standards and consistent expectations were one thing, but bullying and intimidation was something I would never ever allow myself to stoop to. Instead, I would allow boys (and girls) to express their frustrations, their anger, their concerns, fears, and worries in whatever way (within reason) they wanted. Thank goodness I had kind, loving parents who believed me and supported me. My Miss Trunchbull left at the end of that academic year, and the rumours surrounding her departure were gleefully colourful.

A brighter future

Having taught for nearly ten years in two continents, and numerous different schools, I am witness to how the representation and expectation of masculinity has changed. It has mirrored our society. Our little petri-dishes of communities follow the trends that we see at the school gates in the morning. Rewind two decades and in many playgrounds you would have been hard pushed to find a father depositing their most valuable possessions. Mothers stayed at home and fathers went to work. And, when I planned my own future with my nine-year-old friends, these were the foundations we built on.

Rocket forward to the present day and this simply isn't the case. The world has changed and our perception of what is *normal* has with it. I say goodbye to more dads now than I did even five years ago. No longer does a slightly confused child turn to his classmate and whisper *does your dad not work?* Mothers have fought for their rights to go out and work and be the main or joint breadwinner; fathers have fought for their right to carry a My Little Pony rucksack while their little girl swings from their hand on the walk in.

The best footballer I know

During my days as a mediocre football player, my school hosted a mixed football tournament every summer. We had a family friend, a child a year younger than my friends and I, who was that worst of all things: a girl. Boy, could this girl play football. She could *really* play. The other teams laughed, bemused that we'd chosen to field a mixed team when it wasn't mandatory. They questioned why we didn't have enough male friends to make a boys team. Then, they beat us. They were better than us then, but none of them play football at any level now. What happened to her? She went on to play for Charlton Athletic and then moved to the United States where she played professionally. It's funny how things work out.

We must embrace these changes. We must normalise them for what they are and show the children in our lives that this is our new world, offering a chance to forge ahead into an unknown but exciting future.

The things boys can do

So what does masculinity mean in my primary classroom? It means, thankfully, very little. It's almost become a purely scientific term, without the emotional connotations or peer pressure that comes with *being a man*. The boys I teach cry. The boys I teach sometimes miss their mums. The best gymnast in the class? A boy. He also happens to be the best dancer. If a boy had piped up in front of my own Miss Trunchbull with tales of his perfectly executed forward rolls, or talked about his ability to dance the samba, she would have crushed them.

Personally, I don't subscribe to the school of thought that says there are no differences whatsoever between boys and girls. I feel there are: it doesn't make anyone better than anyone else and it doesn't mean that these differences apply to *all* boys or *all* girls. However, these differences should now be viewed as a mere footnote in the understanding of the child. There are still some unconscious biases rolling around: you do on occasion see only boys carrying equipment round school or all-male sports captains. But the presence of boys at dance clubs and the presence of girls in boxing halls show how far we have come.

The need to continue

The journey isn't complete yet. It takes time. Karl Marx described the history of the world in epochs, different stages that shift society throughout time, moving it forward, progressing. This is our new epoch, the freeing up of women from the constraints of male patronage, dominance and limitations, and the realisation that boys can cry, and they do. That boys can be scared, and they are. That it's ok to prefer playing with toys over kicking a ball. Masculinity, at least in primary schools has shifted, it is still shifting and it will continue to do so. And teachers at the chalk face, with the grime, sweat and tears to prove it, will lead the way in supporting this new age.

If you are a teacher out there, watch, listen, and observe. The changes are all around us.

Masculinity and homosexuality in schools, by Hadley Stewart

Hadley Stewart is a freelance writer who has written for publications including Attitude, FS, Out News Global, NBC News, the Nursing Standard, PinkNews, and The Queerness. Specialising in LGBT+ issues and health, Hadley has written about everything from the plight of LGBT+ people in Egypt to sexual health advice. He recently appeared on the BBC Three documentary, Queer Britain. Hadley lives in London and can be found by tweeting @wordsbyhadley.

That's so gay

The first time I heard somebody using the word "gay" to describe me was in the school playground. I was six years old and didn't know what the word meant. I wasn't sure why the older boy was calling me gay, but I know now it was because

I wasn't conforming to how a boy *should* behave. The phrase "that's so gay" and its various iterations followed me throughout most of my school career, meaning that I associated the word with negative connotations for almost a decade. So when I eventually decided to come out, I needed to overcome almost a decade's worth of work by myself.

I went to a primary school in Greater Manchester where I was bullied for most of my time there. The bullying started in 2003, the year that Section 28 was finally repealed. The piece of legislation was brought in by Margaret Thatcher's Conservative government and banned the so-called promotion of homosexuality in schools. The rationale for bringing in such a legislation was to protect young people, but the truth is it did the exact opposite.

Section 28

As a result of Section 28, teachers were unable to discuss LGBT issues. This meant that if you experienced homophobic bullying at school, your teachers were bound by law not to address it. Discussing same sex relationships was simply not an option, and some teachers took the opportunity to express their own homophobic, biphobic, and transphobic views with their class and colleagues. It was an extremely dark time for our education system.

Today, many LGBT people carry the scars of their school experiences. The shame that some LGBT people feel about their sexual orientation or gender identity is doubtless derived from growing up in an environment where being gay, bisexual, or trans was seen to be something that should either be ridiculed or kept a secret. What's more, a lack of discussion about same sex relationships means that many members of the LGBT community left school without the tools to equip them to have healthy and happy relationships.

Although I escaped the majority of Section 28's reign, I was schooled at a time of uncertainty for teachers. Whilst the piece of legislation may have been repealed, the shadow was still looming over schools in the United Kingdom. I remember teachers at primary school telling the children who bullied me to "never use that word again", rather than educating us what "gay" meant. Consequently, I would grow fearful of using that word, meaning that many incidents of homophobic bullying went unreported.

My teachers didn't know what to do

Looking back, my teachers in primary school simply didn't know what to say or do. There was no diversity training for teachers then, nor did Ofsted state that schools should have clear anti-homophobic bullying policies. Charities like Diversity Role Models, that invite LGBT people into schools to talk about their life experiences, weren't even on the radar. The representation of gay men in mainstream media was still fuelled with stigma and prejudice. Even though today I understand there were many contextual factors which influenced my experiences at that school, that doesn't mean that I still don't carry those negative experiences around with me today.

The notion of masculinity was palpable in primary school, but I don't remember it being as noticeable compared with secondary school. In 2007, I sat an entrance exam that would see me going off to an all-boys' school for my secondary education. The first day was odd. I looked around and there were only boys in the class. This "odd" feeling continued throughout my school career, accompanying the conversations about football that evolved into remarks about sex (with girls).

Saved by an English teacher (and Madonna)

I found my safe haven from this "odd" feeling, what the authors of this book now term "non-tender masculinity", in my sixth form English lessons. Here the revolutionary phrase of "gender is a social construct" was uttered and allowed everyone to feel a little closer to being comfortable in their own skin. Our English teacher happened to be a fan of Madonna, so she would play her tunes at the end of term. Madonna frequently rebelled against the status quo, giving me the feeling that it was ok to be effeminate (or camp) and have feelings towards other boys. Going against the status quo of gender is fine, as long as you have somebody behind you in case you fall. In our English classroom, there were no rainbow flags, but I knew that I was safe there.

The school curriculum was also influenced by masculinity and there wasn't any doubt in my mind which subjects we ought to be focusing on. I had three hours of sport every week: PE, swimming, and rugby. Art, drama, and music were on a carousel, with drama dropping off the timetable completely after two years. I vividly remember being told by my head of year to only aim for professions that were going to make me lots of money, with jobs including lawyer, banker, and engineer being suggested.

When I made it to Sixth Form, I was fascinated that the girls' school were always taking part in activities that encouraged more women into male-dominated professions. Girls interested in becoming engineers were invited to conferences and there would be scholarships for female leavers wishing to study sciences at university. The same was not being done to help more men break into female-dominated professions. Why is it that women now outnumber men in many universities in law and medicine, but philosophy and nursing remain female-dominated?

Beyond school

Having now graduated from university, I've met up with a few boys I went to school with. Some of them have even told me they wish that they had applied to study another subject at university, but had felt pressured by societal norms of what career path men *should* take. Schools are not the only drivers with regards to societal norms around gender, but they certainly have the opportunity to dispel archaic workplace gender stereotypes.

Homosexuality and mental health

Of course, masculinity doesn't just influence an individual's career path. Mental health also takes a beating from masculinity, which is perhaps one of the reasons why the leading cause of death amongst men in the UK is suicide. At school I knew a handful of boys who were suffering from poor mental health and who felt unable to seek help from healthcare professionals nor their friends and family. Thankfully we're talking increasingly about mental health and well-being amongst men, which has certainly encouraged some men to talk about what's going on inside. There are still many suffering in silence, which emphasises why talking about mental health in schools is so important.

We know that gay men, and the wider LGBTQ+ community, are disproportionately impacted by poor mental health. Stonewall say in their 2017 Schools Report that bullying is a risk factor for young people experiencing poor mental health, such as depression and anxiety. It's clear that schools have a responsibility to challenge discrimination and prejudice towards LGBTQ+ students, especially due to the fact we know it can have such negative consequences for people later on in life.

I remember sitting in an assembly at school and hearing about Tyler Clementi. He was 18 years old when he jumped from the George Washington Bridge in New York, having been bullied by his university roommate. Our deputy head teacher spoke to us about Tyler, explaining that bullying can have damaging consequences for those who experience it. Tyler is often cited when people talk about the "It Gets Better Project", an American online project that was established following a spike in the number of LGBTQ+ teenagers dying from suicide. The project encourages LGBTQ+ people to make YouTube videos and inspire the next generation that life really does get better.

I spoke about Tyler recently, when delivering a workshop for teachers about LGBT+ visibility in the classroom. It's important to acknowledge that not every LGBT+ young person made it through their education unscathed. Tyler's story is at the thin end of the wedge, but I can't help feeling lucky to have heard the message "it gets better" when I did. It shouldn't have to be this way, of course. Nobody should feel lucky to have survived being bullied during their formative years or have developed resilience as a result of overcoming adversity and discrimination. Young people deserve better than that.

We could get things right

I've come a long way from the six-year-old boy who didn't know what the word gay meant to spending most of my time writing or talking about LGBTQ+ topics. I believe that the opportunities I've been given also come with great responsibility. We may have come on a journey as a society and education system, but the road ahead is still long and bumpy. We need to show those around us and future generations that our differences – be it sexual orientation or gender expression – make us who we are. Previous generations have made mistakes, but we could be the first ones to get things right.

Black masculinity in schools, by Malcolm Richards

> Malcolm Richards lives with his wife and two children in Devon, where he is a teacher. He has worked across adult, secondary, and special education settings and is a trade union activist. Malcolm writes, tweets, and talks about dialogue, race, and equitable futures in education. He is a Philosophy of Education Society of Great Britain teacher scholar and is involved in several cultural education organisations.

Him

It was September, the start of an academic year.

Our small primary school served a large, multi-ethnic council estate in Hackney, London. My fellow class members were friends; everyone lived nearby. Parents knew each other and held positive relationships with school leaders and staff, from the school secretaries to the dinner ladies.

The first time I met him was in a classroom. I have no idea what his background was or what his interests were. This school may have been his first experience of working in a diverse, multi-ethnic setting. I introduced myself in my most polite and eager to please voice, looking forward to learning in his class. Back then, I was never seen without a book. I probably told him what I was reading, Alex Hailey's *Autobiography of Malcolm X* or perhaps *The Count of Monte Cristo*.

I was small for my age back then, lacking in confidence and physically weak. Unlike the other boys in my class, I wasn't good at sport, nor did I possess any physical strength. But what I lacked in size, I made up for in my pursuit, retention, and articulation of knowledge. Ignoring this, he instead focussed on my weakness, offering comparisons between myself and other young black men, while routing me towards physical or musical pursuits.

Me, the anomaly

To him, I was a confusing anomaly: a young black boy who defied the stereotype of young black academic underachievement. This frustrated him and so he sought to position me as worthless because of my racialised, gendered, and cultural identity.

Through his teaching, lesson plans built around colonial perspective and the white gaze, his repeated tropes and catchphrases, he normalised my, and our, position as "less than". In his multi-ethnic classroom, Africa and its diaspora were described as a single underprivileged continent, descended from somewhere other than here. I tried to share my knowledge with him, my language of cultural heritage or histories. These were always dismissed as exotic, imaginative, or uncertified. Although he publically advocated a commitment to defeating hate, oppression, and intolerance, his ignorance repeatedly went unchallenged in his space. He claimed that the best way to fight oppression was to ignore it. I sought action to defeat it.

The unbalanced relationship began placing a taxing toll on my mental health and well-being. I began to navigate with continuous care, developing tactical and strategic astuteness that I would use in classrooms many times over the years, both as a student and later as a teacher. My academic success was limited and ring-fenced. He seemed continually to seek me out. Was he aware of my feelings of powerlessness and alienation? So entrenched were his stereotypical ideas of how I and other black boys should be – full of physical prowess, disinterest, and rhythm – that he couldn't accept an alternative.

Being black

An overwhelming amount of academic literature acknowledges the disproportionate level of success people racialised and gendered as black males have in education. While contested, the reasons for the positioning of black males is complex, wide-spread, and can't be considered in isolation. The outcomes remain. If you are a black boy, you will lag behind your peers academically from primary school onwards and will achieve fewer academic qualifications. You are three times more likely to be permanently excluded. If you are a black teacher, you are less likely to achieve promotion to senior positions. You will be given stereotypical tasks, such as behaviour management or developing diversity projects. You will not be supported by line management and described as a "trouble maker" or viewed as aggressive if you challenge decisions.

Whose British values?

The socio-political intricacies of colonialism and its dominating white British ideal of identity offer much explanation to how racial inequalities remain. Our education policies and legislation have entrenched an idealised identity, which for centuries has continued to wield absolute power and influence. The mandatory British Values, which all schools are obliged to impart on those students who come through their doors, are rooted in this ideal and shape the institutions and history that underpin the nation. The cultural and literary canon on which our National Curriculum remains based upon reinforces this ideal. The black male is one of multiple gendered and racialised identities whose self has been obscured, rewritten, or ignored. There's more to black masculinity than Martin Luther King and Crooks the stable buck. We are more than slavery, segregation, and sit-ins. We are scientists, artists, and writers. We are ignored.

There are clearly no easy fixes.

Decolonising our practice

However, the deep amnesia surrounding the histories of racialised and gendered identities remains. Thus, we must challenge assumptions, motivations, and values. We need a critical dialogue, which can only occur in education spaces based upon universal values, or preconditions of hope, mutual respect, modesty, courage, and love. We can develop an established, emerging, and new cultural canon, using resources from equitable, multi-ethnic, diverse perspectives. We can collectively develop the critical consciousness necessary to transform the way black boys are perceived by others and the way black boys perceive themselves. Only then, can we begin to challenge the endemic inequalities that place (un)conscious barriers to success in their way.

So, are you prepared to decolonise your practice?

Masculinity and leadership in schools, by Hannah Wilson

Hannah Wilson is the Executive Head Teacher of Aureus School & Aureus Primary School, part of the GLF schools trust. Hannah co-founded a grassroots gender equality movement and is a National Leader for #WomenEd. She is a DfE coach for the Women Leading in Education initiative and is an advocate for flexible working.

Gender in the school system

As co-founder and National Leader of #WomenEd, our work on gender and equality gives me an interesting lens from which to view masculinity and the way it manifests itself in schools. When we started our grassroots equality movement, I was deputy head teacher in an established trust. My formative years as a middle leader and assistant head teacher were spent in mixed comprehensive urban schools in socially deprived areas, which were led in a stereotypically masculine way. Would I have been appointed as the only female middle leader, and then become the only female pastoral leader, if I had not been 6'1" and a loud, confident personality? I could most definitely hold my own, physically and vocally, with the hypermasculine leadership model and culture I found myself in. Moreover, would they have appointed me had I not have been trained in, and loved working in, three all boys' schools, which had shaped my teaching in a particular way? As a movement, we feel that for boys to flourish in schools, we must challenge the stereotypically masculine leadership model.

Leading a values-led school

When I became the Head Teacher Designate of a brand new mixed comprehensive school, I was intent on putting the values of diversity, equality, and inclusion at the heart of our school. I wanted to create a space where staff could lead in an authentic way, where staff could work flexibly and not be inhibited in their careers by having a family. I wanted to lead a school where we have a family-friendly culture and our staff are not expected to put the students before their children's needs.

I also wanted to lead a school where leaders could be confident and assertive without the toxic culture I have experienced in other schools. The dog-eat-dog culture is not a healthy model for anyone to thrive in. To address the damaging aspects of traditional masculinity, we also explore the values of kindness, love, and respect at our school. Our values percolate through everything we do. We reward the values being embodied and sanction the values being contravened. If we can teach our boys (and girls) to be kind to themselves and others, to show love to themselves, each other, and our environment, then we will co-create better human beings. We do not have pink and blue values, language, or roles at our school. Emotions and the ability to articulate them are seen as a strength in the boys we teach.

Culture and ethos

Our school is a safe space where male students wear their hearts on their sleeves. The ethical vocabulary our students have developed, their understanding of social equity, their rights as young people is impressive. We are developing their ability to self-regulate their emotions, which regularly run high. As a staff body, we challenge and counter "lad culture" and have slowly unpicked some behaviours, attitudes, and appropriations that we do not want to see in society, let alone in our school. Something we have spent time reviewing and refining is our gender-neutral environment. We have inclusive toilets and changing rooms for our learners to choose from. Following training with Educate and Celebrate on making our school LGBT+ friendly, we took some simple but effective steps. First, we made some adjustments to our uniform and removed all references to male/female garments – it is now a gender-neutral school uniform. We developed our glossary of language; we avoid referring to our students as "girls" and "boys" but as "class" or as "Year 7". Moreover, we challenge each other when we make subtle slips – like proposing a "girls vs boys" bake off – as we recognise there are less divisive ways of splitting classes into teams.

Gender in the classroom

The learning spaces in our school leave learners safe to take risks. This year I have taught drama and have seen gender become fluid and a non-issue for many students. When casting for our schools' Shakespeare production last autumn, we morphed Oberon and Titania into magical transgender beings. So we cast four paired students to bring these characters to life. Hannah and Rhys played Oberon and Ella and Simeon played Titania. This summer we explored *Anne Frank's Diary* and the students felt quite comfortable reading parts from a different gender to their own. In previous schools, boys in particular have been reluctant to temporarily inhabit the skin of a female character.

Stereotyping

In every decision we have made in our school, we have quietly challenged social norms about teaching boys. We collectively believe that feminism liberates boys and men, moreover that we need to work together to shape our boys into fine young men. As part of our Global Citizenship programme, we explore identity and belonging. The Personal, Social, Health and Economic education (PSHE), Spiritual, Moral, Social, and Cultural development (SMSC), Sex and Relationships Education (SRE), and Citizenship curriculum are interwoven into a programme of study to shape our young boys and girls into better citizens, into better human beings.

We are a straight talking school and have the difficult conversations other schools may shy away from. We had workshops on Female Genital Mutilation and our Year 7s boys joined in and created vaginas out of plasticine. We had a guest speaker on Early Child Marriage, where boys also reflected on society's gender expectations. Role models, father figures, and parenting choices are all key topics for our boys and girls, who come from a very mixed background of family dynamics, to reflect on as they mature.

Partnerships

As well as working with Educate and Celebrate, along with Dauntless Daughters – an organisation that promotes female empowerment – we are also collaborating with the Good Lad Initiative. Their sessions deconstruct and challenge social norms. They encourage our male pupils to consider vital questions: what does it mean to be a good lad? What does it mean to be a good man? But I also think that more and more as educators we should be focused on the most important question of all: What does it mean to be a good human?

Interested in finding out more? Suggested Twitter accounts to follow:

■ @TheGenderLab @GLInitiative @GoodMenProject @LetToysBeToys @HeForShe @HeForSheEd

Masculinity in schools: a female perspective, by Natalie Scott

Natalie, TES blogger of the year and TEDx speaker, has been a secondary English teacher for 17 years, is an Specialist Leader of Education (SLE), and was an Assistant Head before leaving the English education system to provide educational aid to children living in refugee camps. Now, back full time in a secondary school in Hertfordshire, she believes firmly in passion over politics, that education is key, and that all children deserve equal and fair access to education.

Stereotypes and leopard print

I'm a female teacher. I wear make-up and stilettos. I always have. I was once told that my make-up would hinder me, when applying for senior leadership roles, and that I should refrain from wearing leopard print to interviews if I wished to be taken seriously. I was told that by a male head. He also told me that my appearance detracted from my intelligence and set a poor example to my female students. I ignored him. And I disagreed. Authenticity is – and always will be – important to me; to thine own self be true and all that malarkey. Why can't a woman be intelligent and attractive? I understand all too well how the stereotypes of my own gender have affected my life. I'm not a dumb blonde. And my male students are not all hormonal lads, testing out chat up lines, trying to be cool, getting into fights.

In the earlier years of my career, before I was older than most of my students' parents, I got a bit of attention. Young and blonde, a few curves. I have always been very careful with my work wardrobe. High neck tops, always. Knee-length skirts, or longer. Ever conscious of my own credibility, conscious too that teenagers are easily distracted by pretty much anything: wind, snow, lawnmowers, weird smells, or simply the way their teachers look. It's not an egotistical comment; I'm pretty sure that most of my female colleagues would agree that it is a factor when deciding on their professional dress.

"Alright miss?"

Co-ed, state schools are where my heart lies. I love teaching boys and girls but I have always been impressed by the ease of teenage lads; reprimand one in a lesson and ten minutes later he will say, "Alright miss", grinning and giving a nod of the head, when he sees you on break duty. Boys, in my experience anyway, are far more forgiving than their female counterparts.

It hasn't always been easy teaching them, but some of the pivotal moments of my career have been associated with male students. Certainly, some of my most

memorable students are boys. I've taught professional footballers, teachers, bas-
ketball coaches, doctors, lawyers, recruitment consultants, marines, writers, and
builders. I've taught bright sparks, cheeky sods, and horny teenage boys, heterosexual and homosexual. I've taught wealthy and privileged boys, neglected and
scruffy boys, polite and timid boys, loud and inappropriate boys. I've learned from
them all. I've laughed with many. I've clashed with a few. This is my chance to tell
the stories of a few moments, in a few lessons, with a few of the boys I have known.
Most of their names have been changed.

Sexual harassment

Sexual harassment. It happens. It happened, years ago now, but I will never forget
it. Teaching for five years and deemed good with behaviour, I was given a "bottom
set". Bottom set Year 10 was made up entirely of lads. Many were bright, but behaviour had been an issue. Ross was one of those students. He was desperate for
attention. He didn't "do English". It was far easier to disrupt than to try and fail.
It was my third lesson with the class. I'd written a whole scheme of work around
football (yes – I now know this was a mistake), even going so far as to source prizes
from the FA, but he was having none of it. I asked him to stop speaking over me.
His snarled reply was, "I'll stop talking when you bend over". I was stunned. I had
never been spoken to that way by a student. I told him to leave my room at which
point he stood, turning to the class, arms out wide, addressing his audience: "Oi,
lads. Don't you reckon Miss looks dirty?" I was utterly livid. Who was this boy and
what right did he have to speak about me like that? Voice raised, I told him to leave
immediately, to which he replied, laughing, "Lads, she looks like she'd take it up
the arse", before strolling out, chuckling as he did so.

Afterwards, I went to the deputy head, who was responsible for behaviour.
Emotionally, I recounted the events. The male deputy listened intently, making notes,
stopping only when I quoted Ross' leaving lines, whereupon he paused, slowly looking me up and down. I was glad for my high collar and tailored trouser suit, for it
seemed he wished to judge for himself. I never saw Ross again. It was his final exclusion and he refused point blank to apologise. His father blamed *Nuts*[1] magazine.

A stick woman with long hair and oversized breasts

As a Newly Qualified Teacher (NQT), years before, I had already suffered sexu-
alisation at the hands of the sexualised attitudes perpetuated by *Nuts* magazine.
A Year 7 boy had drawn a picture of me in which I was little more than a stick
woman with long hair and oversized breasts. My head of department at the time
refused to show it me at first but eventually had succumbed to my insistence and
showed me the labels pointing to where you "put your dick" along with the imaginative labels outlining exactly what "tits" were apparently for. Just as us women
moan about the media and its ideologies and toxic messages about femininity, it

seems that boys are just as vulnerable and just as pressured to behave in certain ways. His parents were mortified that the lads' mags he'd been reading contained such messages.

Not all boys are etched on my memory for these negative, unsettling reasons. Some are there because of their wit, like the lad I told to go and stand outside, who walked out of the room and onto the field. I had told him to go outside after all.

The brave boy who cries

Then there was Matthew in Year 7. He was earnest, diligent and asked a few too many questions. He was an awkward boy, a little too honest, a little unaware of how others in his class perceived him. He wasn't popular, or sporty, and he would hang around at the end of the lesson, desperate to interact with the teacher. Whilst teaching the art of rhetoric and analysing persuasive speeches, I used Emma Watson's "He for She" address to the UN. Afterwards, the class were keen to discuss the issue of gender equality and one passage in particular struck a chord with Matthew. In the speech, Watson uses a series of anecdotes, outlining the fact that gender inequalities affect men too, which mention serious things such as mental health and suicide. As a class, we ended up discussing how and why the boys felt that they had to be brave and sporty, had to pick the blue Kinder eggs. We discussed how it was an insult to them if they were accused of kicking, throwing, or running like a girl. We discussed their emotions and the hard face that they felt they had to show the outside world. I asked the boys if they cried. Total silence.

And then Matthew's hand shot up.

I was expecting a question, but no. Instead, he told me – and the class – that he cries. Suddenly, after his brave contribution, one after another of his peers proudly admitted that they did too. And the girls told them that it was fine. And as a class, we smashed the stereotypes and agreed that we, as females, would box and climb trees if we wanted to and that, as boys, we would challenge these stupid gender roles, show our emotions, talk about our emotions, and go to dance club if we felt so inclined. We'd even have a pink Kinder egg if we fancied one.

They decided as a class that their generation could be the ones to change it all. I told them that all they need to do is challenge, lead, be brave, and ask why. I praised Matt, because he stood up first. His bravery that day blew me away. The other lads knew it too.

The bright lad with the glare

The final lad I need to mention here is Toby. He is in Year 11 now. He thrives on competition. And winning. He is tall, popular, has a killer grin. He is sporty, an athlete, hoody on, hood up. He can glare. He has glared at me.

I first met him in Year 9. His class had been taught mainly by cover. We laugh now at how he used to enter our classes. That flipping glare. It turns out that he was frustrated by cover, by non-subject specialists who didn't challenge him. He is a bright lad. Articulate. He doesn't tolerate fools. I would challenge him, question him, and reprimand him. No excuses. If it wasn't good enough, I would tell him so. If I thought he could try better, I would write it on his report. I would say to the class, "this will help next year," but he didn't believe me. The eyes would roll.

I'll be honest. When he saw my name on his timetable for Year 10, I imagine he groaned very loudly. Actually, it may have been more colourful a response than simply a groan.

We laugh about this now because last week, he gave me a thank you note. This brilliant young man has transformed not only his own attitude, but those of his whole GCSE class and mine. Toby makes hard work, determination, asking for extra work, and an unshamed desire to improve, utterly cool. I am totally in awe of this boy.

Their best shot, always

He challenges me, regularly. I'll be honest (and I have never admitted this to him – although I have agreed to show him this so he will know it before he leaves school), at times he has used the odd word and occasional concept or term, in his home-work, which I have had to look up. He has been unpopular with some teachers on occasion because he wants to know more than us! But I love it. Bring it on, I say, because his grit, resilience and resolve to do well, to do better than his older sister, to be better than me has rubbed off on his peers. Asking for extra homework has become the norm. A desire to do better, commonplace. Trying to trick me out, a constant. I pitch my lessons higher; Toby and his peers give it their best shot. Always.

To date he has only caught me out once in class, a moment that no doubt he will relish forevermore – one that I argue was invalidated by his asking about the use of a word out of context! Besides, once in two and a half years is a bit lame, I laugh at him, "ha, is that the best you can do!"

He grins back. And tries harder each lesson. Because, if you believe in them, and if you challenge them, that's what boys do.

Masculinity in school: a parental perspective, by Ros Ball and James Millar

Ros Ball and James Millar, are founders of the twitter account, @GenderDiary, and writers of the subsequent book *The Gender Diary*, both of which provide detailed insight into how gender inequality is embedded in our society from the earliest years through the lens of their own experiences as parents.

Smashing the egg

We never set out to raise our children gender neutral, at least in part because of school.

What would be the point of putting all that effort to shield your offspring from the pernicious influence of stereotypes for four years only for them to step into the classroom and find the world is not as they had been previously led to believe?

It'd be like carefully making your way to the end of the egg and spoon race with cargo intact only for the teacher to remove the ovoid object at the finishing line and stamp all over it. A pointless exercise ending with a child that is bewildered and upset.

Better to try to equip the kids with a questioning mind and the mental tools to spot stereotypes, challenge them where necessary.

For it's not just or even primarily teachers applying the gender rules, the pupils keep each other in line just as much.

The message that gender matters

So when our eldest child started primary school, the conversation on the walk home invariably went something like this:

> *Parent:* What did you learn today at school, darling?
>
> *Four-year-old:* Oh you know, just the usual reinforcing of traditional gender roles through a complex combination of adults' different treatment of children depending on their gender, and peers who police my behaviour to make sure I don't break out of stereotypical behaviour, and that. Oh, and we did some clay modelling and I made a snail.
>
> *Parent:* Great, did you remember to bring your PE kit home?

ok so she didn't use those EXACT words but you get the point.

From the moment the teacher stands up on day one and addresses the class as boys and girls, difference is emphasised. How come the class teacher is Mrs Smith (and of course in primary school the teacher is invariably a Miss or a Mrs) but the head teacher is Mr Jones? Kids can clock there's a difference. An enquiring mind might wonder why, but a young mind just trying to make sense of the world will conclude that this difference matters in some way.

Because they've been receiving the message that gender matters and the sexes are different from the day they were born and the very first words they heard were not "Welcome to the world" or "I love you" but "It's a boy" or "It's a girl".

Forgotten pink trainers

Our @GenderDiary Twitter project that spawned the book "The Gender Agenda" was dedicated to recording all the tiny ways kids are treated differently according to their gender.

One of the surprises of the @GenderDiary project had been that those differences are as damaging to boys as to girls. We'd started out thinking we were going into battle to achieve equality for our daughter. We soon saw that the restrictions placed on boys were just as limiting but in different ways.

School opened up a whole new frontier.

Boys who were happy to wear pink trainers all summer suddenly shunned them in September. Our son saw the invites to girls' birthday parties quickly dry up. We fumed at the way boys locked our daughter out of their car playing games, told girls the play garage was not for them, and literally packed them off to the (play) kitchen. But we came to realise the boys were suffering too for some of them surely wanted to get stuck in with the pots and pans yet felt they could not. And ultimately learning your way round a kitchen is a more useful life skill than going "vroom vroom".

Fuel to the fire

School fuels gender divisions. It's where kids move on to the next stage of socialisation. If nursery was all about learning not to poo in the sand pit or stick a cucumber stick up your nose, school is where the subtleties of social interaction kick in.

But kids are not subtle. Particularly at age four or five when they are starting school, the discombobulation that accompanies the experience of entering a classroom is as inevitable as it is overwhelming. Gender differences provide a familiar handle.

All those tiny cues kids receive, that we chronicled in The Gender Agenda, come in extremely useful. Take, for example, the Lego sets that have female characters as vets and male ones as ninjas and superheroes. Is your son more likely to pursue a career as an animal doctor or as the Hulk? Boys are having options closed down to them and being directed towards violence and aggression and away from caring responsibilities. (Something that not only ill serves them for a wide-ranging education but that will make their life worse when they become parents themselves.)

No more boys and girls

The excellent BBC2 documentary No More Boys and Girls showed a supposedly enlightened primary school teacher repeatedly referring to boys as "mate" and girls as "love" – a clear difference of tone and approach. The boys in that programme were quicker to put their hand up, fuelled by male entitlement and confidence. Yet there is a flipside to that – they were emotionally far behind their female peers so setbacks were met by despondency and violent outbursts.

It shouldn't therefore come as a surprise that older children learn differently. They've been taught differently. The influence is society not biology and the former is easier to alter than the latter.

So what can be done? With the entire @GenderDiary/The Gender Agenda project, we set out to be positive. To offer solutions rather than whines. Or to offer solutions as well as whines at least.

Model an alternative

The first step is to overthrow the patriarchy. But if that doesn't come off before the bell rings for home time, step up and step in to the classroom. Particularly if you're a man. Model the alternative. Schools flipping love parents getting involved and kids love to see their parents in the classroom (in primary school at least). There's plenty of examples and resources online to lift. It doesn't have to be a hardcore lesson in feminism. In fact, it really probably shouldn't be. Just introducing kids to ideas like "colours are for everyone" so it's ok for girls to like blue and "emotions are for everyone" so it's valid for boys to cry. They are concepts that will help kids cope with the gender policing that goes on in schools. Delivered by a dad, they can offer a powerful alternative outlook to pupils of both genders about what it means to be a man.

And apply a teacher's approach at home.

Reward effort. But don't stress or overload them. They are still kids after all.

For the gender aware parent school is a test. Approach it in the way we tackled tests growing up: do your revision and try your best.

Note

1 A popular "lads' mag" featuring women in various stages of undress. No longer with us.

What next?

Some of you, having read *Boys Don't Try?*, will possess the educational clout or position to enable you to go into school tomorrow and begin making large-scale improvements to the educational and pastoral provision for boys in your school. You can audit the gender split in bottom sets, you can offer staff training dispelling boys' engagement myths, and you can tackle misogyny and sexual harassment in your school by improving your policies.

For others, the opportunity to influence whole school change may seem non-existent. There will be Newly Qualified Teachers (NQTs) who, having read this book, will find themselves grinding their teeth as their mentor advises them to use competition to engage the boys in their Year 8 class; teachers who will find themselves clenching their fists as their head of department tells them 'this term, we're doing war poetry because there's a lot of boys in this cohort'; teachers who will find themselves biting their tongue as they sit through yet another assembly that presents university as the only measure of student success. To these teachers, we say:

Do not worry. Education is a subversive act.

Your classroom is your domain, and in your kingdom *you* make the rules. It's *you* who can encourage the use of homonormative pronouns in your classroom. It's *you* who can ban the phrase 'man up' in your classroom. It's *you* who decides that actually, perhaps boys are bloody sick of war poetry, and today, in this classroom we're going to read a love poem, and after that we're going to talk about the way our heart feels.

If you'll forgive us for bastardising a well-trodden metaphor, the road to gender equity is a bumpy one. It's made more difficult to navigate when the traveller themselves possesses some of the ingrained gendered attitudes and behaviours that they are trying to dismantle. Many of the men who read this book will tell their boys it's okay to cry and yet will never cry themselves. They'll tell boys that violence should be avoided, and yet they'll feel an acute sense of shame as they find themselves walking away in fear from the threat of violence. They'll tell boys that actually, it's okay to be gay and yet be offended when their own sexuality is called into question.

This is ok.

Years of gender socialisation cannot be undone by reading one book. And yet, in reading *Boys Don't Try?* you have made a step towards positive change. Regardless of your job title, experience, or place in the school hierarchy, you have begun considering, examining, and reflecting on your own gender biases. You have embarked on a process of rethinking masculinity in schools. This rethinking process may be ephemeral, or it may be the first step in a longer commitment to ensuring that boys and girls get the education they deserve. An education that enables them to lead happy and fulfilling lives.

Tender masculinity cannot be imparted via the hypodermic needles of assemblies or gimmicky whole school initiatives. Tender masculinity is not a matter of injection but distillation. We need to reflect on our attitudes, our approaches, and our language, and, if need be, to change them. Only then will tender masculinity become simply "masculinity".

Index

Note: Page numbers followed by "n" denote endnotes.

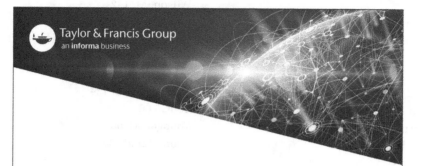